Praise for
Significant Others

"It is never an easy task to explore and explain other faiths, while remaining faithful and dedicated to one's own. Dr. Cox has managed, with a clarity of history, a great deal of humor, and—along with the task—a tone of acceptance, to shed light on traditions other than his deep Christian faith. We are interconnected and valuable as part of the human continent."

—**Barbara L. McBee,** Treasurer, Midwest Buddhist Council

"I really enjoyed reading the chapter on Judaism. It demonstrates academic knowledge and personal experience with Jewish life and living. Overall, it is great, and the style is readable and approachable."

—**Rabbi Feivel Strauss,** Temple Israel, Memphis, TN

"As in the first century Mediterranean world, American Christians are a minority in a pluralistic society. *Significant Others* can help us understand and communicate with our neighbors, friends, and coworkers by providing a concise, readable, and respectful account of major world religions."

—**Sean Todd,** missionary, Chiang Mai, Thailand

"As the world 'shrinks,' and the likelihood of our interacting with people from other countries and cultures increases, it becomes all the more imperative that we understand how adherents of other faiths view what makes us who we are. The easy flowing narrative of *Significant Others* strives to help the reader in getting to know our 'new' neighbors."

—**Anand Pandit,** Hindu Temple of DFW, Irving, Texas

"I love that Monte presents Judaism as personal, and it is clear that his aim is that readers see the others as human, not so different from Gentiles. Monte's understanding of Judaism is apparent."

—**Robert Kallus,** Valparaiso, Indiana

"I appreciate the spirit in which this book is written. To consider others significant is the key to friendship and evangelism. In America, you can be at home and still share the gospel with people from all over the world by reaching out to your neighbors. I think this book can help you do that."

—**Nao Fukushima,** minister, Tachikawa Church of Christ, Tokyo, Japan

"Monte Cox has been teaching religion for some time. What is impressive to me is his commitment to exposing his students to a genuine taste of religions beyond their own. He has annually mounted a student journey to explore all the diverse religious institutions in our very religiously diverse city (Dallas). I have always been impressed with the depth and breadth of his knowledge in the arena of religions and this book will be another vehicle for him to share his knowledge derived from genuine interest and curiosity about 'them.' Based on his writings and having met him personally in my capacity as a professional Buddhist meditation teacher, a former Buddhist monk, and Jewish by birth and upbringing, I unhesitatingly recommend his book, *Significant Others*."

—**Ken Goldberg,** Buddhist Center of Dallas

"One of the biggest benefits for other Christians when they read this book is that they will have a relatively full picture of the religion and cultures of these 'significant others,' which will enable them to evangelize them in a more effective and productive way. I pray this book will be a great blessing to the people who read it and, through them, many others will be blessed as well."

—**Yu Kuang,** Hubei, China

"A delightful guide full of important information for those of us who enjoy the interfaith work. You can either learn from a person who tells you what to do or from a person who is doing it and speaks from their experience. The latter individual is more effective in getting the message across. That is why any person committed to learn about Islam and Muslims will benefit from reading *Significant Others*. Dr. Monte Cox has written a must-read primer for anyone considering learning about Islam. Read this book and learn from one of the best."

—**Nabil A. Bayakly, PhD,** Assistant Imam, Adjunct Professor of Islamic Studies, Memphis Theological Seminary

SIGNIFICANT

UNDERSTANDING OUR NON-CHRISTIAN NEIGHBORS

OTHERS

SIGNIFICANT

UNDERSTANDING OUR NON-CHRISTIAN NEIGHBORS

OTHERS

MONTE COX

LEAFWOOD
PUBLISHERS
an imprint of Abilene Christian University Press

SIGNIFICANT OTHERS
Understanding Our Non-Christian Neighbors

LEAFWOOD
P U B L I S H E R S
an imprint of Abilene Christian University Press

Copyright © 2017 by Monte Cox

ISBN 978-0-89112-464-1
LCCN 2017028575

Printed in the United States of America

Scripture quotations, unless otherwise noted, are from The Holy Bible, New International Version®, NIV®. Copyright © 1973, 1978, 1984 by Biblica, Inc.® Used by permission. All rights reserved worldwide.

LIBRARY OF CONGRESS CATALOGING-IN-PUBLICATION DATA
Names: Cox, Monte, 1959- author.
Title: Significant others : understanding our non-Christian neighbors / Monte Cox.
Description: Abilene, Texas : Leafwood Publishers, 2017.
Identifiers: LCCN 2017028575 | ISBN 9780891124641 (pbk.)
Subjects: LCSH: Christianity and other religions.
Classification: LCC BR127 .C664 2017 | DDC 261.2--dc23
LC record available at https://lccn.loc.gov/201702857 5

Cover design by ThinkPen Design, LLC
Interior text design by Sandy Armstrong, Strong Design

Leafwood Publishers is an imprint of Abilene Christian University Press
ACU Box 29138
Abilene, Texas 79699

1-877-816-4455
www.leafwoodpublishers.com

17 18 19 20 21 22 / 7 6 5 4 3 2 1

To Beth, my partner in the gospel
from the first day until now

CONTENTS

ACKNOWLEDGMENTS

I am indebted to many people who shared my conviction that this project was important. First among them is my wife, Beth, who waived holidays and leisure time with her husband for a year during the writing process. I am grateful to Bill and Doris Fulks, whose endowed chair I occupy at Harding University. Long before this book was written, they understood the need to educate Christians about the religions of our neighbors. The resources they have invested funded a summer sabbatical that enabled me to travel to the homelands of many of the religions I describe in these pages, thus equipping me to better understand through firsthand experience what the faith of these significant others looks like "back home." Dr. Bruce McLarty, President of Harding University, has been unflagging in his support. It was his idea to produce the thirteen-episode video series as a companion to this book, and it was his budget that funded the filming of those lectures. Many other hands contributed to that piece of this project, including Chai Green, Jonathan James, Steve Martin, Marcus Neely, Mark Prior, and David Robison.

More than three thousand students have endured my Living World Religions class at Harding since 1998 and have traveled with me to Chicago, Dallas, Memphis, and, in some cases, Egypt, Greece, Israel, and Turkey, where we have learned together. Their enthusiasm for the content of that course inspired me to make it accessible to others in a non-academic format.

I am more grateful than I can say for the practitioners, past and present, of the non-Christian religions I describe here, as well as for other experts in specific religions who were gracious enough to read the chapters that describe the faith they know so well as insiders. They offered their corrections, critiques, and, in some cases, their endorsements. Their names are sprinkled throughout the book, mostly in the endnotes in each chapter. But their part in this project was so significant that I must name them here in alphabetical order: Aamina Ali-Ahmed, Nabil Bayakly, James Bilagody, Nao Fukushima, Ken Goldberg, Sydney Honyouti, Manoj Jain, Robert Kallus, Eric Kee, Tracy Kee, Yu Kuang, Chirag Lakhmani, Harbans Lal, John Leonard, West Ling, Rajinder Mago, Barbara McBee, Shpendim Nadzaku, Khaled Osman, Anand Pandit, Yossi Paz, Robert Reagan, Hiroko Sando Robertson, Kirpal Singh, Pritpal Singh, Todd Steinberg, Feivel Strauss, Arash Tirandaz, Sean Todd, Chester Whiterock, Renae Whiterock, and Charles Wu. Thank you all! You have made this volume a more useful tool.

I am thankful to Jason Fikes and the team at Leafwood/ACU Press for their encouragement and their refinements. Finally, I thank God for my parents, C. L. and Pat Cox, who introduced me to Jesus and who, I believe, are both enjoying his company now. My mother passed away unexpectedly as I was putting the finishing touches on this book.

PREFACE

This book is about two groups of people: "us" and "them." If I stopped writing long enough for you to ponder those two words, you would likely picture groups of people in your mind without any more prompting. "Us" might be Americans, "them" might be everyone else. If for you "us" were Democrats, "them" would be Republicans. "Us" could be readers and "them" might be writers. "Us" could be football fans, "them" could be soccer fans (or, as the rest of the world calls them, football fans). Or "us" could be Christians, "them" could be Muslims, Hindus, Buddhists, Sikhs, Baháʼí, atheists, and everyone else. The Christian "us" might refer to a more specific group of people, depending on your own affiliation: Presbyterians, Methodists, Pentecostals, Catholics, or Church of Christ members. "Them" would be all the "others."

Paul Hiebert, my mentor in graduate school, once wrote an article entitled, "Are We Our Others' Keepers?"[1] In it he reviews the long and sordid history of "us" versus "them" thinking in the Western half of the world. When Europeans encountered non-Europeans, he writes, they assumed they were less than human. This exotic "other" was a monster, an animal Europeans could use as they saw fit. As explorers' encounters with "others" deepened, they discovered that these "others" loved their families, had a sense of right and wrong, and (more often than not) believed in a single Creator. Those features called for an upgrade: these "others" were no longer "monsters," but "savages" who lacked the trappings of "civilized" societies; but they could (perhaps) be taught European customs and languages. The missionaries who accompanied or followed the explorers to new worlds evaluated the "others" mostly in religious terms, as "heathen" or "pagan." Then, as science came to dominate Western worldviews, evolutionary thought led Europeans to see the "other" as "primitive," like "our" own ancestors. In fact, the field of anthropology was born (a little more than one hundred years ago) partly out of Europeans' fascination with this oppor-tunity to study "us"—these primitive peoples—to learn how "we" used to live. It was as if "we" had been frozen in time, living museum pieces of what "we" were like before "we" became the "sophisticated" and "modern" people "we" are today. Of course, now all such thinking is politically incorrect. It was never Christian.

From the moment God called Abram, it was clear that his purposes for people included "all peoples on earth" (Gen. 12:3). Sadly, Israel hoarded the blessing, earning God's rebuke through prophets like Isaiah who declared, "It is too small a thing for you to be my servant to restore the tribes of Jacob and bring back those of Israel I have kept. I will also make you a light for the Gentiles, that you may bring my salvation to the ends of the earth" (Isa. 49:6). Jonah was the poster child for Israel's inwardness, a living symbol of how God's mediator-nation missed the point.[2] The story of Jonah ends with the anti-hero pouting in the heat under a withered gourd tree and God asking about Nineveh, population one hundred twenty thousand ("and many cattle as well"), "Should I not be concerned about that great city?" (Jon. 4:11). The end. The question is left to echo in the ears of Israel and Israel's spiritual descendants. In other words, God obviously cares a lot about the people of Nineveh, creatures made in his image. Shouldn't we? The question may be more current than we suppose at first. The ancient city of Nineveh lies in ruins just outside of modern Mosul in ISIS-controlled northern Iraq. Does God still care about all of those "others," the inhabitants of that once "great city," including the militant Islamic extremists who now govern it (at the time of this writing)?

Yet "us" and "them" thinking is engrained in us . . . and in them. North Americans and Europeans do not have a monopoly on it. I spent the first decade of my adult life living and working among a people group in Africa for whom the local word translated "people" meant only *their* people—that is, members of *that* tribe. Outsiders were not even "people," though they knew we were human. If the news of the day involved a bus crash, the question might be, "How many 'people' died in that accident?" And the answer might be, "No 'people' died; only twenty-five [insert the name of a neighboring tribe here]." My friends were not being mean, at least not on purpose. This kind of "us" and "them" thinking was embedded in their language.

A generation ago, most of "us"—the North American English-speakers who are reading this book—had little or no contact with Muslims, Hindus, or Buddhists. Some of us may have gone to school with Jewish children. We may have played Little League baseball with some non-churchgoers. But we probably didn't know any Muslims, Hindus, or Buddhists. Now our culture is much more pluralistic. We meet parents of Muslim children at PTA. Our physician (or her parents) emigrated from India. A friend tells us that the convenience store operator we see every time we buy gas is from Thailand. An image—maybe a Buddha statue?—rests on the shelf just below the cigarettes. "We" can often tell by their appearance (or perhaps their accent, depending on when they arrived) that "they" are not from here. Maybe we feel that it is rude to ask, "So where are you from?" Depending on our tone and our intentions, it might actually *be* rude.

In addition to these "others," many Westerners, disenchanted with Christianity, are more inclined than they were a generation ago to sample bits and pieces from a religious smorgasbord filled with "new" spiritual alternatives that were not available here before, except in major cities. Most only "dabble." You overhear a coworker telling others about her weekend meditation retreat at a Buddhist Study Center in the suburbs. A couple at church asks you to pray for their adult son who is considering becoming a "Baha'i." You think to yourself, "a Ba-what?" This is the first time this young world religion (established in Iran in 1844) appears on your radar. Your grown daughter is dating "a really nice man" named "Rog." His full name is Rajpal Prassad. His parents found work in America before Rajpal was born. Your first meeting with them confirms what she tells you: he is moral, with strong family values and a great work ethic. He even attends church with her every Sunday, though he has not yet shown interest in becoming a Christian. You feel conflicted because, in your estimation, he may be the finest marriage candidate she's dated in years. But what do you make of the faith of *his* fathers (and mothers)? Your hesitation makes you doubt your own integrity. "Am I prejudiced?" you ask yourself. Or is it that your understanding of the exclusive claims of Christ means that, in your estimation, your daughter would be "unequally yoked" with an unbeliever if this relationship were to go forward?

I don't believe it is politeness alone that stifles "our" curiosity about our newest neighbors or leaves us confused when our children or friends show interest in these spiritual alternatives. I blame ignorance as the greater culprit. I think many of "us" hesitate to ask questions because we don't know how to respond to the answers we'll get. If our doctor informed us that she did, in fact, have roots in India, would that end the conversation? If we discovered that the parents of our child's friend at school hail from Syria, would we be reluctant to interact with them? Are we intimidated by what we don't know about India and Syria? And do we hesitate to ask the coworker about the Buddhist meditation retreat because we are afraid we might offend? Will they saddle us with that intolerant label—"exclusivists"? And if the goal of faith is a moral life (which, by the way, is *not* the ultimate goal of the Christian life), then isn't Rajpal a good catch for this daughter?

If you can relate to any of these scenarios and you would like to know more about the religious backgrounds of these new neighbors or understand why so many of your fellow-countrymen are considering these religious alternatives, these pages are written with you in mind. If, on the other hand, you have no intention of seeking friendship with "others" like these, you've wasted your hard-earned money on this book. In that case, I would ask that you pass this copy along to a faithful Christian who wants to share their faith in Jesus with "others." Because at the pinnacle of history, God sent his only Son to become *one* of us, One who then laid down his life for *all* of us, so that "we" might become "us" again. That means these "others"—all "others"—are very significant to God.

And with that, I will stop using this annoying "us" and "them" language. You're welcome.

TALKING TOGETHER . . .

1. What dangers accompany "us versus them" thinking?

2. European explorers viewed other races as less than human, even calling them savages. What caused these views to change?

3. What do you think most inhibits you when it comes to making friends with non-Christians? The fear factor? The feeling that you don't know enough about "others"? Something else?

4. Why do you think this book is needed?

5. What parts of Scripture do you think will be most important to review as you begin this study?

Notes

[1] Paul G. Hiebert, "Are We Our Others' Keepers?" In *Currents in Theology and Mission* 22 (October 1995): 325–337.

[2] In fairness to modern Judaism, my Israeli friend Yossi Paz believes this "us and them" thinking in Judaism developed as a defense mechanism during millennia of persecution. He points to many "inclusive" portions of the Hebrew Bible he believes the ultra-Orthodox ignore. In correspondence with the author on January 18, 2017.

CHAPTER ONE

DOES GOD HEAR
THEIR PRAYERS?

On the first day of my undergraduate World Religions class, I read to my class an excerpt from the introduction of a classic textbook first published in 1958 by the renowned comparative religion scholar Huston Smith.[1] Smith was born and raised in China before WWII, the son of Methodist missionaries. His long and deep exposure to the religions of China forced him to ask the question, "How does Heaven hear the prayers of all these God-seekers around the world" as they lift their eyes in his direction? He answers his own question by imagining that in God's ears the chorus of prayers sounds like a great symphony in which the Buddhists play the strings, the Muslims fill the brass section, the Christians provide the percussion, and so on. I admit, I like that image. I wish I could agree with Smith's positive appraisal. But as I read Scripture, I get the impression that to God, all these "prayers"—some of which are not prayers at all, if by "prayer" we mean a petition aimed in the direction of a Divine Being— sound not like a symphony, but more like the junior high band warming up. Their impulse to play their instruments is noble, but they, like I do, have a lot to learn.

Respectful, Informed, Persuasive

Paul's message on Mars' Hill (along with many other biblical stories and texts) leads me in the "junior high band" direction. Paul's street preaching won him an invitation to speak to the prestigious philosophy club that took its name from the rocky outcropping attached to the Acropolis in Athens— the Areopagus. His presentation to them was respectful, informed, and persuasive. He meant to challenge, not just affirm, what these educated elite thought they already knew. Paul began by acknowledging their devotion: "I see that in every way you are very religious" (Acts 17:22). I don't think he's being sarcastic. Paul is applauding them for their spiritual interest. He then proceeds to compare their objects of worship—including the altar erected to "an Unknown God"—with the Living God revealed in Christ. Not once but twice he quotes pagan poets whom he believes support his main points. "In him we live and move and have our being," Epimenides wrote in the original poem Paul is quoting, countering the suggestion of his fellow-Cretans that Zeus had died. "We are his offspring," Aratus (from Paul's home province of Cilicia) had written; the "his" once again referred to Zeus.

Those two quotations tell us at least three things. First, Paul thought it was right to repurpose pagan poetry that praised Zeus and apply it to the one true Creator God. Second, Paul did not feel compelled to slander Zeus, or Athena, or Nike, or Poseidon, or any other "deities" whose images decorated the Acropolis. I am quite certain that Paul didn't believe in any of them. From his perspective they did not exist. But to tweak a borrowed phrase that I'll use again in Chapter Five (on Buddhism), he did not feel like he had to "step on Zeus to lift up Christ." Third, Paul had obviously done his homework long before he ascended Mars' Hill that day. According to several ancient history courses, Epimenides—the one who wrote, "In him we live and move and have our being"—was the hero of an ancient story in which the city of Athens was spared worse damage from a plague that struck around 600 BC. Epimenides was invited to Athens from his native Crete by the city fathers to help them find the spiritual source of the disease that ravaged their city. It was Epimenides who speculated that, though the Greeks had prayed to all the gods of Athens, there must be an "unknown god" they had missed. And it was Epimenides who proposed that they confess their ignorance and make sacrifices to this "unknown god." When they complied, the plague, so say the ancient accounts, ended within a week.[2] Paul obviously knew the story. He did not have to start at square one with that audience on Mars' Hill. He could begin at least at square two or three. He started with what they thought they knew and attempted to lead them to Christ.

Paul's persuasive tone is unmistakable. Of course, we can't be sure that Paul's entire speech is recorded in Acts 17. Luke's account gives the impression that Paul was interrupted when he identified Christ as the one qualified to judge the world because God had raised "him from the dead" (17:31). Paul obviously was convinced that faith in Jesus was a matter of life and death. Sadly, he didn't seem to persuade many, at least not right then and there. Luke mentions just two converts in Athens (17:34). And no "Letter to the Athenians" shows up in the collection of Paul's epistles to churches he planted. Despite that disappointing result, Paul models for us that the right kind of engagement with religious "others" (and all others for that matter) is respectful, informed, and persuasive. Of course, Paul is not the ultimate role model. Jesus is. We imitate Paul as Paul imitated Christ, whose interactions with others were also respectful, informed, and persuasive.

Inclusive Demeanor, Exclusive Claims

One of the qualities I find most endearing about Jesus is his inclusive demeanor toward others, even as he makes exclusive claims about himself and his role. He famously (or infamously from the perspective of his critics) hung out with the "wrong people"—tax collectors (collaborators with the Romans), Samaritans (an "impure" mixed race from a Jewish perspective), women caught in adultery, and lepers (perpetually "unclean" because of that awful disfiguring illness). Simon thought Jesus's warm response to the "sinful woman" who anointed his feet with perfume and wiped them with her hair was a sure sign that Jesus was not a prophet. "He would know who is touching him and what kind of woman she is—that she is a sinner" (Luke 7:39). The problem was not that Jesus did not know this woman's background. The problem was that Simon did not know what sort of Messiah Jesus was and is.

Simon was a Pharisee, a member of the now-infamous Jewish sect that took its name from a Hebrew word many scholars translate as "separate ones." The Pharisees' commitment to ritual purity as defined by the Law meant they had to limit their contact with others who were not likewise committed, even any fellow Jews they deemed too lax in their observance. Their hope was that God would reward them for their faithfulness and send the long-awaited Messiah. By that logic, God should have sent Jesus directly to Qumran by the Dead Sea or to some other community of Essenes, who were way more "separate" than the Pharisees. That ultra-conservative Jewish sect, not mentioned in the Bible, were all about maintaining ritual purity. They took multiple ritual baths each day, wore white clothes as symbols of purity, maintained a strict *kosher* diet, and practiced celibacy. (That last feature helps explain why there are no Essenes today.) If God had been looking for the purest of people (ritually speaking) to welcome the Messiah, the Essenes would have been good candidates, even better than the Pharisees. But Jesus was not so discriminating in his choice of companions. And for that inclusiveness, he was constantly criticized. He was not "separate" enough to suit the religious establishment.

But Jesus also made claims that seem to violate that inclusive spirit, at least from the standpoint of modern pluralistic sensibilities. What did he mean when he said, "I am the way and the truth and the life. No one comes to the Father except through me" (John 14:6)? (We'll unpack that line below.) Or when he declared that unless they believed in him, they would "die in [their] sins" (John 8:24)? Or when he commissioned his disciples to go and make other disciples as if eternity hung in the balance: "Whoever believes and is baptized will be saved, but whoever does not believe will be condemned" (Mark 16:16)?

Exclusivists, Inclusivists, and Pluralists

Diana Eck, a professor of comparative religions at Harvard, poses this question: "Is 'our God' listening to the prayers of people of other faiths?" In other words, how does the God of the universe see religious difference?

Eck outlines the four most common responses to that important question. First, some believe that "one religion (their own) is true and the others are false." (This is the "exclusive" position.) God does not hear the prayers of those outside of their faith. Second, some believe that "one religion is true and other religions may be *partially* true." (This is labeled "inclusivism.") Perhaps God hears the prayers of other religious people, but they do not enjoy the same access to him that "insiders do." A third common answer is that "all religions are true"—that is, all religions attempt to address the divine in one way or another, and all ultimately lead to the same destination. (These days the most popular label for this position is "pluralism.") So from the pluralist's perspective, "God" (whatever term may be used for a Supreme Being in a given religion) does hear the "prayers" (or chants or meditations) of others outside their religion, including those who would say they are directing their "prayers" at no one in particular "up there." Finally, a fourth possible response to the question is that "no religions are true" (atheism). This view has been given new life in the last few decades by astute atheistic or agnostic best-selling authors named Dawkins, Harris, Hitchens, and Sagan, among others. To cling to religious belief in the age of science is to them like maintaining faith in the Olympian gods. Reasonable people, they say, must park their brains to buy into religious faith.[3]

Those of us who follow Christ have to take all of these possible responses seriously. The fourth answer—that no religion is true—is certainly popular in our secular culture, but it is out of bounds among believers. "Exclusivist," "Inclusivist," and "Pluralist" have become fairly standard labels for the first three responses, so we'll go with them.

Exclusivists

These folks believe that only their religion is true. As Jeff Foxworthy might say, "you might be a Christian exclusivist" if you believe that

1. Jesus is the Son of God, fully human and fully divine, in a way that no other character in history has ever been.
2. Salvation is found only in him.
3. The Bible is the true, unique, authoritative revelation from God.
4. Any claims incompatible with the Bible must be rejected as false.

Of course, it is possible to be more exclusive than that simple four-point outline suggests. Some Christians have longer lists. Not all Christians would agree that anyone who accepts these four propositions is, in fact, a true Christian. But if you said "Amen" to all four of those statements, you are probably an exclusivist. Because of these convictions, exclusivists work to evangelize others who are outside of Christ as if their eternal destiny is at stake.

Inclusivists

People in this category prefer Diana Eck's second answer to the question, "Is 'our God' listening to the prayers of people of other faiths?" Yes, only one religion (Christianity) is true, they say, but other religions may be partially true. Inclusivists would agree with the gist of the four statements that define exclusivism but would modify them. Yes, Jesus is the Son of God, fully human and fully divine in a way that no other character in history ever has been. But other religious figures, from Buddha to Krishna, may prepare the soil in which the gospel of Jesus can be heard and understood.

Second, it is true that salvation is found in no one else but Jesus. But those who die before they learn of Jesus or who are faithful to "God" as *they* understand him will be saved *by Jesus* in the end. You should know that inclusivists also quote John 14:6: "I am the way and the truth and the life. No one comes to the Father except through me." But they point out that Jesus does not say they must come to him *before* they die. The Muslim who dies a Muslim will not be surprised to find Jesus at the gates of Heaven; the Qur'an teaches that Jesus will be there. They will be surprised to learn that he is, in fact, the Son of God and not merely a prophet. But Jesus will welcome them in based on their faithfulness to what they thought they knew. In the end, in other words, they still get to the Father *through Jesus* (although, as we shall see in Chapter Three, Muslims do not refer to Allah as "Father").

Fifty years ago, inclusivist Roman Catholic theologian Karl Rahner coined the term "anonymous Christian" to describe the faithful non-Christian "believer" who is, in Rahner's view, a Christian and doesn't know it.[4] That means Rajpal, the faithful Hindu, will be accepted on Judgment Day, saved by Jesus whom Rajpal did not know in this life. Likewise, the devout Muslim will be surprised after death to learn Jesus's true nature, but Jesus will welcome him into Heaven, "reckoning as righteousness" his Muslim faith.

So, do inclusivists feel compelled to evangelize? I know many who do so out of obedience to Jesus's command to "make disciples of all nations." They are more likely to evaluate more positively the religion of those they seek to evangelize, often seeing that religion as "preparation for evangelism." That is, what Sikhs believe about the one true God may actually serve to open their minds to receive the gospel. From that perspective, Sikhism is not so much an enemy of Christian faith as the precursor to it. Could the Sikh Holy Book (*Guru Granth Sahib*) be to Sikhs what the Old Testament is to Gentile Christians? Exclusivists are suspicious that "inclusivism" takes the urgency out of evangelism, given the possibility (as they perceive it) that devout members of other faiths (at the very least) will be saved in the end, even if they do not know Christ in this life.

Pluralists

Those who hold pluralistic views typically do not accept the uniqueness of Christ. All major world religions, they say, have their own mediator figure or figures. Pluralist Christians (like Eck) hold Jesus in high regard, affirming the unique aspects of his life and work compared to founders of non-Christian religions, but not in a way that would suggest that belief in Jesus is neccssary for a meaningful life or for eternal life after death. "Salvation," pluralists also argue, is defined too narrowly by too many Christians as forgiveness of sin and admission into Heaven. On this point we agree. "Salvation" in the full biblical sense means more than those two wonderful things—forgiveness and eternal life. It is nothing less than the complete well-being God intends for all his creatures, a blessing that comes through reconciliation with God through Christ.

Pluralists would argue that all religions offer a path to "salvation" defined according to their own tradition. For Buddhists, the objective is to escape suffering and reach the "Nothingness" of Nirvana. The escape route would be the Buddhist equivalent to the "way of salvation." In Hinduism, the Sanskrit word "moksha," often translated "salvation" in English, means getting off the wheel of birth and rebirth and being absorbed into the

Ultimate Reality which is a force known as "Brahman." Neither Nirvana nor Brahman equates to Heaven, where we who are in Christ expect to experience the fullness of salvation of another kind—to live forever with God.

Third, religious pluralists would not agree that the Bible is "true, unique, authoritative revelation from God"—given that those are all loaded terms from their perspective (and mine). They would offer a more nuanced understanding of each term. The Bible certainly reveals "truths," but those truths are no more true than the truths presented in the Qur'an, the Vedas (Hindu sacred texts), the Granth Sahib (the Sikh Holy Book), or any other sacred text. Exclusivists, inclusivists, and pluralists would also debate the meaning of the terms "unique," "authoritative," and "revelation." To pluralists, the inclusive view of other religions as laying the groundwork for Christian evangelism is condescending toward those other religions and blinds us to what we might learn from them.

Do pluralists evangelize? Generally speaking, the answer is no, if "evangelize" assumes the intention of converting an adherent of a non-Christian religion to Christ. "Interfaith dialogue"—an exercise I value—is more common in pluralist circles, but for pluralists the ultimate goal of such dialogue is mutual understanding, not conversion.

Could We Find a Better Word Than "Exclusive"?

In case I haven't shown my hand already, I am an exclusivist. I embrace those four basic propositions listed above. But, because of the many negative associations that come with it, I cringe when I hear that word "exclusive"—associations that run counter to the inclusive demeanor of the Jesus I so admire. (More on that in a moment.) I don't embrace the exclusive position simply because of the two favorite exclusivist "proof texts": John 14:6 and Acts 4:12. As I mentioned above, John 14:6 is subject to other interpretations (although I believe the exclusive interpretation is correct). In Acts 4:12, Peter boldly declares to the Sanhedrin that "there is no other name under heaven given to men by which we must be saved." Boom. End of discussion, right? Not so fast. Inclusivists quote Acts 4:12, too, for the same reason they quote John 14:6. Does Peter make it absolutely clear that everyone must wear the name of Jesus *before* they die in order to be saved?

The truth is we don't do justice to the exclusivist position when we base it on those two passages alone. I am an exclusivist because first, the whole mission of Jesus, stated in various ways, is described with such gravity that the eternal destiny of the "lost" he came "to seek and to save" is at stake (Luke 19:10). "For I have come down from heaven," Jesus told a crowd, "not to do my will but to do the will of him who sent me. And this is the will of him who sent me, that I shall lose none of all that he has given me, but raise them up at the last day" (John 6:38–39). Why make the trip and pay the heavy price he paid if people could not, in fact, be "lost"? In another exchange with those who were rejecting him, he said, "I told you that you would die in your sins; if you do not believe that I am the one I claim to be, you will indeed die in your sins" (John 8:24). Why would it matter that these people he loves would "die in their sins" if in the end, after death, they would have opportunity to change their minds about Jesus?

Second, Jesus's impassioned pleas for people to repent and enter his Kingdom (John 3:3–5, for example), combined with the dire warnings about the consequences of unbelief, all echoed by his disciples' teaching after him, sound hollow to me if these are idle threats, intended only to cajole people into obedience.

Third, don't the inclusive and pluralist positions amount to an argument for salvation by works? If a pious non-Christian is saved in the end because of their piety, then is that not in direct opposition to the whole idea of "salvation by grace through faith" (Eph. 2:8–9)? As a Christian, I do not believe I am saved because of my good deeds. I am saved only because I am in Christ. In him I do not have "a righteousness of my own that comes from the law, but that which is through faith in Christ—the righteousness that comes from God and is by faith" (Philip. 3:9). To borrow another metaphor from Paul, I am saved only because, through baptism into Christ, I am clothed with Christ (Gal. 3:27). Period.

Now back to this word "exclusive." I sure don't like it. As I mentioned above, my aversion is based on several negative stereotypes associated with the term. Some people imagine exclusivists brow-beating non-Christians, dangling them over the fires of Hell as if they enjoy it. The picture is of a one-sided "conversation," which is no conversation at all. Exclusivists are not known for their listening skills or for their interest in dialogue with those with whom they disagree. Many exclusivists are not well-informed about the religious alternatives they are dismissing with disdain. One author who shares my dislike of this term "exclusivist" prefers as an alternative what he calls the "evangelist paradigm." The evangelist paradigm does stress the importance of knowing Christ personally and in this lifetime. But it is culturally sensitive as well, interested in knowing where non-Christians are coming from so that our interaction will be more meaningful and productive. The evangelist paradigm also rejects the sectarianism within Christendom that usually comes with the exclusivist territory; that is, many exclusivists have longer lists than the aforementioned four criteria that make a person an exclusivist.[5]

I'm not sure "the evangelist paradigm" takes the bad taste out of my mouth. The 2016 book by David Kinnaman and Gabe Lyons explains why. In *Good Faith*, the authors' research suggests that two words capture how most Christians are perceived by non-Christians in North America: irrelevant and extreme.[6] The charge of "extremism" has intensified as the label "intolerant" has stuck. If you think someone else's salvation depends on whether or not they claim Jesus as Lord, in the eyes of the secular world you must be "one of those people"—an irrelevant, extreme, and intolerant Christian. Furthermore, if you believe that eternal punishment awaits unbelievers, even those who never had a chance to hear the gospel, then critics will say you are *really* extreme.

Messenger Mentality

So here's a proposal. Instead of the "exclusive" label or "the evangelist paradigm," why don't we embrace the messenger mentality? Like John the Baptist, who exclaimed when he first saw Jesus, "Look, the Lamb of God, who takes away the sin of the world" (John 1:29), we stand and point others to Jesus, careful not to overstep our bounds. Among other things, this means, first, that we pass on the message that has been passed on to us as best we can, including the dire warnings from Scripture about the consequences of unbelief, minus those judgment calls we are not authorized to make. When I am asked the question, "What about those who have never heard? Don't you believe a merciful God will save them?" I respond, "I certainly hope so!" Of course, I want those people in Heaven, too! I wish them no ill. I want them to know the joys of life in Christ here and now and hereafter. But as a messenger, I am authorized to deliver only the message entrusted to me. And that gospel message, as best as I can tell, comes with serious warnings about the life and death consequences of rejecting it. I take no pleasure in that. In the end, I am very happy to leave that ultimate judgment call to the Judge. But I would be unfaithful as a messenger if I did not mention the consequences of unbelief.

Second, to embrace the "messenger mentality" means we leave behind the combative tone that often characterizes exclusivists, especially when politics seeps into our faith too much (as opposed to our faith seeping into our politics). I'm thinking of a time I invited a Muslim acquaintance to our campus for a conversation about "Islam in America." Someone took a picture that appeared in a national church newspaper with a simple caption about the event. Soon after that, I received a letter in the mail from a woman in another state chastising me for hosting that dialogue. In her view, there is no point in having conversations with "Moslems." "All they want to do is kill us. . . . They are devils, not worth the time of day." In the margins of her letter, I scribbled, "You mean devils (like me), not worth the time of day, for whom Christ died, right?" I wondered what sort of "gospel" she has heard proclaimed in her church and for how long.

Note, too, that messengers embrace dialogue as an indispensable part of finding mutual understanding and building friendships. I choose the word "dialogue" deliberately. Gordon Smith says it's disingenuous (at best) to have a "dialogue" that is really only about you teaching them.[7] I agree. True dialogue is a two-way street and cannot be manipulative. Yes, we can learn from others. But I do not agree that if I hold on to my conviction that this non-Christian with whom I'm in conversation is lost outside of Christ, then our "dialogue" is irreparably tainted by my "hidden agenda."

At the beginning of that public conversation with my Muslim friend, I informed the audience what both he and I knew about each other—that he would love to convince me that Jesus is merely a prophet, take my confession of faith ("There is no God but God, Muhammad is his prophet"), and witness my conversion right then and there, and that I would love nothing more than to persuade him to confess that Jesus is Lord and baptize him into Christ. After I made it clear that we both know that about the other, I said, "But we sit here tonight as friends."

I believe real dialogue *is* possible, even (and maybe especially) between two people of conviction. I will also testify that studying world religions most of my adult life has only deepened my appreciation for the uniqueness of Christ. "Dialogue" is not a betrayal of Christian commitment; true dialogue is a mark of discipleship.

Let me pose a fourth reason for us to see ourselves as messengers. As messengers we are not surprised to find truth in other world religions and affirm it as truth when we find it. God is the author of all truth. If, as David believed, "the heavens declare the glory of God," and, as Paul taught, even Gentiles know something of God from creation and in their own conscience, evidence of such truths should neither surprise us nor threaten us.[8] Paul, preaching this time to a rural, pagan audience in Lystra (as opposed to the sophisticated philosopher types on Mars' Hill), said: "He has not left himself without testimony." And what did Paul consider to be "testimony"? "He has shown kindness by giving you rain from heaven and crops in their seasons; he provides you with plenty of food and fills your hearts with joy" (Acts 14:17). Building on that point of contact, Paul began to preach about the Christ who had just healed a lame man in their town before their eyes. Boldly, he begged them to turn from their "worthless idols" to the living God. In that same spirit, messengers don't simply "shoot down" at point-blank range religious ideas that are incompatible with Scripture. Instead, we find those points of contact between what others believe and practice and the gospel—not in a manipulative way, but in a way that affirms that these truths originate with the God we serve, who, we believe, speaks a better, final Word in Christ.

A fifth reason to adopt this self-identity is that messengers know that meaningful relationships start with listening. That's why this book matters. Most of us don't know where to begin to plug the holes in our knowledge of the different faiths of our newest neighbors. But messengers are not interested in caricatures that demean people and their beliefs. We care about getting our information straight. Accuracy matters. This is one reason that before publication, I have shared each chapter of this book with friends and acquaintances of mine who practice these religions. You'll find their names in the Acknowledgments.

Finally, messengers pray fervently that God will put us in the path of people who are seeking him and give us opportunities to engage in conversations this book might inform. We cling to God's promise: "Seek and you will find" (Matt. 7:7). The Gospels and Acts offer testimonies of seeking people whom Jesus and his followers encountered, not by chance, but by providence. Jesus declared, "I have other sheep that are not of this sheep pen. I must bring them also. They too will listen to my voice, and there shall be one flock and one shepherd" (John 10:16). God is looking for those lost sheep, his creatures made in his image. This means God is looking for those who are looking for him (and may not even realize it).

Humility and Confidence

To be a "messenger" is a high calling. To be effective, we must communicate—in word and in deed—with humility and confidence, a combination I find too rare among us. Humility is required of those who know we don't know everything. Even the Apostle Paul, under the inspiration of the Holy Spirit,wrote, "Now I know in part; then I shall know fully" (1 Cor. 13:12). Obviously, God has not spoken about everything! Much about the universe and our journey through it is mysterious. Like many of you, I have studied the Bible most of my life. Yet I find that I still have much to learn. Our role as messengers is cause for humility as well. We usurp the authority of the One who sends us if we overstep our bounds and make judgment calls we are not authorized to make. Finally, we are called to humility because we are followers of One whose earthly life embodied humility, from the manger to the cross.

But this is also a call for confidence. I repeat Paul's line: "we know in part" (1 Cor. 13:9). Some of my students (and their parents, I would imagine) hear that phrase and throw up their hands in surrender, as if we don't know anything worth sharing, at least not definitively enough to share what we think we know. But this is Paul writing that line. He devoted the rest of his life post–road-to-Damascus to proclaiming what he believed he knew, though he only knew it in part. And he proclaimed it confidently with the conviction that souls were at stake. He was commissioned as a messenger, just as you and I have been. There is much the King did not tell me. But I am honored that he entrusted to me (and you) a "treasure in jars of clay," a message that is of such consequence that sharing it with others is worthy of a lifelong commitment. Finally, I testify about Christ with confidence because I am a follower of One who, before he was laid in a manger, was conceived in a miraculous way no one else has ever been conceived. And I testify about One who, after dying a humiliating and public death, emerged from the tomb less than seventy-two hours later as no one else has. He is our source of humility and confidence and our role model for both.

Here's the Plan

This book is written for a Christian audience in North America. Since my purpose is to equip Christians to engage non-Christians in meaningful conversations, informed by the basics of each of these faiths, I have not included a chapter on Christianity. I am assuming that it is your faith in Christ and your interest in sharing that faith with others that brought you to this book. To any non-Christians who may read this book, like my friends and acquaintances with whom I shared specific chapters prepublication (so they could fact-check), I trust you will appreciate this narrow focus. This is a primer for beginners.

I have included chapters on the "world religions," mostly those with the largest numbers of adherents. By "world religions," I mean those whose adherents don't live in only one corner of the globe. Census data shows there are approximately thirty million Sikhs in the world, and twenty million of them live in Punjab State in northwestern India. But the Sikh diaspora is so widespread that chances are you have already encountered Sikhs in this part of the world. For example, former South Carolina Governor Nicki Hailey grew up in a Sikh family. On the other hand, Zoroastrians number fewer than one hundred thousand; most of them live in India and Iran, though a faithful few continue to worship in "fire temples" in the United States. Many academic textbooks on world religions no longer include a chapter on Zoroastrianism. I mean no disrespect to that ancient religion by not writing about it here. I have also omitted any mention of what scholars call "New Religious Movements" such as Mormonism and Scientology, even though those groups (and others) get a lot of attention in the press.

Each chapter to follow will begin with a brief snapshot of those religious adherents as they practice their faith in North America. Then I will outline in brief the story of how that religion was "born," its most significant figures, basic beliefs and practices, and the divisions that developed as it spread. Finally, I will name some significant "points of contact" and "points of contrast" in each religion compared to Christian faith.

TALKING TOGETHER . . .

1. How do you think God hears all these prayers of non-Christians? Do they sound more like a symphony or like a junior high band? Is there a choice in-between?

2. What biblical examples other than Paul's message on Mars Hill offer insights into how we ought to interact with adherents of non-Christian faiths?

3. What are the challenges of imitating Jesus's inclusive demeanor toward others while also upholding his exclusive claims?

4. Is the "messenger mentality" more appealing to you than the "exclusive" position? If so, why?

5. How would you answer this question: "If I had been born in _____ and had little or no access to the gospel, would I be lost?"

IF YOU WANT TO READ MORE . . .

Eck, Diana L. *Encountering God: A Spiritual Journey from Bozeman to Banaras.* Boston: Beacon Press, 2003.

Kinnaman, David, and Gabe Lyons. *Good Faith: Being a Christian When Society Thinks You're Irrelevant and Extreme.* Grand Rapids: Baker, 2016.

Netland, Harold A. *Encountering Religious Pluralism: The Challenge to Christian Faith and Mission.* Downers Grove, IL: InterVarsity Press, 2001.

Newbigin, Lesslie. *The Gospel in a Pluralist Society.* Grand Rapids: William B. Eerdmans Publishing, 1989.

Richardson, Don. *Eternity in Their Hearts, Revised Edition.* Ventura, CA: Regal Books 1981.

Strange, Daniel. *Their Rock Is Not Like Our Rock: A Theology of Religions.* Grand Rapids, MI: Zondervan, 2014.

Notes

[1] Huston Smith, *The World's Religions: A Completely Revised and Updated Edition of The Religions of Man* (New York: HarperCollins, 1991). Originally published as *The Religions of Man* in 1958.

[2] I like Don Richardson's description of the background for Paul's sermon on Mars' Hill which Richardson pieced together from ancient sources. See *Eternity in Their Hearts,* Revised edition (Ventura, CA: Regal Books, 1981), 9–25.

[3] Diana L. Eck, *Encountering God: A Spiritual Journey from Bozeman to Banaras* (Boston: Beacon Press, 2003), 167.

[4] "Anonymous Christian," *New Catholic Encyclopedia* (2003), accessed March 17, 2017, http://www.encyclopedia.com/religion/encyclopedias-almanacs-transcripts-and-maps/anonymous-christian.

[5] Charles Van Engen, "The Uniqueness of Christ in Mission Theology," in *Christianity and the Religions: A Biblical Theology of World Religions,* edited by Edward Rommen and Harold Netland, 184–217, Evangelical Missiological Society Series, Number 2 (Pasadena, CA: William Carey Library, 1995), 195–200.

[6] Davd Kinnaman and Gabe Lyons, *Good Faith: Being a Christian When Society Thinks You're Irrelevant and Extreme* (Grand Rapids: Baker, 2016), 21.

[7] Gordon T. Smith, "Religions and the Bible: An Agenda for Evangelicals," in *Christianity and the Religions: A Biblical Theology of World Religions,* edited by Edward Rommen and Harold Netland, 9–29 (Pasadena, CA: William Carey Library, 1995), 20.

[8] Psalm 19:1; Romans 1:18–21; 2:14–15

CHAPTER TWO

OUR JEWISH NEIGHBORS

Ben and Sarah Goldberg and their two children are settling in for their every-Friday-evening routine. Just before sunset, Sarah lights two Shabbat candles, covering her eyes as she recites a blessing in Hebrew, in keeping with the ancient tradition. At dinnertime, Ben and Sarah sit down with their two young children. Ben reads Proverbs 31 (the "worthy woman" chapter) in English to honor his wife. Then together they pronounce a blessing on their children. Their weekly Shabbat observance has begun. For twenty-five hours, until the sun sets Saturday evening, they will enjoy each other's company—read books, take naps, short walks—but they will not text, surf the Internet, talk on the phone, watch TV, cook, or do any other work. They may or may not attend the Sabbath service at the synagogue Saturday morning; that depends on how well their children sleep tonight. But each week, as they "take their hands off the world" for this one night and day, they will feel the blessing of rest ordained by God himself.

Ari Kaplan, on the other hand, will attend the Shabbat service in the morning as he has virtually every Saturday for as long as he can remember. As an active member of a conservative congregation in Raleigh, North Carolina, Ari is responsible for recruiting his fellow members who will receive "honors" during the Shabbat service; that is, they will be asked to "ascend" ("aliyah" means ascend, like the "Psalms of Ascent") to the stage (called the "bema," pronounced "BEE-mah") to either help open the Ark (the much-decorated closet on stage that houses several Torah scrolls), remove the scroll and place it on the podium, recite one of the blessings in Hebrew before a section of the Torah is read, or read from the Torah themselves (in Hebrew). For three hours, the Rabbi and Cantor will emcee the service, but many others will participate, with Ari directing the traffic to the bema.

Jeff and Denise Cohen will not be resting tonight, nor will they attend a synagogue service in the morning. Jeff, a lawyer, and Denise, a family practice physician, live in suburban Chicago, where they look forward to dinner tonight at a favorite restaurant, followed by a long Saturday bike ride and an afternoon of napping and reading. Jeff grew up in a "non-observant" Jewish home; his family did not attend synagogue, Jeff was not "initiated" ("bar mitzvah") at age thirteen, he cannot read Hebrew, he rarely celebrates Jewish holidays, and he has never been to Israel.[1] He met Denise in college. She was raised in a nominal Episcopalian family. When she and Jeff fell in love and moved in together, they rarely talked about their religious upbringings. It simply wasn't an issue. Until now. They have just started talking about getting married and starting a family. What kind of wedding should they have—Jewish or Christian? Or should they plan a civil ceremony, then host a reception for their family and friends? And should they introduce their future children to spiritual traditions, both Jewish and Christian? If so, what do they teach their children about the significance of those traditions?

In some ways, it is difficult to paint a picture of a "typical" Friday evening for "typical" American Jews. Even the label "Jew" (short for Judah, the largest of the twelve ancient tribes) is problematic, laden with almost two millennia (if not more) of anti-Semitism that those of us who are not Jewish cannot fully appreciate. Any description of Judaism in North

America is not one and the same as a description of a typical "Jewish" experience in North America. Based on 2015 numbers, nearly fifteen million people of Jewish background exist worldwide; six million of them reside in the United States. Another six million call Israel home. The rest are part of the wider Jewish diaspora scattered around the globe.

Not all people of Jewish ethnicity embrace the religion we now call "Judaism." Christian readers may be especially susceptible to confusing modern Judaism with "the religion of the Old Testament."[2] In fact, I have wondered how many readers might be tempted to skip this chapter altogether, thinking, "I have been in Sunday school my whole life. I already know about Judaism." Yes, religious Jews read the "Old Testament," which in this chapter we will refer to as "the Hebrew Bible," as my Jewish friends do. Yes, they speak of God, Scripture, covenant, and salvation. Yes, they repeat the Bible stories we have learned since childhood. But many of those words and some of those stories are interpreted in ways that differ significantly from Christian understandings. That is why Norman Solomon observes, "The two religions [Judaism and Christianity] are divided rather than united by a common language."[3] So don't skip this chapter! Tell your friends who did to come back and read it. Because this chapter focuses on the religion of Judaism in its various forms, emphasizing what is most common to most "observant" Jews.

Significant Figures

The central figure in Judaism is God, of course, a Being like no other. Equating anyone or anything with God is blasphemy. The Patriarchs Abraham, Isaac, and Jacob (pronounced "Avram," "Yitzak," and "Yakov" in modern Hebrew) played key roles in the establishment of "the children of Israel" as a distinct people group, as did Kings David and Solomon. Their names are mentioned frequently in synagogue services. God gave Moses the Law, or "Torah" (pronounced "Toh-RAH," emphasis on the last syllable) on Mount Sinai. But "Torah" no longer refers simply to the first five books of the Bible, nor to the Hebrew Bible itself. Over the centuries, the term "Torah" has expanded to mean "teaching" or "instruction." That teaching includes the interpretations of the first five books handed down from one generation of rabbis to the next since ancient times. Many (though not all)

Jewish sects trace the origins of these rabbinic interpretations back to Moses himself. In other words, Moses not only received the "Written Torah" on Mount Sinai, God also revealed the "Oral Torah" ("Oral" because it wasn't written down initially). Those interpretations were eventually put in writing in the encyclopedia-like volumes known as Talmud. When people speak of "Torah study," they are including the study of these writings. For that reason, those rabbis ("teachers") involved in the transmission of these oral traditions are key figures in Judaism. That is why scholars often use the expression "Rabbinic Judaism" to distinguish between modern Judaism and "the religion of the Old Testament."

Famous Rabbis

In the ancient world, rabbis Hillel (d. 10 AD) and Shammai (d. 30 AD) were foremost among those teachers. They were partners in Torah study and contemporaries of Jesus. Hillel was born in Babylon but immigrated to Palestine, where he devoted the rest of his life to Torah study. Eventually, the Sanhedrin, the governing religious body, named him President. The most famous anecdote about Hillel reflects his reputation for wisdom. A Gentile once challenged him, saying that if Hillel could explain to him (the Gentile) the whole Torah while standing on one foot, the Gentile would convert. Hillel, balancing on that one foot, replied, "What is hateful to you, do not do to your neighbor. That is the whole Torah; the rest is the explanation of this—go and study it!"[4] When the same Gentile posed the same question to Hillel's friend, Shammai, he is said to have chased him out of his house with a stick. (Let's just say that Shammai was not known for his patience.) He and his students ("the House of Shammai") were regarded as stricter in their interpretation of the Law than the "House of Hillel," though the two leaders were friends.

Their descendants dominated Torah interpretation for generations after them; both schools survived the destruction of Jerusalem and the Temple in 70 AD. Gamaliel, whom Paul identified as his own teacher and who makes a cameo appearance in Acts 5, was the grandson of Hillel. (The sect of the Pharisees to which he belonged was perhaps the forerunner to modern Rabbinic Judaism.) Gamaliel's grandson, known as Gamaliel II or "Gamaliel of Yavne," reconvened the Sanhedrin in the city of Yavne south of Jaffa ("Joppa" in the Bible) after the catastrophe of 70 AD and helped ensure the continuity of Torah study.

Rabbi Akiba (pronounced "Akiva") ben Joseph lived in the same period. From humble origins, he herded the sheep owned by a wealthy man whose daughter took notice of Akiba. After they married, he had the resources to dedicate the rest of his life to Torah study. In time he gathered a following of several thousand students. One of his most famous sayings was, "All that God does he does for the good."[5] He held firmly to that conviction despite the hardships he suffered late in life. As an old man he believed Simon Bar Kochba to be the Messiah who would liberate Israel from Roman occupation and rebuild the temple. Rabbi Akiba, like Bar Kochba, was captured and executed by the Romans in 135 AD.

Other Key Figures

Through all this history, the commentaries of the rabbis were passed down orally, some believe, going all the way back to Moses. Judah the Nasi ("Judah the Prince," or "Judah the President," circa 135–219), a resident of Galilee, led the effort to preserve those oral traditions in writing. The finished product was called "Mishna," from the Hebrew word for "repetition," a reference to the method by which these commentaries had been received and continue to be learned in modern times. Students in modern Yeshivot (plural of "yeshiva," a Torah study center) spend much time memorizing by rote and "repeating" out loud the biblical texts and the rabbinical interpretations of those texts.

Other rabbis of note include Shlomo Itzchaki (that is, "Solomon son of Isaac"), more commonly known by his nickname, Rashi (1040–1105). His *Commentary on the Pentateuch*, the first book ever printed in Hebrew (in 1475), is still read today, and Torah students still study in the school he established in Worms, Germany. A century after Rashi, Moses Maimonides (1138–1204), nicknamed "Rambam," would leave his mark on Judaism. Born in Cordoba, Spain, under Muslim rule, Moses's family fled to Cairo when a more puritanical Muslim leader assumed power and threatened Christians and Jews. Equipped with a gifted mind and great curiosity, "Rambam" devoted himself to the study of science, medicine, philosophy, and religion. His "Thirteen Principles of the Faith" became something of a creed in Judaism; they are still cited today.

Rabbi Yisrael ben Eliezer (1698–1760) came to prominence, not for his keen mind, but for exuberant devotion to God in prayer, song, and dance. Known by his honorific title, Master Baal Shem Tov ("Master of the Good Name"), Eliezer led a spiritual revival of "Chasidim" (pronounced "Kha-si-deem") or "piety" in what is now the Ukraine. To this day, Chasidic Jews sing and dance as an expression of the joy of living in the presence of God, to the chagrin of their critics, who prefer more serious Torah study over such displays.

Moses Mendelssohn (1729–1786) lived at the opposite end of this spiritual spectrum. As a secular teacher in Berlin, he doesn't really belong on this list of rabbis who perpetuated Torah study and, thereby, Judaism, down to the modern era. On the other hand, Mendelssohn's advocacy for Jewish participation in the wider culture as much as their religious scruples would allow, his efforts to advance what we would today call "the separation of church and state," and his general credibility in German society as a thinker, addressed the issues that were critical to the survival of people of Jewish heritage in the centuries that followed.

Finally, Theodor Herzl's (1860–1904) name belongs on this list of significant figures, not because of his faith in God—he was not a religious man—but because of his role in helping establish the State of Israel. A Hungarian socialist, Herzl published a pamphlet entitled "The Jewish State" in 1896 which put in writing the message he proclaimed around Europe to anyone who would listen. The Jewish people, he argued, should be granted a Jewish State in their traditional homeland, the land of Palestine. Because of his efforts, though he did not live to see them bear fruit, he is known by many as the "Father of Zionism." Given the importance of the State of Israel in modern Judaism, Herzl deserves this honorable mention here.

Significant Beliefs

No universal creed encapsulates the basics of faith for all Jewish believers in God. Jewish texts and websites often refer to Maimonides' "Thirteen Principles of the Faith," even though eight hundred years have passed since he wrote them. The first five, all about God, are common convictions among observant Jews I know:

1. The Creator is Author and Guide of everything that exists.
2. The Creator is One. His unity is unlike that of anything else. He is our God and exists eternally.
3. The Creator has no body or physical characteristics, and cannot be compared with anything that exists.
4. The Creator is first and last of all things.
5. It is right to pray to the Creator, but to no other being.[6]

In orthodox circles, it is common to see the name of God written with a missing letter, as in G_d. The practice is an attempt to avoid violating the third commandment, "You shall not misuse the name of the LORD your God" (Ex. 20:7). It is more common these days to see the name of God written and spoken in all but Orthodox synagogues in North America.

The centrality of faith in God is affirmed in the confession, "Shema Yisrael" ("Hear, O Israel"), usually referred to in short as "the Shema." The full statement (from Deuteronomy 6:4–5) is familiar to Christians as well: "Hear, O Israel: The LORD our God, the LORD is one. Love the LORD your God with all your heart and with all your soul and with all your strength." The confession is chanted in Hebrew near the beginning of every synagogue service. In keeping with the instructions that follow (in Deuteronomy 6:6–9), adherents of Judaism do "tie them as symbols on [their] hands and bind them on [their] foreheads." Called "phylacteries" in English, *tefillin* are small boxes males attach to the arm (the one they don't write with, so to the left arm of a right-handed person and the right arm of a left-handed person) and to the top of the forehead, with leather straps holding them in place. Four passages written on four tiny pieces of parchment—Deuteronomy 6:4–9, Deuteronomy 11:13–21 (which essentially repeats Deuteronomy 6:4–9), Exodus 13:1–10 (about Israel's deliverance from bondage in Egypt), and Exodus 13:11–16 (instructions to teach children that redemption story)—are placed in the boxes. Tefillin are worn during synagogue services and during individual daily prayers. Based on that same command in Deuteronomy 6, people also affix "mezuzot" (literally "doorposts," singular is "mezuzah") to the doorframes of their houses. Mezuzot contain the two passages from

Deuteronomy 6 and 11 that command this practice. Inhabitants of the house touch the mezuzah when they enter, then kiss the hand that touched the box as a reminder that loving God with heart, soul, and strength is paramount.[7]

I do not want to leave the impression that all religious Jews who are serious about their faith wear phylacteries, adorn their doorposts with mezuzot, or keep the Sabbath and kosher food laws. What about Jewish folk you meet who seem to question the very existence of God? I have many such friends. Some of them show little patience for the "Ultra-Orthodox" traditions described below. Many are frustrated by what they perceive to be one-sided politics in Israel that continue to turn a blind eye to the establishment and embellishment of Jewish settlements in Palestinian territories and hinder peace talks with the Palestinians. I am reminded (by my Jewish friends) that "Israel" means "wrestles with God." While Christians and Muslims emphasize submission to God, Judaism encourages lament, which includes at least an element of complaint. We hear it in the rants of Job, in the arguments of prophets like Habakkuk, and in the "Lamentations" of Jeremiah, to name just a few. We should not be surprised when we meet Jews who do not seem "faithful" by our standards (or by the standards of many observant Jews), but who are still proud of their Jewish heritage.

Scripture

God reveals himself in Scripture, the Hebrew Bible, identical in content to what Christians call the Old Testament. But the thirty-nine books of the Christian Old Testament are divided differently in the Hebrew Bible. For example, 1 and 2 Samuel, 1 and 2 Kings, 1 and 2 Chronicles are each combined into one book—Samuel, Kings, and Chronicles—though in daily Torah study rabbis and students alike may refer to "Kings One" or "Kings Two." The twelve minor prophets are combined into one book, "The Book of the Twelve," which begins with Hosea and ends with Malachi. Furthermore, Ezra and Nehemiah are combined as one book, which brings the total number of books to twenty-four, not thirty-nine. The Hebrew Bible as a whole is called "Tanakh," an acronym formed from the first Hebrew letters for each genre of books. The "T" stands for "Torah" (technically the first five books), the "Na" for the prophets, and the "Kh" for the "Writings," that is, everything else. Just as in broadly-defined Christian circles, in Judaism a spectrum of thought exists regarding how literally to interpret the Bible, with a quite literal reading on the most conservative ("Orthodox") end and a more liberal interpretation on the other.

Covenant Loyalty

Judaism places greater emphasis on practice than on theory, on obedience than on belief. Covenant loyalty, perhaps the highest virtue in Judaism, is demonstrated by Torah study and by compliance with Jewish law ("*halakhah*"). The foundation of the law is the Ten Commandments; the details are spelled out (to some extent) in the 613 commands (by the rabbis' count) that follow in the rest of the Pentateuch. But what about those matters about which the law is unclear? It is here that the "Oral Torah" mentioned above comes into play. According to the Mishna, God revealed these interpretations to Moses to serve as a "fence around the law."[8] That is, to guard against inadvertent violations of God's commands, the faithful must observe rules even more stringent than the commands written in the law. Once again, those interpretations were passed down an unbroken chain of command through the rabbis. Many practices in Judaism—like typing the name of God as G_d— trace their roots to that "fence."

The "kosher" practice (which we will explore below), for example, of separating meat and dairy, preparing meat dishes in one kitchen and dairy dishes in another, and so on, is inspired by the prohibition, repeated three times in the Bible, against cooking "a young goat in its mother's milk" (Ex. 23:16; 34:26; and Deut. 14:21). To be sure, the practice (of boiling the off-spring of an animal in the milk of its own mother) offends our modern sensibilities. But why all this fuss? What might be the back story behind such a law? Does it have something to do with Canaanite animal sacrifices? Is this a case of God preparing Israel to keep her distance from her neighbors when the people enter the Promised Land? Those may be good reasons for this law. But for many people, the more important question is, "How do we obey?" With the multiple layers of tradition that developed in response to this rule that include the many restrictions about mixing meat and dairy products, the "fence around the law" comes into view. In restaurants in Israel, officials hired to enforce such food laws make sure, for example, that consumers don't eat a hamburger and ice cream at the same table.

I should also mention that many Israelis—polls suggest it may be a majority now—oppose the imposition of such rules on the public. Likewise, it would paint the wrong picture to suggest that even the majority of adherents to Judaism are this meticulous about observing the law. Rabbis in the largest Jewish sects in America (Reform and Conservative congregations) are not so legalistic about the 613 commands. They are more concerned about finding the principle behind the law, its contemporary application, and the blessing that comes to those who abide by it.

The Talmud

In the centuries after the Mishna was compiled in written form, rabbis who lived and taught after the destruction of the Temple in 70 AD interacted with their ancient counterparts in lively debates. Their commentaries on the Mishna were called "Gemara" from the root of the word for "study" (in Aramaic). Those comments were added to the margins of the Mishna and published together in what is now called the Talmud. There are two versions of the Talmud, one produced in Babylon called the "Babylonian Talmud" and the other compiled in Jerusalem and called the "Jerusalem Talmud." The former is considered by many to be more authoritative since it is older. Both versions are divided into six parts based on six broad topics: Agriculture, Appointed Times, Women, Order of Damages, Holy Things, and Purities.

The After-Life

Proper motivation for obedience is also a common theme in Jewish teaching. "Wanting to go to Heaven" is not the most compelling reason to obey. Reward-driven obedience strikes my Jewish friends as childish. It is enough that God loves us by offering guidance through the Torah, and it is enough for us to show our love for him by our compliance.

As many have noted, the Hebrew Bible says little about the after-life. And some of what is written is not reassuring. The author of Ecclesiastes wonders out loud if the soul of man is different than the soul of an animal. "Who knows if the spirit of man rises upward and if the spirit of the animal goes down into the earth" (3:21)? Did a moment of despair find its way into the author's spiritual journal? By the end of Ecclesiastes, the writer sounds more confident: "the dust returns to the ground it came from, and the spirit returns to God who gave it" (12:7). Still, it is fair to say that the Hebrew Bible reveals less about Heaven than the New Testament does.

The Messiah

Many (but not all) observant Jews believe that the Messiah ("Mashiach"), the "Anointed One," will come. He will be a charismatic hero, but not a divine being. His agenda will include rebuilding the Temple in Jerusalem and re-establishing proper worship there (Ezek. 37:18–28), returning all Jews to Israel (Jer. 23:8), and ushering in an age of world peace where "nation will not take up sword against nation, nor will they train for war anymore" (Isa. 2:4). From a Jewish perspective, Jesus could not have been the Messiah, mainly because he failed to do all of those things. Furthermore, Christian claims that Jesus was God (not just Messiah) are blasphemous, since the fundamental conviction, affirmed every time the Shema is recited, is "The Lord is one." Jewish sects on the liberal end of the theological spectrum do not necessarily expect a human Messiah to come but understand those biblical prophecies as metaphors.

Significant Practices

I described above the priority of Torah study as the primary way of showing devotion to God. Torah study ranks as the most significant practice in modern Judaism. The Torah is read in its entirety in synagogue services every calendar year based on a reading schedule. Synagogues follow the liturgical calendar of their larger national association and read the designated "Torah portion" each Saturday, beginning with Genesis in the New Year ("Rosh Hoshanah") and ending with Deuteronomy by year's end. Synagogue services open with a series of blessings read from the Psalms. Then the Torah scrolls, covered with very decorative materials, are taken from the Ark and carried around the room with great respect. Congregants touch the scroll with their prayer book (the book that contains the blessings and prayers recited throughout the service), then kiss the book that touched the scroll. The scroll is then "undressed" and laid on the podium.

The assigned Torah portion is then read in Hebrew, usually by a member of the congregation, not by the rabbi. Readers are careful not to touch the scroll itself with their hands, but use a pointer to keep their place as they read.

After the Torah portion is read in Hebrew, an excerpt taken from the rest of the Bible (usually the prophets) that is thought to be related to that Torah portion is read. This excerpt is called the "Haftarah" reading, from the Hebrew word for "conclusion."[9] The rabbi will then preach a brief sermon expounding on the reading for the day and making contemporary application. Toward the end of the service, the Torah scroll is returned to the Ark, prayers and blessings are pronounced for the nation, for the State of Israel, and for those in mourning. The service concludes with "Kiddush," a blessing over special bread and wine.

Attendance at synagogue services is not the mark of true commitment that church attendance tends to be in Christian circles. Faithfulness to Torah is measured in many other ways, including keeping the Sabbath, observing food laws, life cycle rituals, and feast days, as well as a commitment to charitable giving with the goal of "repairing the world."

Keeping the Sabbath, Keeping Kosher

The fourth commandment requires Israel to "remember the Sabbath day by keeping it holy" (Ex. 20:8). The details of Sabbath observance are based on the traditions handed down from generation to generation. The opening paragraph of this chapter provides a brief sketch of a typical Shabbat meal as Sabbath begins on Friday evening. Many observant Jews adhere to a "kosher" diet; "kosher" comes from a mispronunciation of the Hebrew word "kashrut" meaning "proper." The foundation of what is "proper" and what is not is found in the Bible in the distinction between "clean" and "unclean" foods (in Leviticus 11, for example). Kosher guidelines also include proper ways to prepare food.

Some Bible scholars (not just Jewish ones) speculate that health concerns in the context of an ancient environment shaped these laws. Others believe what was "proper" had more to do with putting distance between the people of Israel and pagan customs. The Bible does not explain these rules. Observant Jews say they do not need an explanation. The details of kosher dietary restrictions are worked out in the Talmud.

Life-Cycle Celebrations

In Judaism as in other religions, there are important life-cycle rituals. Male infants are circumcised on the eighth day after birth. The ceremony, called "Brit Milah" ("Covenant of Circumcision"), or "Bris," is based on the original covenant God made with Abraham (Gen. 17:10–14). The surgical procedure is performed by a "mohel" (rhymes with "oil"), and a blessing is offered by a rabbi. The child is given a Hebrew name, regardless of what other name is written on his birth certificate. He will be called by his Hebrew name at any time in the future when he is called to the bema during a synagogue service. Female infants are blessed and given a Hebrew name the first time their father makes "Aliyah" ("ascends" to the stage during a synagogue service) after her birth.

Traditionally, fathers are held accountable for their children's sins until their thirteenth birthday for boys; twelfth birthday for girls. On that birthday, they automatically become a "son" or "daughter of the covenant," a "bar mitzvah" ("bar" means "boy," "mitvah" means "commandment") or "bat mitzvah" ("bat" means "girl"). In modern times, the ceremony that marks the occasion has become quite elaborate. The most important part of it takes place in the synagogue on the Saturday morning in the week of the child's birthday. The "bar" or "bat mitzvah" reads part of the Torah portion (in Hebrew) and offers a brief interpretation and application of the text they have read. Blessings from parents and extended family members follow, along with gifts from the synagogue and a reception. Bat mitzvah ceremonies (for girls) occur only in Reform and Conservative congregations, not in Orthodox ones. But in all Jewish sects, the child is now responsible for his or her own sins; the male child can be counted toward the quorum ("minyan") of ten men (or women in some synagogues), the number required before a formal prayer service can take place.

The Talmud gives few instructions about wedding ceremonies. Traditionally, brides are veiled (like Rebecca was veiled when she met Isaac). The ceremony takes place under a canopy ("chuppah"), a symbol of the home they are forming. Blessings are recited by the bride and groom, and rings are exchanged. At the end of the ceremony, the groom smashes a glass (sometimes only a small piece of glass) under his foot in memory of the destruction of the Temple.

At death, the body is washed and wrapped in a prayer shawl. Cremation is forbidden, as are open-casket funerals.[10] After the burial, tradition dictates that the immediate family members gather in the home of the deceased to "sit shiva" for seven days. ("Shiva" means "seven.") They are not permitted to work or bathe during that period. Of course, practices vary in modern Judaism, depending on the level of strictness of the sect to which the family belongs.

Holy Days

The observance of Holy Days is significant for many Jews, even for the less observant. The Jewish calendar counts years from creation forward. The traditional year of creation was 3760 BC on the Gregorian calendar; that is the year zero on the Jewish religious calendar. I am writing this chapter in the year 5776 AM (for "Anno Mundi" or "Year of the World"). "Rosh Hoshanah" marks the "Head of the Year," that is, the Jewish New Year, which usually takes place in September or October on the secular calendar. It is followed days later by Yom Kippur, the "Day of Atonement." Those ten days are known as "Days of Awe" or the "High Holy Days," underscoring the importance of the season. Synagogues in the United States are more full than normal on Yom Kippur, like many churches are more filled with worshipers on Easter and Christmas. The Day of Atonement is a day of humble penitence before God; observant Jews fast on this day.

Sukkot (pronounced "sue-KOAT") or "The Feast of Tents" follows on the calendar, commemorating the Israelites' wandering in the wilderness. In sympathy with their ancestors, Jewish families build temporary shelters in their backyard, eat meals in them, and often sleep in them. Simchat Torah (literally "rejoicing in the Law") is celebrated on the first day after Sukkot, marking the point where the entire Torah has been read and the cycle of readings for the new year begins again in Genesis.

Hannukah often coincides on the calendar with the Christmas holidays, but it celebrates the victory of Judas Maccabee over the Syrian invader, Antiochus IV, and the rededication of the Temple (that the intruder had defiled) in the year 164 BC.

Pesach ("Passover") comes in the spring of the year (around Christian Easter; Jesus was crucified during Passover Week). It is arguably the most important of all Jewish holy days, given the pivotal historical significance of Israel's release from Egyptian captivity in ancient times. The meal served on the first night (sometimes the first two nights) of Passover is called "Seder," from the Hebrew word that means "order." The word itself suggests the importance of eating the meal in the prescribed way. Usually prepared and served in a private home, the Seder menu includes symbolic foods like "bitter herbs," a boiled egg, unleavened bread, and a sweet mixture of walnuts, honey, apples, cinnamon, and wine called "charoset" (HA-ROT-zet). Four cups of wine are also drunk, each in turn, according to the guidebook, called "Haggadah." Not all guidebooks are identical; Jewish traditions vary depending on the families' cultures of origin. But every Haggadah includes a retelling of the story of the Exodus and God's initial instructions for the Passover meal (in Exodus 12). Shavuot (literally "Weeks"), like Pentecost, comes seven weeks after Passover and, in modern Judaism, celebrates God's gift of Torah to his people.

Tikkun Olam

The expression "repairing the world" ("*tikkun olam*") points to the goal of charitable giving in modern Judaism. To be sure, the phrase, which does not appear in the Hebrew Bible, was used in the Mishna to either encourage the faithful to abolish idolatry (and thereby "repair the world") or to defend the rights of the marginalized (including women).

A more mystical understanding of "repairing the world," originating in the Kabbalah (see "Sects and Developments" below), has provided something of a rallying cry for some socially-minded adherents of Judaism. On the other hand, Orthodox commentary on "tikkun olam" is often somewhat cynical, blaming left-leaning Jews for repurposing this phrase to suit their social agenda.

Sects and Developments

The history of the Jewish people is a history of exile and return. Often, the "children of Israel" did not return after periods of exile but settled permanently in lands far from the Middle East. Settlement patterns created two broad divisions or subcultures known in Hebrew as "Ashkenazim" and "Sephardim." Traditionally, Ashkenazi Jews populated mainly France,

Germany, and Eastern Europe, while Sephardic Jews were predominant in Spain, Portugal, North Africa, and the Middle East. Many Ashkenazim spoke Yiddish (some still do), a mixture of German, Hebrew, and Aramaic. Sephardic Jews once spoke a combination of Hebrew and Spanish called Ladino, though it is virtually a dead language today. Ashkenazic Jews trace their name to Ashkenaz, one of Noah's great grandsons (Gen. 10:3) while the label "Sephardim" likely comes from a reference to Sepharad (Obad. 20) which was mistakenly identified as Spain. Though most of the early Jewish settlers in the United States were of Sephardic descent, 80 percent of the world's Jews today are Ashkenazim. In terms of theology, there is little difference, though Sephardic Jews gravitate in larger proportions to the Orthodox end of the spectrum. Otherwise, the two groups differ in style of dress, music, foods, and in other cultural incidentals.

The Enlightenment in Europe drove a wedge between Jews who wished to blend in with the wider culture and those who resisted. Theological debates over the proper interpretation of the Bible also led to divisions that persist in our day. The largest body of Jewish congregations in the United States is the Reform movement. Conservative Judaism ranks second behind Reform Judaism in the number of U.S. adherents. Orthodox adherents constitute the third largest Jewish sect in America.

According to a recent study by the Pew Research Center, about six out of ten Orthodox Jews in America identify themselves as "Haredim," literally "those who tremble" at the word of God.[11] Called "Ultra-Orthodox" by outsiders, the Haredim distinguish themselves from other Orthodox Jews by their strict separation from all things secular. Reconstructionist Judaism constitutes the fourth largest Jewish sect in America. Its mission is to focus on the relevance of the Jewish religious and cultural heritage for our time.

Reform, Conservative, and Reconstructionist groups are not allowed to operate in Israel, at least not legally. A young couple who hosted us for a Shabbat meal in Jerusalem one evening described their synagogue as "far, far, far left Orthodox." Both of them were born in North America in observant families who were members of Conservative synagogues. They represent many like-minded Israelis when they complain about the power of the "Jerusalem Rabbinate," the Orthodox authority recognized by the secular government to make judgments about religious matters, including the enforcement of kosher dietary laws, the licensing of rabbis, and the functioning of synagogues.

The number of "Messianic" congregations in the United States may be increasing. For obvious reasons, they are not included in lists of other Jewish organizations or associations. They are the subject of much controversy in Israel. Jews of other affiliations or no affiliation are allowed to immigrate to Israel, even offered financial support for the first few years to encourage more to make that move. But those who claim to be "Messianic" are not allowed to immigrate.

In addition to these sects, other movements with large numbers of followers include the Chasidim mentioned above, the spiritual descendants of revivalist Rabbi Yisrael ben Eliezer (1698–1760), better known by his nickname, Master Baal Shem Tov, "Master of the Good Name." Followers express their devotion through song and dance. They are subdivided into other groups as well. Kabbalah (from a Hebrew word that means "receiving," as in the way a tradition is "received" from those who pass it down) is a form of Jewish mysticism based in part on an ancient Aramaic text known as "Zohar" (literally "Radiance") which contains allegorical interpretations of the Hebrew Bible. Kabbalists emphasize themes like "universal energy," "reconnecting with the Light," the "law of cause and effect," and astrology, apparently borrowing from Eastern religions. Kabbalah has garnered media attention in North America thanks to celebrities' interest in it.

The Holocaust

Historians estimate that the six million Jews who died in the genocide perpetrated by Nazi Germany between 1933 and 1945 constituted as much as two-thirds of the Jewish population of Europe at the time. The "Holocaust" (Greek for "burn completely"), also known as the "Shoah" (Hebrew for "catastrophe"), was the horrific culmination of centuries of institutionalized hatred toward people of Jewish descent.

Jewish people struggle to explain it. Some wonder if somehow Jews bore the sins of the world, like Isaiah's "suffering servant." Others suggest that perhaps the tragedy was like "birth pangs" that will give way to a new world of redemption and peace. Still others believe the faithful must, like

Job, live on without any explanation, but with resolve to never allow them-selves to be so vulnerable and defenseless again.

"Zionism" and the State of Israel

The State of Israel was officially established with a declaration by its first President, David Ben Gurion, on May 14, 1948. But decades of "Zionism"—the push among Jews to establish a state in their traditional homeland—made it possible. Ongoing persecution of Jewish people in Europe drew many to immigrate to Palestine in the late nineteenth century. By 1914, when World War I began, the population of Palestine was six hundred fifty thousand; only sixty thousand, or 9 percent, were Jews. Under Ottoman control at the time, much of the land in the region was owned by absentee Arab landlords, not by the Palestinians who lived there. Jewish people found it relatively easy to purchase land from those foreign owners. The British governed the region after the collapse of the Ottoman Empire at the end of the war. The pace of Jewish immigration from Europe and Russia increased significantly, as more and more Jews responded to the popular slogan, "A land without a people for a people without a land."

For obvious reasons, the local Arab population took offense. Attempts by foreign governments to slow the flow of Jews into Palestine didn't stop the momentum for statehood. By 1947, people of Jewish origin still owned only 6 percent of the land in Palestine, but they constituted 27 percent of the population. That year, the United Nations Partition Plan proposed to create two states: a Jewish State would be home to half a million Jews and the same number of Arabs and would occupy 55 percent of the land. The Arab State would be established on the remaining 45 percent of the land and would be home to seven hundred fifty thousand Arabs and fewer than ten thousand Jews. The Arab population and all of Palestine's neighbors rejected the plan. The British, weary of the conflict, withdrew on May 14, 1948, the very day Israel declared its sovereignty as a nation. War broke out immediately as Israel's neighbors simultaneously attacked the new state, intent on destroying it. Three more wars have followed in subsequent years, with many more violent conflicts, attacks, counter-at-tacks, and protests in between.

Significant Points of Contact

I have taken my students to a Shabbat service at a synagogue at least twice a year for nearly twenty years. Every time I am reminded that, as a Gentile, we who are Christians have been "grafted in" to a vine from which we were estranged (Rom. 11:23). I think of Paul's words to the Gentile believers in Ephesus: "Remember that at that time you were separated from Christ, excluded from citizenship in Israel and foreigners to the covenants of the promise, without hope and without God in this world" (Eph. 2:12). I feel this kinship deeply when I am there, a kinship based on shared convictions about the God who reveals himself in Scripture, who enters into covenant with his children, and who intervenes in history for salvation's sake. Although it can be offensive to voice those feelings too loudly, because of the long, tragic story of "Christian" bigotry and anti-Semitism, I feel that common ground.[12]

My students and I can participate fully in the synagogue service, except for the fact that most of us can't speak or read Hebrew. The words that are read, sung, and prayed, we can read, sing, and pray. On occasion, when I am called to the bema to read the "Prayer for the Nations" ("nations" meaning Gentiles), I feel honored. Who better to read a "Prayer for the Nations" than one of those Gentiles on whose behalf the prayer is prayed?

Christian assemblies are another point of contact. They are actually patterned after synagogue services, with the public reading of Scripture, singing, prayer, and an exposition. Even Kiddush—the blessing of bread and wine at the end of the service—bears much resemblance to the Lord's Supper. The similarities should not be surprising, given that most of the earliest Christians were Jews who continued to attend the synagogue. The desire to "repair the world" as it is understood in all but the most conservative Jewish circles draws from the same spirit as "the ministry of reconciliation." The idea that the pristine world God created was broken by human sin and, therefore, stands in need of repair is perhaps *the* story of the Bible. The difference—and it is a significant one—is in the rest of that story.

Significant Points of Contrast

The differences are not hard to identify. Our conviction that Messiah did come, that the Kingdom he established was not of this world (and still isn't), is one of many reasons we believe he did not fail in his mission. He renewed his covenant with his people, a covenant that includes Gentiles like me. But it is a new covenant, even a new kind of covenant, written not on stone, but on the human heart. It is a covenant that comes with the promise that the Spirit of God will live inside us and empower us to obey and live submissively under the Lordship of Christ. From the standpoint of this new covenant, the Law and the many traditions inspired by rabbis' commentaries passed down from generation to generation in some ways obscure God's intentions. Jesus said, "You have let go of the commands of God and are holding on to the traditions of men" (Mark 7:8). And he's actually quoting Isaiah. I write this with fear and trembling, because I know most of us are tempted to do the same thing.

So when we have opportunity, we do our best to listen and understand these significant others—our Jewish friends and neighbors, religious and non-religious, observant and secular. We listen with respect, as if the story we're hearing is our own. Because it is. And we pray that God will give us another chance to share—without condescension, without a patronizing tone, without even a hint of the bigotry of the past, but share, with grace and truth—the rest of the story.

TALKING TOGETHER . . .

1. How do the stories of the Goldbergs, Cohens, and Ari Kaplan connect with you? How do their spiritual journeys compare with those of people you know from Jewish backgrounds?

2. What surprises you about the differences between Modern Judaism and "the religion of the Old Testament"?

3. How have the Holocaust and Zionism caused adherents of Modern Judaism to read Scripture in new ways?

4. Some Christians characterize Jewish practices, such as Sabbath-keeping, kosher food laws, and other rituals, as legalistic. Which of these practices do you find admirable in some way, and why?

5. What did you learn in this chapter that you had not understood until now about the conflict between the State of Israel and the Palestinian people?

6. The earliest Christian assemblies took place in synagogues, and the earliest believers drew on the patterns of the synagogue as they planned their assemblies. How is a Jewish synagogue service like a Christian assembly, and how are these assemblies different?

IF YOU WANT TO READ MORE . . .

Damkami, Jacob. *Why Me?* Jaffa, Israel: Jacob Damkami, 1997.

Gertel, Elliot B. *Over the Top Judaism: Precedents and Trends in the Depiction of Jewish Beliefs and Observances in Films and Television.* Lanham, MD: University Press of America, 2003.

Solomon, Norman. *Judaism: A Very Short Introduction.* Oxford: Oxford University Press, 1996.

Tolan, Sandy. *The Lemon Tree: An Arab, a Jew, and the Heart of the Middle East.* New York: Bloomsbury, 2006.

Websites: http://www.jewishvirtuallibrary.org/, http://www.reformjudaism.org/, and http://www.conservativejudaism.org.

Notes

[1] I will follow convention in using the term "non-observant" to refer to a person of Jewish lineage who is not actively engaged in the religion of Judaism.

[2] To borrow the language of Norman Solomon in *Judaism: A Very Short Introduction* (New York: Oxford University Press, 1996), 4.

[3] Ibid., 3.

[4] In the Talmud, Shabbat 31a, as translated by Shoshannah Brombacher, in "On One Foot: Tales from the Past," accessed January 16, 2017, http://www.chabad.org/library /article_cdo/aid/689306/jewish/On-One-Foot.htm.

[5] Berel Wein, "Rabbi Akiba," adapted by Yaakov Astor, www.jewishhistory.org, accessed March 18, 2017, http://www.jewishhistory.org/rabbi-akiva-2.

[6] Excerpted from Maimonides' *Commentary on the Mishnah* as translated by Norman Solomon, *Judaism*, 4. See also Edward Hoffman's *The Wisdom of Maimonides: The Life and Teachings of the Jewish Sage* (Boston: Trumpeter Books, 2008), 100–101.

[7] For the curious who took the time to read the endnotes, the Hebrew letter "shin" is inscribed on the outside of the mezuzah box; "shin" is the first letter in "the Name." And why are mezuzot placed at an angle? The most common answer is that the rabbis could not decide if it should be attached vertically or horizontally, so the angle was a compromise. The anecdote is also typical of some Talmudic debates, though others are of greater weight.

[8] Aboth 1:1 in the Herbert Danby, *The Mishnah: Translated from the Hebrew, with Introduction and Brief Explanatory Notes* (London: Oxford University Press, 1933), 446.

[9] Rabbi Feivel Strauss believes the practice of reading the Haftara may have begun when non-Jewish majorities forbade the public reading of the Torah. In correspondence with the author February 2, 2017.

[10] Strauss says cremation is performed in some Reform communities, but is still strongly discouraged. In correspondence with author February 2, 2017.

[11] "A Portrait of American Orthodox Jews," Pew Research Center website, August 26, 2015, accessed July 9, 2016, http://www.pewforum.org/2015/08/26/a-portrait-of -american-orthodox-jews/. My friend, Yossi Paz, an Israeli and native Hebrew speaker, says the better translation of "Haredim" is "fearings," as in "God-fearers." Correspondence with author January 18, 2017.

[12] My Jewish friends and acquaintances who proofread this chapter said they are not offended by this expression of kinship.

CHAPTER THREE

OUR MUSLIM NEIGHBORS

Rachel fell in love with Ahman when they were in college in California. Ahman was from Pakistan; he was a good and moral man, committed to his family and to his faith, and outspoken against extremists who, he said, do not represent true Islam. Rachel's parents referred to themselves as "lapsed Roman Catholics." Her own religious training as a child was minimal at best. Two years after meeting Ahman, she decided to convert to Islam, changed her name to Rashil (the Arabic equivalent of Rachel), then married Ahman. Together with their two children, their family invests much time and money at the Islamic Center near their home in Sacramento.

Aisha grew up in a Muslim home in Wichita, attended public schools, and in high school, as a statement of renewed commitment to her faith and without any pressure from her parents, decided to start wearing a *hijab*.[1] At first her friends were taken aback by her new look, but she felt they respected her for her commitment.

Gustavo found himself out of work and homeless in Atlanta when he wandered into a mosque downtown, not realizing it was a mosque. There he was fed and befriended. Eventually, a building contractor who regularly prayed at that mosque offered Gustavo a job. Impressed with the man's honesty, work ethic, and devotion—especially during the Ramadan fast—Gustavo began to study Islam. Later that same year, in front of a small audience of witnesses, he repeated the words in Arabic: "There is no God but Allah; Muhammad is his prophet."[2] With that simple confession, Gustavo became a Muslim.

These composite sketches of American Muslims represent the faith of a worldwide community of 1.5 billion people. It may come as a surprise that only 20 percent of the world's Muslims are Arabs. In fact, the most populous Muslim nations are, in order, Indonesia, Pakistan, India, Bangladesh, and Egypt. Only in Egypt is there a large Arab population, and even there the "Arab" identity is a controversial subject.[3] At last count, there are at least fifty nations with Muslim majorities. In the United States, an estimated 65–70 percent of Arab-Americans identify themselves as Christian.[4]

Significant Figures

From a Christian and Jewish perspective, the story of Islam begins in the Bible. Abram was clinging to God's promise that through him and his seed, all the nations of the earth would be blessed (Gen. 12:3). But he and Sarai weren't getting any younger and still had no offspring. Impatient with God's timetable, Sarai suggested (and Abram agreed) that they should produce an heir with Sarai's Egyptian servant, Hagar (Gen. 16:1–6). Trouble started as soon as Hagar found out she was pregnant with Ishmael. When Ishmael was thirteen years old, God required both him and his father to be circumcised as a sign of the covenant he had made with Abram (Gen. 17:23–27). When Sarai, now called Sarah, finally gave birth to Isaac, she feared that Ishmael might threaten her own son's status as the heir apparent, since Ishmael, not Isaac, was Abraham's oldest son. Hagar was driven into the desert, where she despaired for Ishmael's life. But God promised to make of Ishmael and his descendants a great nation that would inhabit the desert regions of Sinai (Gen. 21:17–21; 25:12–18).

Muslims believe that this whole account is the corrupted Jewish version, showing favoritism toward Isaac (the ancestor of the Jews) over Ishmael (the ancestor of the Arabs). In fact, Muslims believe it was Ishmael, not Isaac, who was almost sacrificed by his father when God called out to Abraham at the last minute and provided a ram as a substitute.[5] Muslims *do* believe in the Torah, but, they say, not this twisted version of it. Unfortunately, the uncorrupted version has been lost to history.

Allah and Muhammad

From a Muslim perspective, the most important figure in Islam is the one true God. Known as "Allah" in Arabic—the name Arabic-speaking Christians also use to refer to the Father of Jesus—he is the one and only. God has spoken in history through thousands of prophets including Adam, Abraham, Moses, and Jesus. But most recently he spoke through Muhammad, the "Seal of the Prophets." Muhammad's words were not his own. Muslims believe he was merely the messenger to whom Allah revealed the Qur'an through the angel Gabriel (Jibril in Arabic).

Muhammad was born in 570 AD in Mecca (Makkah in Arabic) in what is now Saudi Arabia.[6] Orphaned in childhood, Muhammad was taken in by a grandfather and uncle who were in the caravan business. His travels with them exposed the young boy to life beyond Arabia, including the religion of Christians and Jews. Polytheism and tribal warfare ruled Arabia at the time; most tribes worshiped multiple deities, and many Bedouin clans did not get along with each other. The Ka'aba (meaning "cube" in Arabic), the stone monument now draped in black cloth in Muhammad's hometown of Mecca, was a center of pagan worship. Pilgrims made their way there regularly to pay homage to the 360 gods said to be enshrined in the Ka'aba. Among them was a female "goddess" represented by a black stone (a meteorite).

Muhammad, on the other hand, was drawn to the monotheism of his forebears, like other *hanifs* ("pious ones") who traced their spiritual heritage to Ishmael (Ismail), Abraham's (Ibrahim's) oldest son. When he was twenty-five years old, Muhammad attracted the attention of a wealthy widow named Khadijah. They married in 595 and together had four daughters who survived into adulthood, but they had no sons.[7] I have heard some

Muslims speculate that if a male heir had lived to succeed him, his followers might have descended into worshiping Muhammad and his heirs instead of worshiping Allah alone.

In the year 610, while he was meditating on Mount Hira just outside of Mecca, Muhammad said that the angel Gabriel appeared to him, bathed in bright light. Gabriel said, "Recite," intending for Muhammad to repeat after him. Faithful to the command, Muhammad committed to memory everything Gabriel said.[8] It was the twenty-seventh day in the month of Ramadan, remembered by Muslims now as the "Night of Power" or the "Night of Destiny."

This was the first of the many revelations he would receive over the next twenty-two years, all of them delivered orally to Muhammad, who would eventually repeat them to those around him. These 114 messages comprise the Qur'an, which means "Recitation," the noun form of the first word Muhammad heard Gabriel say.[9] In the year 619 his beloved wife, Khadijah, died. While she was alive, Muhammad took no other wives, though customs at the time permitted polygamy. After her death, Muhammad married as many as eleven women (though the number of his wives is the subject of some debate within Islam), but apparently fathered no more children.[10]

The next year Muhammad made the famous "Night Journey" from Mecca to Jerusalem on a winged horse named Buraq. From Mount Moriah where the Jewish temple once stood, Muslims believe Muhammad miraculously ascended into Heaven, leaving his footprint on the large boulder now covered by the building known as "The Dome of the Rock." Ascending to the seventh heaven, Muhammad had an encounter with God that would reinforce his credibility as God's messenger.[11]

Still, he had his opponents in Mecca, some of whom felt threatened by his message of monotheism, fearful that it could undermine trade with the pagan pilgrims who frequented the city. As opposition grew, Muhammad felt guided by Allah to leave his hometown. The move from Mecca to Yathrib some two hundred fifty miles to the north, accompanied by the community of those who believed that the revelations he was receiving were from God, is known as "the Hijra" ("Migration"). The journey began on July 22, 622 AD. So significant was this moment in Islamic history that the Muslim calendar was recalibrated, and now counts the year 622 on the

Gregorian calendar as the year 0. I am writing this chapter in the summer of 2016, the year 1437 AH ("Anno Hijra") on the Muslim calendar.[12]

Muhammad's charismatic personality made him quite popular in Yathrib, later renamed Medina ("City of the Prophet"), where Muhammad succeeded in resolving disputes and uniting the local population.[13] Believing he had been wronged by his hometown, he engaged in many armed conflicts with Meccans. He was often outnumbered but usually successful. Those victories enhanced his reputation as a messenger of God, and the Muslim community grew.

He continued to receive revelations in Medina as he had in Mecca. In 630 he had won enough support to return to Mecca in triumph and gain control of the city. He destroyed the idols worshiped at the Ka'aba and made peace with all who were willing to live peaceably with Muslims. For non-Muslims, he required only that they not oppose him, that they abstain from supporting his enemies, and that they pay a tax for their own protection. Two years later, in 632, after a short illness, Muhammad died and was buried in Medina. Disagreements over who should succeed him divided the community and constitute the main division within Islam to this day. But in many ways, Muhammad had succeeded in uniting the different tribes of the region through a common faith.

Significant Beliefs

Arguably the most important concept in Islam is submission—submission to God who reveals his will for humankind in the Qur'an. In fact, the word "Islam" means submission; a "Muslim" is "one who submits."[14] The religion is Islam; Muslims are those who practice it. The ideal of submission is evident in Muslim prayer posture—bowing before God with the forehead pressed to the floor. The submission of the faithful is apparent in all of the "Five Pillars" (outlined below) and in many other ways.

Six Articles of Faith

Muslim teachers list six "articles of faith" as foundational. First is belief in God, in his oneness and his greatness. To say "God is one" suggests that he has no equals or partners. Christians are in view in this text in the Qur'an: "Say not 'Trinity': desist. It will be better for you, for God is one

God—Glory be to him. Far exalted is he above having a son" (Qur'an 4:171; 19:35). The oneness of God, as well as the status of Muhammad, is affirmed in the confession of faith repeated by every new convert and recited by the faithful throughout the day (either aloud or in one's mind): "There is no God but God; Muhammad is his prophet." To say, "God is greater" (*Allah-hu-akbar*)—a declaration repeated in the call to prayer—is to say that he is like no other being. Idolatry—equating anyone or anything with God—is the worst sin.[15]

The second article of faith is belief in God's angels. Muslims believe there are thousands of angels. Most prominent among them is Gabriel (Jibril), through whom they believe the Qur'an was delivered to Muhammad.

Third, belief in God's holy books is fundamental. Those holy books include the Torah (the first five books of the Old Testament), the Psalms, the "Gospel" (singular, *Injil* in Arabic), and the Qur'an. But both the Torah and the Gospel have been corrupted by Jews and Christians respectively, Muslims are taught. The former went astray with the story of Abraham, following Isaac's lineage to the exclusion of Ishmael's, as we noted earlier. The "Gospel" in its present form is full of blasphemy, since it includes references to Jesus as God, passages which Muslims believe were added to the stories of Jesus long after his death. Actually, the only parts of the Bible that can be trusted are those passages repeated in the Qur'an. (I'll say more about the Qur'an below.)

The fourth article of faith is belief in God's prophets and God's messengers. These include Adam, Abraham, Isaac, Moses, and Jesus. Muhammad is believed to be God's final messenger.

Fifth, Muslims believe in a Day of Judgment in which all the dead will rise to answer for their deeds. The main criterion by which all people will be judged is their belief in God and his prophet. "If anyone desires a religion other than Islam (submission to God), never will he be accepted of him, and in the hereafter he will be in the ranks of those who have lost all spiritual good" (Qur'an 3:85). A few verses later, "As to those who reject faith, and die rejecting, never would be accepted from any such as much gold as the earth contains, though they should offer it for ransom. For such is in store a penalty grievous and they will find no helpers" (Qur'an 3:91).

Believing that Christ is God is considered blasphemy; such believers will be hell-bound. "They do blaspheme who say, 'God is Christ, the Son of Mary.' But said Christ, 'O Children of Israel! Worship God, my Lord and your Lord.' Whoever joins other gods with God, God will forbid him the Garden [Paradise] and the Fire [Hell] will be his abode. There will for the wrong-doers be no one to help" (Qur'an 5:72). In fact, Jesus himself will stand as witness against Christians on the Day of Judgment (4:159).

To be sure, other passages in the Qur'an sound more inclusive. For example, "Those who believe in the Qur'an, and those that follow the Jewish scriptures, and the Christians and the Sabians [an ancient Christian sect]— any who believe in God and the last day and work righteousness shall have their reward" (Qur'an 2:62). This is why opinions vary among Muslims about the fate of "People of the Book" (Jews and Christians) on the Day of Judgment.

The sixth article of faith is belief in God's divine will, what some Christians might call "predestination." God knows all future events. He has already recorded the death date of every person. Non-Muslims often ask, "What do Muslims say about their fellow-Muslims killed by other Muslims in terrorist attacks?" The answer is that, although God does not condone terrorism, it was their day to die. Had they not been killed in that violent way, they would have died by some other means on that day. Confidence in the will of God is expressed in the word *inshallah*, "if God wills," which punctuates many sentences when Muslims speak about the future.

The Qur'an

Of all the books Muslims consider holy, the Qur'an is the most authoritative, not only because it is considered to be uncorrupted, but also because they believe it is the oldest. Muslims refer to the Qur'an as "the book of heaven." It was written by God, they believe, before human beings were created. God dictated the contents of the book word for word to Muhammad through the angel Gabriel, beginning on that most auspicious night in 610 AD. So they consider the Qur'an to be the very words of God, not the writings of Muhammad. Muslims would never say, "Muhammad says in Chapter 6, verse 25." In fact, part of the miracle of the Qur'an from a Muslim perspective is that Muhammad could neither read nor write; he merely repeated every message he received to those around him who believed the messages came directly from God. Furthermore, the Qur'an was revealed in Arabic; Muslims believe that it must be read in Arabic to be properly understood. Translations of the Qur'an into other languages are encouraged, but translations are considered "interpretations" of the Qur'an; the true Qur'an is in Arabic only.[16]

The Qur'an is about fourth-fifths as long as the New Testament. Of the 114 chapters or *surahs* (Arabic) in the Qur'an, Muhammad was said to have received eighty-six of them in Mecca and the remaining twenty-eight in Medina. The chapters are not arranged chronologically from beginning to end but according to their length, from longest to the shortest. The exception is the first chapter, called "The Opening" (*Fatiha*), which is recited either in whole or in part in daily prayers. This arrangement makes it difficult for the non-Muslim to place the revelations within the timeline of Muhammad's life.[17] But from the perspective of Muslim believers, the historical context of each message is mostly irrelevant, since these are the dictated words of God. Many entries do reflect events that were current at the time the message was revealed. For example, when Muhammad took as his wife a former daughter-in-law, this unusual move caused enough of a stir to warrant a message from God that essentially chastises Muhammad for second-guessing himself.

> More fitting that thou shouldst fear God. Then when Zaid [Muhammad's adopted son] had dissolved his marriage with her [Zainab] with the necessary formality, we joined her in marriage to thee in order that in future there may be no difficulty to the believers in the matter of marriage with the wives of their adopted sons when the latter have dissolved with the necessary formality their marriage with them. And God's command must be fulfilled. (Qur'an 33:37).

The collection of stories called the *Hadith* (see below) includes an explanation of the incident that gave rise to this revelation.[18]

For the most part, the Qur'an does not consist of narratives, though there are a few. For example, chapter 12 is entitled "Yusuf," the Arabic name for Joseph, and repeats the basic details of the Genesis account of Joseph's life. Instead of stories, the Qur'an addresses recurring themes, including God's divine will, proper ways to submit to him through confession (of belief in God and his messenger), prayer, fasting, and charity, and his blessings to those who obey. It also includes warnings about the Day of Judgment, the consequences of unbelief and evil deeds.

Jesus (called *Isa* in Arabic) is mentioned by name in the Qur'an twenty-five times. The Qur'an affirms his virgin birth (3:42–55), his miracles and the work of the Holy Spirit through him (2:87, 253), and his miraculous ascent into Heaven (3:55). But Jesus's divine status is denied. "It is not befitting to the majesty of God that he should beget a son" (19:35). The Qur'an is also adamant that Jesus did not die on the cross as Christians profess, but that only someone "who looked like him" was crucified in his place. "They killed him not, nor crucified him. But so it was made to appear to them" (4:157).[19] No, Jesus was taken up into Heaven by God, never having tasted death, and will return to Earth at the Day of Judgment. Jesus also foretells the coming of another messenger who will follow him: "Jesus, the son of Mary, said, 'O children of Israel! I am the apostle of God sent to you confirming the Law which came before me, and giving glad tidings of an apostle to come after me, whose name shall be Ahmad" (Qur'an 61:6). "Ahmad" means "one who is praised." Another way to say the same name? Muhammad.

Finally, convinced that the Qur'an is the dictated word of God, many Muslims devote themselves to committing it to memory in its entirety. Those who can recite it by heart are honored as *Huffaz* or "guardians."[20] Muslims also show great respect for printed copies of the Qur'an. The Qur'an is never laid on the floor, but placed on special book stands; no other books or objects are placed on top of it. A Muslim would never write in the Qur'an the way Christians write in our Bibles, nor would they purchase a "pocket edition" and carry it in their back pocket. That, too, would be considered disrespectful.

Significant Practices

Muslims introduce non-Muslims to Islamic practice by explaining the Five Pillars of Islam, usually listed in the following order.

First is the "confession of faith" or *Shahada*, repeating the statement (in Arabic), "There is no God but God, Muhammad is his prophet."[21] These are the first words whispered in a newborn baby's ear; they are the words a dying person hopes to utter with their final breath. These words are inscribed above the entrance to every mosque in the world, usually in Arabic and often in the local language as well.

The second pillar is prayer (*salat*). Faithful Muslims pray five times per day at set times—dawn, midday, mid-afternoon, sunset, and at night before bed. Of course, the times vary within the different time zones around the globe. For example, the midday prayer should be exactly halfway between sunrise and sunset. Therefore, midday will not be uniform on the clock around the world. Muslims in various regions publish the set times of prayer in advance, based on calculated times for sunrise and sunset.[22]

When the time for prayer is approaching, the "call to prayer," chanted by a *muezzin* (often recorded and played electronically in the United States), can be heard from the minaret, the tower that often identifies a worship center as a mosque. Those who pray must first purify themselves through ritual washing known as *wudu*. Ablution involves very specific instructions for washing the face and head, hands and wrists, and feet and ankles. Once purified, the person prepared to pray must not use the restroom or do anything else to nullify the cleansed state.

Those who gather at the mosque (*masjid*) to pray first remove their shoes, then wash in the washrooms provided. They then assemble in the prayer hall shoulder to shoulder in rows starting at the front facing the niche (*mihrab*), which is oriented toward Mecca. New rows are formed as needed, going toward the back of the room, as the set time for the prayer approaches. The words and movements that follow are all uniform. The leader recites certain portions of the prayer, and the congregants respond in a series of recited words and specified postures, from standing, to kneeling, to a prostrate position with the forehead touching the floor and the hands flat on the floor beside one's head.[23]

A typical Friday midday prayer lasts about fifteen minutes; it is usually preceded by a sermon. Since Friday is to Muslims what Sunday is to Christians, attendance at the mosque is usually higher on Fridays and during the month of Ramadan. But prayers are said there five times a day every day of the year. In North America, more employers are accommodating their Muslim employees who ask for time off on Fridays to participate in midday prayers. In most mosques, women assemble and pray separately, either in a balcony or behind a screen. The reason for the separation is due to the nature of the physical prayer postures; praying "shoulder to shoulder and foot to foot" (in the words of my Muslim friend Nabil Bayakly) with a person of the other gender is considered distracting.[24]

The third pillar is almsgiving (*zakat*). Muslims are expected to give at least 2.5 percent of their surplus income to the poor as a minimum level of charity. In North America, many Islamic Centers host private K–12 schools or seminaries and provide other services for the needy, caring for their own and for non-Muslims. The offerings are often solicited for such causes as well as for supporting the other expenses of the mosque (such as the salary of the *imam*, the local cleric).

The fourth pillar is fasting (*sawm*) during Ramadan, the month on the Islamic calendar when the Qur'an "came down."[25] The purpose is spiritual reflection and rededication. Children and the sick are exempt, although children believe they are honoring their parents when they volunteer that they think they are old enough to attempt to fast with the adults for the first time.[26]

The fast begins each day at dawn and ends each evening at sunset. During the day for the entire month, faithful Muslims abstain from food and drink, from smoking, and from sexual relations. Typically, families wake up early for a pre-dawn breakfast, then celebrate the end of the day with a family meal. Lailat al-Qadr on the twenty-seventh day of the month marks the "Night of Power" or "Night of Destiny" described above—the first revelations delivered to Muhammad—and is an especially important time for Muslims to gather.

I wrote portions of this chapter in Jerusalem during Ramadan. Israeli news agencies reported that an estimated three hundred thousand Muslims gathered on the Temple Mount to celebrate the Night of Power.[27] Eid-al-Fitr is the three-day feast that marks the end of Ramadan. Families exchange greeting cards and gifts; children and parents alike sport new outfits.

The fifth pillar is the pilgrimage to Mecca or *Hajj* that every able-bodied Muslim who can afford it is required to make at least once in their lifetime. Some people make the journey more than once; after their first Hajj, they can fulfill the obligation for someone else who cannot go themselves.

Muslims believe the pilgrimage pre-dates Muhammad, that it extends in time as least as far back as Abraham, whom they believe built the Ka'aba with his son Ishmael.

The pilgrimage includes a number of prescribed movements in and around the two holiest cities of Mecca and Medina, all meant to reenact key moments in the life of Muhammad or his forebears. Many Muslims report that the pinnacle of the experience is walking around the Ka'aba seven times. They also say the emotional impact of joining two to three million fellow-Muslims, all dressed in simple white garb and going through the same motions, is tremendous. The Hajj takes place on the first ten days of the last month in the Islamic year. Due to crowd control logistics, the Saudi government limits the number of pilgrims through a quota system.[28] Non-Muslims are not allowed to enter Mecca at all in order to preserve the purity of the holy city (Qur'an 9:28).

Jihad

A minority of Muslims (only some Shi'as) refer to *jihad*—"holy war"—as the "sixth pillar" of Islam.[29] But most do not have armed struggle in mind. The word "jihad" means "struggle" or "exertion." The emphasis is usually on the "jihad of the heart," that is, the spiritual struggle against evil, especially within one's own soul, not the "lesser jihad" that involves physical conflict with opponents of Islam. The Qur'an makes it clear that "lesser jihad" is justified when

1. armed struggle is necessary for self-defense
2. a non-Muslim force overtakes territory formerly held by Muslims (2:190–191)
3. a non-Muslim group or nation supports those who fight against Muslims (60:7–9)
4. a non-Muslim force encroaches on Islamic holy sites in Saudi Arabia or, for Shi'ites, in Iraq or Iran.

These guidelines explain why many Muslims believe jihad is necessary to support the Palestinians who were forced out of their homeland in the Israeli "War of Independence" in 1948–1949. In fact, Muslims refer to that event as "al-Nakba," "the Catastrophe," and many work to reverse the result. But most Muslim scholars agree that physical violence is never to be used to spread Islam; the religion itself should be advanced only by reason and persuasion.

Holy Days

Islamic holy days include fasting during the month of Ramadan, the "Night of Power" (Lailat al-Qadr) that occurs on the twenty-seventh day of Ramadan, and Eid-al-Fitr, the celebration that marks the end of Ramadan. Eid-al-Adha ("Feast of Sacrifice") takes place on the tenth day of the month of the Hajj and commemorates the near-sacrifice of Ishmael by his father Abraham. Muslims celebrate by feasting and by feeding the less fortunate.

Ashura ("tenth") takes place on the tenth day of the first month of the Muslim calendar, that is, ten days after New Year's Day (Ra'as assanah), much like the Jewish Day of Atonement. For Shi'ites, on the other hand, Ashura is a sad occasion, because it marks the anniversary of the martyrdom in 680 AD of Shi'a leader, Hussein, the grandson of Muhammad, who was assassinated by the Sunni caliph when Hussein refused to submit to his authority.

Islamic Law

In many Muslim-majority nations, there is no separation of "mosque and state." Laws in those countries are based on the Qur'an. Where the Qur'an does not address a specific matter, scholars turn to the Hadith, the traditions about the life of Muhammad, for guidance. If no precedent is found in those accounts, Islamic jurisprudence turns to the elders of a given Islamic region for rulings—scholars in Cairo for Egyptian Muslims or experts in Shari'a in Ankara for Turkish Muslims.

Islamic law distinguishes between practices that are required (such as the Five Pillars), recommended (like extra prayer and fasting), permitted (like growing beards or drinking coffee), disapproved but not forbidden (including celibacy, divorce, and card-playing), and practices that are forbidden (*haram*, including murder, theft, gambling, disobedience to parents, and fornication, to name a few).

Significant Sects and Developments

Disagreements over who should succeed Muhammad as the leader of the young Islamic community have divided Islam since the day Muhammad died.

Sunni Muslims believe that, as he lay ill, Muhammad told his three closest associates to choose from among themselves who would serve as caliph ("successor") in his place. This successor would not have the same spiritual authority as Muhammad himself, since he would not be a prophet. But this leader should be charged with following the way of Allah as revealed in the Qur'an and exemplified by Muhammad. The term *sunna* means "way" or "form," and is often used as a synonym for the *Hadith*, the collection of stories about the life and sayings of Muhammad. Sunni Muslims take their name from this term, believing that they adhere to the "way of Allah" as passed on to them by Muhammad.

Shi'a Muslims, or Shi'ites, on the other hand (whose name derives from a shortened version of the phrase "followers of Ali"), believe that Muhammad appointed Ali, his cousin and son-in-law, to succeed him, based on a revelation he received from God before he died. That revelation, Shi'ites believe, was suppressed by the first Sunni caliphs who, from a Shi'a perspective, had a vested interest in protecting their own status. Shi'ites believe that the rightful heir to Muhammad's role should be a direct descendant of Muhammad. Since Muhammad had no sons, Ali, his son-in-law was the most qualified. Ali eventually was named as the fourth successor to Muhammad, but he was killed by his fellow-Shi'as in 661 near Najaf (in modern Iraq) when they thought he was too willing to compromise with Sunni rivals. Further sects (described below) emerged from this initial disagreement.

Despite all of this division, attempts were made to maintain an unbroken caliphate—a lone spiritual and political leader of the Islamic world. That ended with the Mongol invasion of Baghdad in 1258. Thereafter, sultans in the Ottoman Empire occasionally used the title "caliph" themselves, but they were not internationally recognized as caliphs by all Muslims. The caliphate was officially ended by Ataturk, the founder of modern Turkey, in 1924. The movement that calls itself the Islamic State of Iraq and Syria (ISIS) represents a current attempt—utterly rejected by the vast majority of Muslims worldwide—to restore a single caliphate that would govern all Muslims.

Compiling the Qur'an

The oral revelations Muhammad received he repeated to his followers who would recite them often in order to retain them. Around the time of his death, the Muslim community recognized the need to write them down. Predictably, not all written versions were identical. The mention of Ali, for example, as the rightful successor to Muhammad, was omitted in some written copies (according to Shi'ites). Seeing the need for a single authorized text, Uthman, the third caliph after Muhammad, collected all copies he could find, burned all but one, and published that one as the authoritative Qur'an.[30] Muslims familiar with the process whereby the Christian New Testament was preserved and copied often point to "textual variants" in the Greek manuscripts as evidence that Christians do not have a sacred text as reliable as the Qur'an. Islamic publications do not typically include details about the transmission process, but instead claim that,

> the Qur'an is a record of the exact words revealed by God
> through the Angel Gabriel to the Prophet Muhammad. It
> was memorized by Muhammad and then dictated to his
> Companions, and written down by scribes, who cross-checked
> it during his lifetime. Not one word of its 114 chapters, *Suras*, has
> been changed over the centuries, so that the Qur'an is in every
> detail the unique and miraculous text which was revealed to
> Muhammad fourteen centuries ago.[31]

Muslim scholarship also developed the concept of "abrogation" to explain alleged discrepancies within the Qur'an. The principle of "abrogation" holds that a later revelation (from God) trumps an earlier one. The Qur'an itself mentions this possibility. "None of our revelations do we abrogate or cause to be forgotten, but we substitute something better or similar. Knowest thou not that God hath power over all things" (2:106), and, "We substitute one revelation for another—and God knows best what he reveals in stages" (16:101).

Compare, for example, those passages mentioned above (regarding the Day of Judgment) that make it clear that Jews and Christians will not be saved (such as 3:85) with those that imply that they will be saved (2:62). Note that the "Chronological Qur'an" lists Chapter Two as revelation no. 87

(out of 114) and Chapter Three as no. 89. From a non-Muslim perspective, it appears that Muhammad's attitude toward Jews and Christians changed over time, especially when he made the move from Mecca to Medina (after revelation no. 88). Some of the harshest words against non-Muslims appear in Chapter Nine, which was revelation no. 113 (out of 114). In other words, these strong words come toward the end of Muhammad's life.

Sunna and Hadith

Two hundred years after the death of Muhammad, Muslims were troubled by spurious stories being circulated about his life and teachings. These accounts were being used to justify interpretations of the Qur'an that were at odds with each other. An effort was launched to compile and publish these sayings in written form. The result was six collections of "Hadith," the Arabic word for "accounts" or "records," which together constitute the "Sunna" ("tradition" or "consensus") about the life of Muhammad.

Each story in the collections begins with the history of its transmission; that is, who was the original source of the story (someone close to Muhammad himself) and how it was passed down through the centuries. The anecdotes are rated, based on whether they are "authentic," "good," "weak," or even "fabricated." Obviously, the ones considered "authentic" carry more weight.

These stories are second only to the Qur'an in importance, given the role of Muhammad as the exemplar of submission to God. For example, the Qur'an mentions each of the Five Pillars of Islam, but the Hadith offer more specifics about those practices. Rules of jihad when the term applies to armed conflict are drawn largely from the battles Muhammad himself led. Not all Muslims agree on the place of the Hadith in Islam. Some reject these accounts entirely; Shi'as have their own collection.

Expansion

In the first one hundred years after the death of Muhammad in 632, and despite significant infighting among Muslims that led to the assassination of at least five of the first six of Muhammad's successors, Islam spread rapidly. By the end of the seventh century AD, Muslims had conquered and converted the Persian Empire (Iraq and Iran), Egypt, Palestine and Syria, and North Africa. By 732, Muslim armies had crossed the Mediterranean Sea into Spain. Their advance was halted only at the Battle of Tours in France that year.

Historians debate the reasons for their quick success. Surely some of the factors that made Islam appealing to people in those lands they conquered were

1. the simplicity of Islam compared to the complicated theological debates that divided the Christian world at the time;
2. the charge that Christians were, for the most part, prejudiced against people of Arab descent;
3. the fact that Muslim armies were adept at desert fighting; and
4. there was at the time in these regions a political and religious void that Islam filled, just as it had in Arabia.[32]

Sects

The primary division within Islam is between Sunni and Shi'a. Of the world's Muslims, 85 to 90 percent are Sunni; only 10 to 15 percent are Shi'a. The Shi'a population is heavily concentrated in Iran (where 90 percent or more are Shi'as) and Iraq (with between 65 to 70 percent Shi'a). These sectarian tensions have flared into outright war throughout Islamic history and are driving the current conflicts between Muslims in the Middle East. A complete list of the major sects is beyond the scope of this book.

Readers should know that many Sunni sects were formed based on disagreements over how to interpret and apply the Qur'an in our time. "Salafiyas" (outsiders call them "Wahhabis"), for example, are conservative in their interpretations, heirs to a "Back to the Qur'an" movement initiated by a Muslim scholar named Ibn Wahhab in the eighteenth century in what is now Saudi Arabia. His desire was to purge Islam of what he considered Christian influences, including the use of religious art, pilgrimages to tombs of saints, and the like, and to return to Islam as practiced by his ancestors.[33] The infamous Osama bin Laden, mastermind of the attacks on United States soil on September 11, 2001, was influenced by this movement.

Shi'a sects derive their origins from disagreements among themselves over the line of succession of caliphs. They agree that Ali should have followed Muhammad, but various branches parted ways as history unfolded. For example, "Twelvers" (also called "Imamis") believe that the twelfth imam after Ali, Muhammad al-Mahdi, born in 869 AD, mysteriously disappeared after the death of his father, the eleventh imam. Twelvers believe he is still alive and living in hiding in an undisclosed location, and that he will one day return and signal the end of the age. The line of imams officially ceased with his disappearance.

For Seveners ("Ismailis"), the line of imams was broken with the death of the seventh imam, whom they believe should have been Ismail, the oldest son of the sixth imam. But since Ismail died before his father, other Shia's recognized Ismail's surviving brother Musa as the rightful successor. So Ismailis and Imamis parted company at that juncture. Seveners refer to their leader as the Aga Khan. Large numbers of Ismailis live in India.

Some Muslim sects are considered heretics by other Muslims. The Alawites, for example, practice a kind of syncretistic faith that honors Ali, Muhammad's son-in-law and first successor (according to Shi'as) as a deity, which is blasphemy to other Muslims. Alawites consider the Five Pillars of Islam to be largely symbolic; historically, they have not observed them. Many of their practices are secret. Most Alawites live in Syria where one of their own, Hafez al-Assad, seized political power in 1971, succeeded by his son, current Syrian ruler Bashar al-Assad, when his father died in 2000. When civil war erupted in Syria in 2011, only an estimated 12 percent of the Syrian population were Alawite; 74 percent were Sunni Muslims, and 10 percent were Christian. In other words, al-Assad's status as an Alawite has not helped garner support for him in the wider Islamic world.

Other Islamic movements such as ISIS (Syria and Iraq), the Muslim Brotherhood (mainly in Egypt), al-Qaeda (in many countries), the Taliban (in Afghanistan), and Boko Haram (in Nigeria) are not sects of Islam. Instead, they constitute political movements driven in part by ultra-conservative Islamic ideology.

Significant Points of Contact

Christians agree with Muslims that God is one and he is great. Although some Muslims and Christians may find it objectionable, the Arabic word for God, "Allah," is the same word Arabic-speaking Christians use when they pray to the Father of Jesus. I realize that some Christians reading this book react negatively to the notion that "Allah" is the same God to whom we Christians pray. Many have made the case that Allah is a totally different "god" because of the way he is portrayed in Islam. Likewise, many Muslims will argue that Christians don't teach that God is one, but three. They would also object that we cannot say we believe God is great and at the same time call him "Father." That intimate, human label for the divine being amounts to bringing God down to our level.

Paul on Mars' Hill used the Greek term "theos" as a point of contact to introduce his audience to the one true God who reveals himself in Christ. He was not depending on the term itself but on his more complete descriptions of this God, contrasted with their common convictions about deities, to make the case. "Allah" is a similar point of contact for Christian witness.

At a debate with a comparative religion professor at a public university, I made the case that I (as a Christian believer) have more in common, in some ways, with my Muslim friends than I do with my secular colleagues. When one of my Muslim friends speaks about the Qur'an as if God himself spoke to Muhammad, at least some of my secular friends think this Muslim is deluded. As a Christian, I too believe that God has spoken. No, I don't believe he has spoken in the Qur'an. But I do believe that God has revealed himself in history in the written word (and more). We share with our Muslim friends a commitment to faith based on revelation, as well as the sense of obligation we both feel to obey what God has revealed.

The desire of faithful Muslims to submit to God is admirable. I know many Muslims whose submission is humble and unpretentious. We, too, are commanded "to obey everything" Jesus has commanded us (Matt. 28:20). "If you love me," Jesus said, "you will obey what I command" (John 14:15). It is also this spirit of submission and the commitment to obedience that can make conversations between Muslims and Christians (and anyone else) possible and productive.

Significant Points of Contrast

The debate about whether or not "God" and "Allah" are the same Being gets some people riled up (on both sides). Polls consistently show that 90 percent of Americans believe in God. But what sort of "God" do they believe in?

For some, surely this "God" is a vague "higher power," "the personification of love," or "the energy that fills the universe." In that case, I am not comforted by the 90 percent figure. In other words, many Americans who say they believe in "God" are not referring to the One you and I worship, who reveals himself in Scripture and in the Word made flesh. In fact, this God we serve is too exclusive for many of our countrymen to warm up to him. So the term "God" itself is insufficient to communicate to non-Christians what we really mean when we speak that name. Instead, we rely on descriptions of God's nature and character—the attributes that distinguish him from anyone and everyone else in the universe.

Meaningful discussions with Muslims focus on the commonalities and the differences in the way God is portrayed in Islam and in Christian faith. In Christ we believe we see the Father. We call him "Father" because Jesus told us we could. "This, then, is how you should pray," he said. "Our Father in heaven, hallowed be your name" (Matt. 6:9).

The Incarnation and Crucifixion

The Christian conviction that Jesus is God is more than offensive to Muslims; it is idolatry. Given the greatness of God, as Muslims understand his greatness, he is far too exalted to have entered human flesh as we believe he did in Jesus. It is also impossible that God would have abandoned a great prophet (Jesus) to suffer a humiliating death, the death of a common criminal, on the cross. So, the Qur'an teaches, Jesus himself was not crucified, but only someone who looked like Jesus. In fact, Christ crucified is as much a "stumbling block" to Muslims as it was to Jews in Paul's day.

Through the centuries, Christians have struggled to explain the relationship between God the Father, God the Son, and God the Holy Spirit. The term "Trinity," found nowhere in the Bible, became the shorthand for this complex theology. I'm not complaining about the term. But we Christians do better to focus on Jesus's claims of deity and the miracles he performed before eyewitnesses that support those claims rather than to try to explain through reason how the Godhead "makes sense." I am following Jesus's own words when he said, "Believe me when I say that I am in the Father and the Father is in me; or at least believe on the evidence of the miracles themselves" (John 14:11). Jesus speaks of his own crucifixion in ways that focus on obedience. The night he was betrayed, Jesus told his disciples, "The world must learn that I love the Father and that I do exactly what my Father has commanded me" (John 14:31). He predicted his own violent death, but also announced with confidence that it would be followed by his resurrection (Mark 8:31–36). Humble obedience inspired Jesus to accept the shame and pain of the cross (Philip. 2:5–11).

The Nature of the Bible and the Qur'an

Christians by and large reject the "dictation theory" of inspiration. I believe the Bible is the inspired word of God. But I recognize that God worked through human authors—their different languages, personalities, and contexts—to produce what most Christian teachers call a "divine-human book," a cooperative effort between the Spirit of God and those the Holy Spirit inspired to write it.

At the pinnacle of history, "The Word became flesh and made his dwelling among us" (John 1:14). Jesus is the embodiment of what God wants to say to the world. The Old Testament foretells his coming, the Gospels offer eyewitness accounts of his birth, life, death, burial, resurrection, and ascension. Acts of the Apostles gives us a sketch of what happened next as the gospel message spread around the Mediterranean world, the letters give us insight into what it meant to follow Christ as a group, in clusters of disciples known as churches, and Revelation offers a glimpse of the ultimate victory still to come.

All of this means that the Bible we read is like a road map that points us to Jesus as the center of our faith, the ultimate Word of God. Jesus once said to Jews, to whom the Qur'an refers as "People of the Book" (along with Christians), "You diligently study the Scriptures because you think that by them you possess eternal life. These are the Scriptures that testify about me, yet you refuse to come to me to have life" (John 5:39–40). The bottom line is we do not follow a book; we follow this Word made flesh who is revealed in this divinely inspired book. That is why I *do* make notes in my Bible and underline passages; that is why my copy is worn and torn like a well-used road map. Jesus, not the Bible, is to me what the Qur'an is to Muslims—the final word of God.

The Kingdom of God

Most (though not all) Muslim-majority nations find it hard to understand the American commitment to the so-called "separation of church and state." Where there is little religious pluralism, theocracy makes sense. "Separation of church and state" sounds to Muslims like an excuse to not practice in public what we believe in private.

From the beginning of the Islamic community (the beginning from a Christian point of view, when Muhammad and his followers first migrated from Mecca to Medina in 622 AD), society was ordered by Islamic law. Christianity, on the other hand, began as a tiny minority religion. The movement's very survival was threatened by the Roman Empire that was hostile to its non-conformist ways. None of this came as a surprise to early Christ-followers. Jesus taught that his Kingdom was not of this world and that his followers would be hated as he was (John 18:36; 15:18–19). They were "aliens and strangers in the world," wrote Peter, and surely did not entertain the possibility that one day they would achieve political power in Rome (1 Pet. 2:11). This all changed when Emperor Constantine legalized Christianity in 313 AD. In a relatively short time, Christianity became the predominant religion of the Empire. A much more cozy relationship between "church and state" was formed, one that endured in many Western countries for the next nineteen centuries.

The pluralism that now makes the United States "the most religiously diverse nation on earth" many Christians find disorienting.[34] Our Muslim friends are grateful for the freedom of religion they experience here. We, too, should be grateful. In another time and place, this conversation we hope to have between Muslims and Christians—a conversation that includes points of contact as well as points of contrast—would be virtually impossible.

TALKING TOGETHER . . .

1. In what ways do the stories of Rachel, Aisha, or Gustavo match with your own encounters with Muslims in North America?

2. What, if anything, surprises you about the connections between the Bible and Islam?

3. What do you think some non-Muslims find appealing about the Six Articles of Faith or the Five Pillars of Islam?

4. Have you read passages from the Qur'an? How would you compare the composition and content of the Bible and the composition and content of the Qur'an? How are these books similar, and how are they different?

5. What is your response to the discussion about the limitations of the use of the word "God" in pluralistic North America to describe the Creator?

6. In what ways has this chapter changed your view of Muslims?

IF YOU WANT TO READ MORE . . .

Geisler, Norman L. and Abdul Saleeb. *Answering Islam: The Crescent in the Light of the Cross*. Grand Rapids: Baker Books, 1993.

Ibrahim, I. A. *A Brief Illustrated Guide to Understanding Islam,* 2nd edition. Houston, TX: Darusssalam Publishers and Distributors, 1997.

Qureshi, Nabeel. *No God but One: Allah or Jesus? A Former Muslim Investigates the Evidence for Islam and Christianity*. Grand Rapids: Zondervan, 2016.

Ruthven, Malise. *Islam: A Very Short Introduction*. Oxford: Oxford University Press, 2000.

Taber, Shirin. *Muslims Next Door: Uncovering Myths and Creating Friendships*. Grand Rapids: Zondervan, 2004.

Notes

[1] A *hijab* is the modest head-covering that hides the hair but leaves the face exposed. The garment that covers the entire body and face, with an opening only for the eyes, is a kind of *burqa* or *chadri*. An *abaya* does not necessarily cover the face.

[2] My friend, Nabil Bayakly, believes the first half of the Islamic "confession of faith" is best translated into English as, "There is no deity rightfully worshiped other than Allah." In correspondence with the author February 1, 2017.

[3] For example, Shahira Amin wrote an article on Egyptian self-identity in *Daily News: Egypt*, September 6, 2012, entitled, "Are Egyptians Arabs or Africans?" Accessed on July 10, 2016, http://www.dailynewsegypt.com/2012/09/06/are-egyptians-africans-or-arabs/.

[4] According to *Arab Americans: An Integral Part of American Society* (Dearborn, MI: Arab American National Museum, n.d.), 13.

[5] The account of the binding of Ishmael is mentioned in the Qur'an (37:99–109), but only mentions Abraham's "son," and does not name him. Islamic tradition is unanimous that it was Ishmael. All references to the Qur'an are from Abdullah Yusuf Ali, *The Holy Qur'an: Text, Translation and Commentary*, 4th U.S. edition (Elmhurst, NY: Tahrike Tarsile Qur'an, Inc., 2002).

[6] When a Muslim speaks or writes the name of Muhammad, it is always followed with the blessing, "Peace Be Upon Him." That practice is based in part on a line in the Qur'an that calls on the faithful to "salute him with all respect" (Qur'an 33:56). To my Muslim friends reading this chapter, I mean no offense by not following that practice in this chapter. Obviously, I am honoring my Christian convictions.

[7] Qur'an 33:40

[8] Muslims believe that this first revelation is recorded in Qur'an 96:1–5. See below (endnote 17) for an explanation for the organization of the Qur'an and why this first one (chronologically) is not listed first in the Qur'an.

[9] Nabil Bayakly translates "Qur'an" as "Perpetual Recitation." In correspondence with author February 1, 2017.

[10] According to Moulana Muhammad Ashiq Elahi Bulandshehri, *The Wives of the Prophet* Muhammad, translated by Mohammad Akram (New Delhi, India: Islamic Book Service, 2001). The Qur'an (4:3) allows men to marry up to four wives at a time, provided that the husband is able to "deal justly" with each of them. God permitted Muhammad, on the other hand, to marry as many wives as he saw fit: "Prophet, we have made lawful for thee thy wives to whom thou hast paid dowers and those whom thy right hand possesses out of the prisoners of war whom God has assigned to thee [the widows of enemies he and his army had defeated in battle] and daughters of thy paternal uncles and aunts and daughters of thy maternal uncles and aunts who migrated from Mecca with thee, and any believing woman who dedicates her soul to the Prophet if the Prophet wishes to wed her. This only for thee and not for the believers at large. We know what We have appointed for them as to their wives and the captives whom their right hands possess, in order that there should be no difficulty for thee" (Qur'an 33:50).

[11] The Qur'an (17:1–2) mentions this "Night Journey," but the details of what happened there are found in the collection of accounts about Muhammad's life known as the *Hadith*. It should also be noted that Muslims are divided over whether or not this journey was an actual journey or a vision. See Ram Swarup, *Understanding the Hadith: The Sacred Traditions of Islam* (Amherst, NY: Promotheus Books, 2002), 23. According to testimony from Muhammad's youngest wife, Aisha, Muhammad never left his bed on the night in question. In Ishaq, *The Life of Muhammad*, a translation of *Sirat Rasul Allah*, by A. Guillaume (Karachi, Pakistan: Oxford University Press, 1955), 183. Ishaq (who died in 768 AD) claims to be quoting a relative of Abu Bakr, Aisha's father.

[12] The Muslim calendar is lunar and is not adjusted to fit the Gregorian calendar. Consequently, even though 1394 years have passed since the Year of the Hijra, years pass more quickly in the lunar calendar. That is also why Muslim months move around the calendar from a Western point of view. For example, Ramadan was in June this year, but will begin a week earlier next year, a week before that in the following year, and so on. So Ramadan may occur in June or in January.

[13] The full name of Medina was "Medina-tu-Nabee" or "City of the Prophet," later abbreviated to Medina. Nabil Bayakly in correspondence with author February 1, 2017.

[14] Some say "Islam" means "peace." The Arabic word for peace is "salaam," and derives from the same root word as "islam." From a Muslim perspective, submission to God is the only path to peace.

[15] The word for "idolatry" in Arabic is *shirk*, now in the English vocabulary, as in "shirking one's responsibilities."

[16] I. A. Ibrahim, *A Brief Illustrated Guide to Understanding Islam, 2nd edition* (Houston: Darussalam Publishers, 1997), 54.

[17] I find it helpful to consult versions of the Qur'an arranged chronologically—that is, in the order in which Muslim scholars believe the revelations were received. See https://wikiislam.net/wiki/Chronological_Order_of_the_Qur'an. Accessed July 12, 2016.

[18] According to Ram Swarup, *Understanding the Hadith*, 76, Muhammad happened into the tent of his daughter-in-law, Zainab, while her husband, Zaid was away, and saw her half-dressed. The awkwardness was resolved when Zaid offered to divorce his wife "with the proper formality"—meaning he repeated three times, "I divorce you," then she waited three months and was eligible to marry her former father-in-law.

[19] Nabil Bayakly prefers the translation "it looked as if he had died" over the translation I have used here, "who looked like him." In correspondence with the author February 1, 2017. No one is named in the Qur'an as the one who was crucified in Jesus's place, but some Islamic literature suggests it was Judas, others say Simon of Cyrene. Former Muslim Nabeel Quresh mentions this "Substitution Theory" popular among Muslims in his book *No God But One: Allah or Jesus?* (Grand Rapids: Zondervan, 2016), 172.

[20] Singular form is *Hafiz* for male, *Hafiza* for a female "guardian" or "memorizer."

[21] Again, I should mention that my friend Nabil Bayakly's preferred translation is, "There is no deity rightfully worshiped other than Allah." In correspondence with the author February 1, 2017.

[22] Nabil Bayakly pointed me to www.islamicfinder.org for the calculations of prayer times. In correspondence with author February 1, 2017.

[23] The Arabic word *masjid* (from which we derive the word "mosque") literally means "to prostrate oneself."

[24] In correspondence with the author February 1, 2017.

[25] For reasons explained in the section on the Qur'an, Muslims would not say Ramadan is the month when the Qur'an "was written."

[26] Karen Katz, *My First Ramadan* (New York: Henry Holt and Company, 2007).

[27] The Al-Aqsa Mosque, built on the Temple Mount in the seventh century, is the venue of this gathering. The size and location of the assembly is not intended to insinuate anti-Jewish sentiment.

[28] The quota is based on an estimate: one pilgrim slot for every one thousand Muslims in each country.

[29] Abu Amina Elias acknowledges that some scholars refer to Jihad as "the Sixth Pillar of Islam," but refutes that claim based on the passages from the Qur'an. "Some scholars have designated jihad as the sixth pillar of Islam, but there is no evidence to support this opinion." In "Is Jihad the 6th Pillar of Islam?" *Faith in Allah* online publication, August 2, 2014, accessed on January 16, 2017, http://abuaminaelias.com /is-jihad-the-sixth-pillar-of-islam.

[30] Malise Ruthven, *Islam: A Very Short Introduction* (Oxford: University Press, 1997), 22; also Zafar Ullah Khan, *Islamic Religious Knowledge* (Nairobi, Kenya: Longman Kenya, 1985), 27.

[31] No author, *Understanding Islam and the Muslims* (Washington, DC: The Islamic Affairs Department, The Embassy of Saudi Arabia, n.d.), 8.

[32] As outlined by Winfried Corduan, *Neighboring Faiths: A Christian Introduction to World Religions, 2nd edition* (Downers Grove, IL: InterVarsity Press, 2012), 145–146.

[33] The term "salifiya" in Arabic means "ancestors."

[34] That is the subtitle of a book by Diana Eck, *The Pluralism Project: How a 'Christian Country' Has Become the World's Most Religiously Diverse Nation* (San Francisco: HarperSanfrancisco, 2001).

CHAPTER FOUR

OUR HINDU NEIGHBORS

Ajit and Chadna Agarwal live in Maryville, Tennessee, where Ajit works as a computer programmer and Chadna directs Human Resources for a local company. Ajit grew up in Northern India, but studied at the University of Tennessee Knoxville. After graduation, he accepted his current position and began saving money. Some years later, he traveled back to India where he married Chadna, a childhood friend whose family was close to the Agarwals. Together they raised three children who all live and work in the States. Ajit and Chadna reserve most of their vacation time each year to visit their families in India. In addition to her day job, Chadna is also serving a term as the current Chairman of the Board of the Indian Cultural Center in Knoxville, which houses a temple, classrooms for after-school Indian-language programs, and a large meeting hall for holiday gatherings, weddings, and funerals.

Lakshmi Prasad was born and raised near Austin, Texas. After attending Texas A & M, then UT Medical School in San Antonio, she works as an allergist in an underserved community in rural Texas. Her parents, both second-generation immigrants from India, worry that Lakshmi, now thirty-one years old, works too much and does not leave enough time in her life for romance.

Krishna Swaminathan calls himself "Kris" at the accounting firm in Minneapolis where he made partner by age thirty-five. He has distinguished himself by his strong work ethic, his even temperament, and his business savvy. When his parents visited for the first time three years ago, Kris introduced them to Chloe, his girlfriend. Chloe grew up in a nominal Lutheran home, but was fascinated by what she was learning about Hinduism through reading about India. To her surprise, Kris seemed to be learning as much as Chloe was about the religion of his homeland. They recently got married in a civil ceremony and are now planning a trip to South India, where they will be married in a traditional Hindu wedding. Chloe's parents love Kris; they are nervous about traveling to India for the wedding, but look forward to experiencing exotic sights and sounds.

These are just a few of the more than one billion Hindus in the world, comprising 15 percent of the world's population. Ninety-seven percent of all Hindus live in India, Nepal, and Mauritius, a small island nation off the coast of East Africa. The rest make up the Indian diaspora which stretches around the globe. More than two million Americans of Indian origin identify as Hindus. Yet the term "Hindu" is more complex than readers might imagine. With no single founder, no sacred text common to all of them, and no standard set of teachings, the term "Hindu" was coined by outsiders to describe the varied religious beliefs and practices of the people who lived in the "Indus" (Indians call it "Sindhu") river valley in Pakistan and India. So not only is the label "Hindu" problematic, "Hinduism" defies description as a single, unified religion. Typically, Hindus take pride in the fact that "Hinduism" resists the neat, clean categories our Western minds prefer.

Significant Figures

Religion scholars trace the origins of what we call "Hinduism" to two main sources—the Harappan culture that was native to the Indus valley, and the Aryans, people of European descent, who migrated to India more than one thousand years before Christ. Long before then, sages whose names we do not know composed and compiled hundreds of hymns directed to thousands of deities as well as hundreds of sacred "mantras" (incantations) to be chanted on specific occasions, often as remedies for specific illnesses. Eventually, the hymns and mantras were collected in written form and are known today as the *Vedas*. Hindu priests still sing these hymns and chant these mantras when they conduct religious "pujas" ("acts of worship") for lay Hindus.

Beginning perhaps as early as 600 BC, reformers (around the time of Siddhartha, or "Buddha") wrote volumes of philosophical commentary on the nature of reality—writings known as the *Upanishads* ("sittings near a teacher"). The *Bhagavad Gita*, the most famous portion of the *Mahabharata* epic, is said to have been written by a legendary figure named "Veda Vyasa," the same author credited (by some) with compiling the *Vedas* and other sacred texts. Hindu scholars agree that all of these texts began as oral traditions handed down from one generation to the next. Those wise men who eventually preserved them in written form are considered less important than the truths the texts reveal.

Hindu Deities

Those truths derive from the thousands of deities, all considered to be manifestations of the one ultimate reality that many Hindus call "Brahman." In the *Vedas* themselves, Indra, the god who controls the weather, is one of the deities mentioned most often. Another is Agni, the god of fire, who conveys all offerings to the other deities when the sacrificial flame is ignited. The popularity of these two deities gives the correct impression that the worship of the gods in ancient times was especially tied to nature.

Vishnu, who some would say is the deity worshiped by more Hindus than any other, appeared as an animal in the first four of his nine incarnations—a fish, a tortoise, a boar, and a lion, in that order. Given the fragility of life in an agrarian society, it is not surprising that people would see a close connection between the divine and the natural world and seek the blessing of the gods on their food supply.

In modern India, an element of nature worship is preserved, for example, in the veneration of "Mother Ganga," the Ganges River that flows across the northern half of India. From a boat on the Ganges in Varanasi, India, I once witnessed the annual Mother Ganga Festival, which marks the occasion when Hindus believe Mother Ganga was incarnated as the river, a river that has been an important source of life to India for millennia. The "sacred cows" that wander the streets of India untended and unharmed may also reflect this ancient nature-worship phenomenon. Of course, none of that is too different than the Canaanite preoccupation with Baal, the thunder god, or other forms of nature worship that the Israelites found so alluring in ancient times.

Today Hindus focus more on the gods Vishnu and Shiva (sometimes spelled "Siva") than those deities who receive more attention in the *Vedas*. Vishnu is considered the god of love and benevolence, the one who sustains the world. Shiva, on the other hand, is the god of reproduction and destruction, perhaps a contradictory portfolio unless you consider that there is a degree to which reproduction always involves destruction. (In John 12:24, Jesus said, "Unless a kernel of wheat falls to the ground and dies, it remains only a single seed. But if it dies, it produces many seeds.")

A third deity, Brahma, not to be confused with *Brahman* (with an –n), is responsible for creating the world. Given that the present world has already been created, there isn't much for Brahma to do at the moment. When Shiva decides to destroy this world, Brahma will then create a new one which Vishnu will once again sustain. Vishnu, Shiva, and Brahma are sometimes called the "Hindu Trinity" ("Trimurti"), especially by Indians who have had more encounters with the West. But among the deities, Vishnu and Shiva are central. Most Hindu temples in North America are devoted to one or both of these deities; none are dedicated to Brahma. In fact, even in India fewer than ten temples are dedicated to Brahma worship.

The Hindu pantheon includes other popular deities including Ganesha, the elephant-headed god; Rama, the hero of the other famous Hindu epic, the Ramayana; Krishna, the hero of the Bhagavad Gita; and female deities such as Parvati, Lakshmi, and Saraswati. But all of these figures are associated with Vishnu, Shiva, and Brahma, either as their spouses (the female deities), their offspring (like Ganesha), or as their incarnations ("avatars") in other forms (like Rama and Krishna, believed to be the seventh and eight incarnations of Vishnu respectively).

Gurus and Reformers

Gurus or teachers are leading figures in Hinduism. Many Hindus can name the guru whose teachings they embrace the most. Several gained and maintained prominence in the West beginning in the 1800s. (See "Significant Sects and Developments" below.) Another important historical figure in the religious landscape of India is reformer Ram Roy (1772–1833), who, like many others, tried to reconcile his traditional Hindu beliefs with Christian faith and the British imperial rule he lived under. He is credited with challenging longstanding traditions such as the caste system and the now-outlawed practice of "widow-burning" (*sati*, whereby a widow would throw herself on the funeral pyre of her husband to honor him).

Mohandas Gandhi (1869–1948) was India's most famous modern reformer, politically and religiously. He championed civil rights for all Indians and independence from the British through nonviolent civil disobedience. He was inspired by Hindu and Jain ideals, and, he said, by Jesus's Sermon on the Mount. His success earned him the title "Mahatma" ("great soul"). Martin Luther King Jr. said Gandhi's example informed the nonviolent protests of the American Civil Rights Movement. Not everyone was enthralled with Gandhi's reforms. He angered Hindu nationalists who thought he compromised too much with Muslims after the partition of India and Pakistan in 1947. One of them assassinated Gandhi on January 30, 1948.

Significant Beliefs

Many key Hindu beliefs are clear in the sacred Hindu texts, such as the ones I named above. The *Vedas*, the four-fold collection of ancient hymns and mantras (sacred words chanted on specific occasions) are used in religious services, including life-cycle rituals (at birth, puberty, marriage, and death), and in healing encounters between a worshiper and a priest.[1] Hindu priests in training master one or more of the *Vedas*, committing the content to memory. The *Upanishads* have a more philosophical flavor, explaining to the reader the nature of reality. The two major epics, *Mahabharata* and *Ramayana*, convey in narrative style not only myths about the many deities, but the basic tenets of the Hindu worldview, including the notions of karma, reincarnation, and virtue.

Brahman and Atman

Given the diversity of opinions and teachings that are all grouped under the heading "Hinduism," offering an accurate summary of Hindu beliefs is difficult. With that disclaimer, let me tell you it is common to say that Hinduism points to 330 million gods. That is not a misprint. The number is perhaps intended to astound the mind. I believe it is accurate to say that most Hindu teachers believe in a single and ultimate reality known as "Brahman," of which the "330 million gods" are but manifestations.

The fact that "Brahman" is often translated "God" in English creates confusion for Christians trying to understand what their Hindu friends mean when they say "Brahman." Especially for Indian-Americans, it is simple enough to say, "There is only one God—Brahman—who is in all of us and manifests [himself] in many different ways." The analogy makes sense in our context.

But Hindu scholars (more than Hindu lay persons) debate the nature of "Brahman" (just as Christian scholars debate the nature of God more than the average Christian does). For the most part, Brahman is presented in Hindu literature as an impersonal force, not as a personal being. Human beings, trying to approach this Ultimate Invisible Reality, resort to creating images—thousands of images—that feature different attributes of this Ultimate Reality. But the images should not be mistaken as the Reality itself. In fact, according to ninth-century Indian guru, Shankara, the images are a concession to "weak" people who needed to think of the divine in more personal terms.[2]

Every living being houses a measure of Brahman, called "Atman" (or sometimes "atma"). Some refer to this Atman as the "divine spark" within the soul. Yoga practitioners end their sessions with the Sanskrit greeting, "*Namaste*," best translated, "I bow to the divine in you." Atman is that "divine" invisible part of living beings that continues to exist from one birth to the next. Hindus compare the Brahman-Atman concept to electricity. Brahman is like the electricity that runs invisibly through the wires of our electrified buildings. The lamps, toasters, and hair dryers we plug into the electrical outlets all operate on the strength of that unseen force. Furthermore, some light bulbs glow more brightly than others, depending on their wattage.[3] In the same way, some human beings are aglow with Atman, while in others the evidence of Brahman is not so obvious.

Atman is also compared to a drop of water that is absorbed into the ocean. The Atman is recycled through many reincarnations until it finally becomes one with Brahman. It would not be accurate to say "the drop becomes *part* of Brahman." That language still describes one thing—the drop—as if it is separate and apart from the Ultimate thing—the ocean. It is better to say the drop of water simply becomes ocean. Likewise, the final goal for Hindus is not to one day be "dissolved" into Brahman (as if "they" no longer exist), but to simply *be* Brahman, undifferentiated from all other drops.

Karma and Reincarnation

In the meantime, living beings are locked in a cycle of birth and rebirth—a cycle Hindus call *samsara*—ascending and descending the scale of existence, from more pleasant to horrible circumstances, based on *karma*. Karma is the link between deeds and consequences. "Good" deeds produce positive karma and lead to an improved condition in one's next incarnation. "Bad" behavior generates negative karma and leads to a worse circumstance in one's next life. Very bad people may be reborn as animals. (This is the main reason for vegetarianism.) As I was told in a Hindu temple in New Delhi, "The chicken you eat may one day eat you." Suicide is considered a great evil. "Such an action [suicide] will condemn the soul for thousands of years," writes one Hindu author, "and it will be forced to start life all over again from the lowest level of the evolutionary ladder."[4]

Although Westerners, even some Christians, have developed a fascination with reincarnation, Hindus believe reincarnation is neither desirable nor glamorous, but simply inevitable. Hindus do not know "who they were" in their former lives. (So let's not ask our Hindu friends that question.) They can and do assume that they have achieved their current status—whether good or bad, rich or poor, successful or not, healthy or sick—not only because of their karma in this current life, but because of the total effect of their cumulative deeds over countless past lives.

The law of karma explains the inequities of life—why one person lives a long life of ease while another endures poverty, pain, and suffering and dies young. "Unluckily," writes one Hindu author, "many souls whose past Karmas were very bad are born together in the deserts of Ethiopia, but they are not destined to suffer forever."[5] Karma is at work. In the end, the goal remains the same: to get off this merry-go-round of birth and rebirth and be absorbed into Brahman. The assumption is that it will take hundreds, even thousands, of lives to achieve such liberation from birth and rebirth. That ultimate experience is known as "moksha," often translated "salvation" in English. From a Christian and a Hindu perspective, that translation is problematic. (See "Significant Points of Contrast" below.)

Every semester at least one of my undergraduate World Religions students asks me a question that goes something like this: "So how do Hindus explain the growing world population?" In other words, how do Hindus account for population increases over time, if every person is reincarnated in some other form? It is a "gotcha" question for some, as if reincarnation is so illogical that this mathematical question will dismantle it. But most of my students, like my readers, assume a one-to-one relationship between human (or animal) bodies and the number of available souls. The assumption is a reflection of the individualism at the core of Western culture. For Hindus, Brahman is an infinite source of "souls" (or atman). As an analogy, if the question were, "How many drops of water are there in the ocean?" the answer might be, "As many as you'll ever need."

Reality or Illusion?

Not only is Brahman the Ultimate Reality, it is the only reality. Nothing else in life is "real." Our physical existence including the world of matter all around us and our own bodies themselves are all *maya* or "illusion." To Hindus, death proves that truth. The human body is obviously temporary for all of us; therefore, the body cannot be real.

So why, you ask, would Hindus take the physical world seriously at all? Why not walk in front of the illusory bus barreling down the illusory road and end one's own illusory life if in fact this life is all illusion? The Hindu response is that it is one's duty (the word is *dharma*—remember the TV sitcom "Dharma and Greg"?) to play along, to perform the tasks one is assigned, tasks traditionally determined by one's caste at birth, and thereby to progress up the spiral staircase of reincarnation through many lives. One should do his or her duty while resisting the temptation to invest too much in this illusory world.

Some may choose instead the life of a "renouncer," usually a retired person who renounces his possessions, his position, even his own family, conducts his own funeral, then flees to a remote region where he spends the rest of his days meditating in isolation, enduring extreme self-deprivation. A "renouncer" illustrates an ideal response to the world of illusion, a response relatively few Hindus (and virtually no Indian-Americans) choose these days.[6]

Caste System

What do Hindus believe about the caste system? The question is legitimate and controversial, since "Untouchability" was officially outlawed by the Indian Constitution in 1950. Broaching the subject of caste might make some of your Indian friends defensive. They may assume you have derived your information about modern India from watching the movie *Slumdog Millionaire*. (I can imagine that non-Americans seeing in the news ample evidence of lingering racial strife in the United States would develop a negative impression about ongoing discrimination here.)

The word "caste" actually comes from the Portuguese word *kaste* (*casta* in Spanish), which means "lineage" or "race." Indians use the term *varna* ("color" or "type") to refer to the ancient system of social classification. According to the ancient Hindu text the *Laws of Manu*, the Indian social hierarchy was fixed when the first man was made from the body of "Brahman." From the mouth came the highest caste, the Brahmin (not to be confused with the concept of Brahman), whose main role in society is spiritual leadership. From the arms came the Kshatriyas, who serve as the rulers and warriors. The Vaisyas were drawn from the thighs and serve society as farmers and merchants. The Sudras were born from the feet of Brahman and do manual labor for the other higher castes.

The *Laws of Manu* are clear: those born outside this four-caste system are the "outcastes" or "untouchables," known more commonly in our time as "Dalits" ("downtrodden" or "oppressed"), and not considered Hindus.[7] The same *Laws of Manu* prohibit intermarriage between castes, as well as many types of social co-mingling. For example, only Brahmins may drink from a Brahmin well or fish in a Brahmin lake. Kshatriyas and Vaisyas should not eat together. Dalits are not even allowed to enter Hindu temples. Violations are often met with hostility and violence.[8]

These four broad "castes" are further subdivided into *jati*, a social classification typically tied to one's occupation as well as to the larger caste one belongs to. Of course, it is not true that everyone in the carpenter *jati* works as a carpenter or that all Brahmins are priests. But traditionally, one's duty is heredity: those born into the washerman *jati* should wash clothes, those born into military families should join the military. The expression "doing what you were born to do" has roots in Hindu thought.

To be fair—and we must be fair—Hindu scholars often argue that the caste system was intended to organize Indian society in ways that were appropriate at the time, but the *Laws of Manu* should not be cited as justification for discrimination in India today.[9] The Indian government has, with some success, tried to enforce laws that prohibit discrimination based on caste. In 1950, before the American Civil Rights movement got much traction in our own country, the Indian government established a quota system whereby lower castes and even "untouchables" would be more integrated into the wider society. Despite these efforts, abuses persist, so much so that Philip Jenkins, professor of history at SMU, refers to the Indian caste system as "simply the largest single case of institutionalized injustice in the world today."[10]

Bhagavad Gita

Perhaps no single Hindu text captures the practical implications of these beliefs better than the *Bhagavad Gita*. The story goes that Arjuna, a warrior born into the Kshatriya caste, was hesitant on the battlefield one day when, across the battle lines, he saw his own relatives armed and ready to kill him. In that moment, feeling the pointlessness of fighting over territory, he put down his weapons, sat down in his chariot, and refused to fight. Krishna, his chariot driver, scolded him for his cowardice. "Stand up and fight like a man!" Krishna urged.

When Arjuna would not change his mind, Krishna launched into a lengthy speech explaining to the reluctant warrior the essence of duty (doing what he was born to do since he was born into the warrior caste), the nature of karma (that the best way to earn karma was through doing one's duty), and reincarnation (that even those he may kill in battle will not be "gone"—they will simply leave the lifeless body and enter another one, much as a person takes off one old set of clothes and puts on a new outfit—Krishna's illustration, not mine).

Arjuna eventually takes up the fight, then learns that Krishna, his humble driver, is none other than the god Vishnu in disguise. Krishna's message continues to resonate with millions, making the *Bhagavad Gita* the second most-translated book in the world (second only to the Bible).

Significant Practices

An overview of Hindu practices begins with "puja" ("act of worship"). Three types of pujas are common: those conducted at home, those conducted at temples every morning and evening, and those conducted at the temple on special Hindu holy days. The home puja is usually brief; the mother of the household may light sacred fire or incense, wave it in front of the image of the deity—whichever deity the family is especially devoted to—and chant a brief mantra or hymn. The most well-known (and shortest) mantra is the sound "Om" (pronounced "ohh-mmm"), considered the sacred syllable. Hindu texts explain "Om" in many different ways: as a representation of the Ultimate Reality (Brahman-Atman), "the song of the universe," "the past, present, and future," "the earth, heaven, and sky," and so on. The single syllable is considered so powerful that it is often used to punctuate mantras—at the beginning and the end—both when written and spoken.

Christians are usually surprised the first time they visit a Hindu temple and witness people worshiping idols. What do they believe about them? The images made to represent the gods are not the deities themselves. When the idol is first crafted, delivered to the temple, and installed, priests conduct the rituals whereby they invite the deity to inhabit the image. Once consecrated, the image is treated as if it were the deity. Of course, Hindus are well aware that the image is replaced, sometimes once a year, and that it is the image, not the deity it represents, that is "disposable."

Worship and Meditation

Daily temple pujas are conducted by priests every morning and evening. Temples in America usually include a dozen or more deities, each one enshrined in a separate space larger than a walk-in closet, with all the shrines under one roof in the temple proper. More often than not, the image of Vishnu is front and center, with Lakshmi (Vishnu's "consort") in a shrine to one side and a representation of Shiva in a shrine on the other side.[11] Images of other deities are housed in similar small structures around the perimeter of the room. The morning and evening sacrifices are dedicated to each image in turn and include prayers, hymns, and offerings of food. In India where there are nearly one billion Hindus and thousands of temples, it is more common to find whole temples dedicated to a single deity.

Only the priests may enter the innermost shrines that house the idols, though the idols are visible to all. Worshipers stand or sit in the main hall facing the images, ringing bells to draw the attention of the deities, and joining the priests in chanting hymns or mantras. Families request special pujas at the temple on occasions such as the birth of a newborn, a child's first haircut, the birthday of an eight-year-old boy (for members of the Brahmin caste, as a kind of initiation into Hinduism; for other castes, the ceremony takes place on a later birthday), a wedding ceremony, or after cremation. Worshipers bring offerings of food—fruit, vegetables, milk, but no meat—and present them to the priest, who lays them before the idol and leads them through the ritual in the Sanskrit language in "repeat-after-me" style (since Sanskrit is spoken only by priests). Worshipers are invited to draw some of the sacred fire toward themselves (by pulling the smoke of the flame toward themselves with their hands) and to eat some of the offering as well, in communion with the deity.

Hindu devotees seek to "empty the mind" through meditation. There are too many forms of meditation to enumerate here. But most forms have in common a focus on one's own breath as the beginning point. By slowly breathing out and breathing in, concentrating on each breath and nothing else, practitioners say they can eventually detach themselves, even for hours at a time, from this illusory world of sensation. Some meditation sessions involve long stretches of silence punctuated at certain intervals by mantras the worshipers chant together.

Holy Days

Hindus are not expected to attend temple worship services regularly, but only on special occasions. And with a pantheon of thousands of deities, the Hindu calendar is full of special occasions. A short list of the most important ones includes Diwali (also spelled "Divali" or "Deepavali"), the "Festival of Lights." Inspired by the *Ramayana* epic, Diwali celebrates the victory of light over darkness and knowledge over ignorance. On Diwali, Hindus decorate their homes and businesses with bright lights (that resemble Christmas lights), shoot fireworks, and exchange gifts.

The celebration known as "Holi" marks the coming of spring when the demoness Holika is defeated (thus the name "Holi") and the faithful rededicate themselves to Vishnu. Participants parade through streets, spraying colored powder and water on each other, which has, in turn, inspired "Color Runs" in America (though I assume most American participants are unaware of the origins of the practice).

"Kumbh Mela" is the famous pilgrimage to Allahabad on the River Ganges that takes place every twelve years. (A similar event takes place at other cities on the Ganges every three years.) Because the gods are believed to drop sacred nectar in the water on the occasion, bathing in the river during Kumbh Mela is said to bring an extra potent level of purity. The official Kumbh Mela website estimates that between 80 and 120 million participated in the last major Kumbh Mela in 2013.[12] Even if that estimate is exaggerated, the organizers are correct when they claim that Kumbh Mela is easily the largest religious gathering in the world.

Significant Sects and Developments

Hindu scholars speak of "the three ways of Hinduism," referring to three different ways one might pursue the ultimate objective—oneness or "union" ("yoga") with Brahman. (Fun fact to share with your friends: the English word "yoke" derives from the Sanskrit word "yoga.") Many consider the "the way of works" ("Karma Yoga") to be the original way. In other words, the faithful Hindu does her duty as prescribed by her birth, and does it without complaint or resistance. She participates in religious rituals on the right occasions, showing proper reverence for the gods, and is not overly entangled with worldly pursuits other than meeting the needs of those she loves. By such submission, she will amass sufficient karma to return in the next life to a better, higher station.

To reform-minded Hindus in the sixth century BC, such a path was dominated by priests. There was little room for curiosity, for questioning the nature of reality, or for dissent. Those feelings may have given rise to the second "way," the "way of knowledge" (Jnana Yoga). On this path, the faithful pursue "union with Brahman" through knowledge and understanding, not just ritual observance. The movement inspired the collection of writings known as *Upanishads*.

Eventually, a third "way" emerged that overlaps with the first two: "the way of devotion" ("Bhakti Yoga"). To follow this "way," devotees identify one deity above all others and commit themselves to that one. That does not mean they stop worshiping other Hindu gods. But they henceforth identify themselves as "devotees of Shiva" or of Vishnu, of Krishna, and so on. Hindu scholars believe this third "way" gained momentum when the *Bhagavad Gita* grew in popularity in South India around 1500 AD.

YOGA IN AMERICA

The form of yoga most familiar in America is Hatha Yoga. The various stretching exercises in different postures ("asanas") are said to release the free flow of "hatha" (literally "force") throughout the body. That energy is said to travel along the spine through seven key junctures called "chakras," the first at the base of the spine and the seventh at the top of the head. The sixth chakra which lies between the eyebrows is considered "a spiritual eye" and is often marked by a colored dot. (Married women also place a decorative red dot on their forehead in the same spot; widows must remove theirs.) The hatha yoga positions are given names, sometimes based on what the human form resembles when in that position. So there is the "body twisted like a bird" position, the "sitting like a hen" pose, and many more. In addition to health benefits, some "yogis" (teachers of yoga) emphasize the spiritual advantages of hatha yoga, namely the relaxation that comes from such exercise and enables the practitioner to meditate.

Should a Christian practice yoga? I was afraid you would ask. I do not find it objectionable to do physical stretching like hatha yogis do. (I do find it painful, since no one would mistake me for a physically flexible person.) It is cause for concern when people embrace a practice that is inspired by a particular piece of worldview—as hatha yoga is—without knowing about that worldview. If your yoga instructor goes down that road and explains the power of yoga in terms of chakras and "energy flow," then the Lord may be giving you an opportunity to have a spiritual conversation with your instructor. On the other hand, if your yoga instructor is a Christian and speaks about yoga in these same terms, then the two of you certainly need to broach this subject. We do not want to "dabble" in the religious practices of others in ignorance. Whenever we borrow a quote, a thought, or practice from a source outside of Scripture— as Paul did on Mars' Hill—we need to make sure we shine light on it and not embrace it uncritically.

Gurus in North America

Hindus place high value on the role of a personal guru or teacher. That has led to the proliferation of thousands of sects, most of which still huddle under the umbrella of "Hinduism." Some of the gurus and sects that have significant numbers of followers in the United States include Swami Ramakrishna (1836–1886), for whom Ramakrishna Missions take their name. Ramakrishna never traveled outside of India, but his message of "God-consciousness" won a hearing in North America after the visit of his disciple Vivekananda, one of the keynote speakers at the World Parliament of Religions in Chicago in 1893.[13]

Maharishi Mahesh Yogi (1918–2008), an advocate of "Transcendental Meditation," caught the world's attention when he became the guru to the Beatles and subsequently gathered a large following in the United States. Chandra Mohan Jain (1931–1990), also known as "Osho," became famous, then infamous, in North America in the 1980s as Bhagwan Shree Rajneesh, teaching a form of meditation mixed with philosophy and politics. Having outgrown the "ashram" (a Hindu study and retreat center) in his native

Pune, India, he and his followers settled on sixty-four thousand acres near the tiny Oregon town of Antelope, which they renamed "Rajneeshpuram." Legal trouble led to their leader's arrest and deportation and eventually the closing of the ranch.

Abhay Charan De (1896–1977), known by his honorific name Bhaktivedanta Prabhupada, achieved global recognition in the 1960s when he founded the International Society for Krishna Consciousness (ISKCON). Operating more than fifty centers in the United States and hundreds around the world, ISKCON members are famous for chanting the mantra "Hare Krishna, Hare Rama" both in private and in exuberant public worship gatherings.[14]

Mata Amritanandamayi is better known as "Amma, the Hugging Saint" ("Amma" means "mother") for her practice of hugging all who attend her events on her world tours. According to her website, she has hugged more than 34 million people worldwide, believing that the essence of religion is love and compassion.[15]

At age eleven, Nilkanth Varni (1781–1830) began a long journey (more than seven thousand miles) across India after the death of his parents. His spiritual dedication earned him the nickname "The Teenage Yogi." At the age of thirty, he encouraged a gathering of followers in Gujarat (India) to chant the mantra "Swa-mi-na-ya-ra-n" ("teacher Narayan"), invoking the name of Narayana, another incarnation of Vishnu. Many reported that chanting those six syllables led them into a deep trance in which they realized that Nilkanth was actually a deity himself, sent to cleanse Hinduism of impure elements. From that point on, he was called Swaminarayan. Many adherents of the sect hail from Gujarat State in India where it began. The sect's BAPS organization has built nearly one hundred temples in the United States and Canada, including the largest Hindu temple on the continent, scheduled to open in Robbinsville, New Jersey, in 2017.[16]

HINDU NATIONALISM AND CHRISTIANITY IN INDIA

The tug of war between religion and politics in India may have little impact on our Hindu friends in North America, but it certainly affects the Christian population of India. According to Indian Government data, 25 million people in India say they are "Christians," a little more than 2 percent of the total population. Hindus make up 79 percent, Muslims 14 percent, Sikhs 2 percent, and Jains comprise less 1 percent.[17]

Reported incidents of persecution against Christians have increased with the election in 2014 of the current Prime Minister Narendra Modi, the leader of the BJP, a Hindu Nationalist Party. The party advocates what it calls "Hindu Nationalism," though they claim that they do not intend to discriminate against the millions of non-Hindus in India. The rhetoric and the on-ground experience has seemed scarier to religious minorities.

Significant Points of Contact

The Hindu notion of Brahman, depending on how it is explained, sounds like something the Apostle Paul might endorse, for "in him we live and move and have our being." Hindus are taught that Brahman pervades everything as the only true reality. Everything else, including the physical world around us, our own bodies included, is illusory. Practically speaking, the Hindu who is convinced of this truth is more likely to focus on spiritual realities than earthly ones. Paul also wrote that "we fix our eyes not on what is seen, but on what is unseen." Why? "For what is seen is temporary, but what is unseen is eternal" (2 Cor. 4:18). At the very least, we agree that the ultimate truths of life are found in the invisible realm and help us interpret what is happening in the physical world.

The concept of karma has merit, too. (Yes, the play on words is intended.) Paul also said, "God cannot be mocked. A man reaps what he sows. The one who sows to please his sinful nature, from that nature will reap destruction; the one who sows to the please the Spirit, from the Spirit will reap eternal life" (Gal. 6:7–8). Deeds do indeed have consequences.

Many Hindus demonstrate great affection for their spiritual teachers and a willingness to submit to them. We, too, are students (the meaning of the word "disciples") of the Greatest Teacher and need to model humble submission to him.

Significant Points of Contrast

Most Hindus (with some notable exceptions) view Brahman as an impersonal force or all-pervading energy. But the God who reveals himself in the world, in the word, and in the Word flesh is personal. He is no vague, universal energy or "vital force." We are made in his image. The biblical prohibition against idols is tied to this truth: God himself has already crafted images of himself, and we are it! We are not permitted to fashion god substitutes to somehow convey some truth about the invisible God. Worshipers tend to bow to the image and not to the deity they say the image represents. We are told to worship the Creator and not created things.

Yes, it is true that deeds have consequences. But the concept of karma goes beyond this simple connection and attributes our station in life now and in the future to past deeds, deeds that can never be erased, only counterbalanced by positive deeds. As a result, in Hinduism there is virtually no understanding of grace or mercy. Certainly there are compassionate Hindus, but the fundamentals of the faith inform a Dalit or a leper that the law of karma allows no shortcuts. It is good to show kindness to such people, but only as a way to gain merit for ourselves, not because it will help those people in the long run. The only real hope for them is to work off the effects of negative karma by doing what they were born to do, no matter how menial or demeaning the duty.

We believe that because of his love for us, God removes our sins "as far as the east is from the west" (Ps. 103:12). The promise of forgiveness is for those who have "put on Christ" (Gal. 3:26–27). In Jesus I have a righteousness that is not "my own that comes from the law, but that which is through faith in Christ—the righteousness that comes from God and is by faith" (Philip. 3:9). "There is now no condemnation for those who are in Christ Jesus, because through Christ Jesus the law of the Spirit of life set me free from the law of sin and death" (Rom. 8:1–2). In Christ, I am set free from the law of karma and the endless cycle of birth and rebirth.

This grace we share in Christ is what tears down walls that divide, regardless of race, gender, socioeconomic status . . . or caste. In Christ there is "neither Jew nor Greek, slave nor free, male nor female," neither is there any Brahmin or Dalit, black, white, Asian, or Latino, "for you are all one in Christ Jesus. If you belong to Christ, then you are Abraham's seed, and heirs according to the promise" (Gal. 3:28–29)—the promise God made to Abram long ago that through him and his seed all the nations of the earth would be blessed (Gen. 12:3). To be sure, our Christian witness is diminished when we do not live up to this high ideal, when our newest non-Christian neighbors can point to evidence that we have not fully embraced and lived this truth ourselves. But there is no equivalent in the Bible to the Hindu *Laws of Manu* that justify discrimination.

Someone might object, "Doesn't God show favoritism toward Israel as 'the chosen people'?" The Bible teaches that God called the people of Israel for a pragmatic reason, so that they might serve as a mediator nation, so that through them, and eventually through Christ, all nations might know the Lord. He even cautions them against thinking that they were chosen because they were somehow more righteous than others.[18]

The willingness of many Hindus to submit to their teacher or guru runs counter to the rugged individualism that is considered only and always a virtue by too many American Christians when, in fact, such self-reliance is considered a spiritual handicap in Scripture. To that extent, there is something to admire here as I noted above. On the other hand, Hindu gurus generally make no claim that what they teach is based on any revelation from on high. Instead, their insights are the product of searching the depths of their own souls. Hinduism is based on intuition, not revelation. As Christians we learn to "submit to one another out of reverence for Christ" (Eph. 5:21). We may hold Christian teachers or other leaders in high esteem, but we do so cautiously, careful that we pledge allegiance to God and not to the "jars of clay" that serve him.

Finally, we must think more deeply about the "exclusiveness" of Christian faith (there's that word "exclusive" again) compared with the much-celebrated "inclusivism" of Hinduism. A popular line Hindus often quote says, "There is only one truth, men just describe it in different ways."[19] Hindus emphasize this tolerance toward all religions as a point of contrast with monotheistic faiths like Christianity. Krishna told Arjuna (in the *Bhagavad Gita*), "In whatever way I am approached, in that way do I respond. All men, by whatever path, come to Me."[20] The Ramakrishna disciple, Vivekananda, drew applause when he quoted and explained that concept in Chicago in 1893.

The truth is that Hindus think you and I are mistaken to believe that Jesus alone is the unique Son of God, fully human and fully divine. But our error will not condemn us to eternal punishment, only because we will have another opportunity to learn the truth about the universe in the next life. If we are faithful Christians, we can expect a better incarnation next time around. It is this conviction that makes Hinduism (and most of the other Eastern religions described in this book) appear to be more inclusive than it is. What is different is not their belief that "everyone is right" and that "all roads lead to heaven," but their confidence that only a few, very dedicated souls escape the endless cycle of birth and rebirth and are absorbed into Brahman *in their next lifetime*. So there is no need for urgency or even for persuading non-Hindus to convert. From their perspective, we'll have our chance down the road in lives to come.

The Christian conviction that "man is destined to die once, and after that to face judgment" (Heb. 9:27), along with the commitment to take Jesus at his word and make disciples of all nations, inspires us to share our faith with all people in a way that is respectful, informed, and persuasive.

TALKING TOGETHER . . .

1. What kinds of experiences have you had with people of Indian origin? Do they match the profiles of the Agarwals, Dr. Prasad, or Kris and Chloe?

2. Why do you think the concepts of reincarnation and karma have grown so popular in Western culture? How do the Western versions of these Hindu beliefs differ from the original Hindu ideas?

3. How do Hindus use the teaching of *dharma* to avoid fatalism?

4. Are you surprised that the *Bhagavad Gita* is the second-most translated book in the world, second only to the Bible? What do you think accounts for its appeal?

5. What is your reaction to the word of caution in this chapter about "hatha yoga"?

6. How would you respond to the claim that Hinduism is more "inclusive" than Christianity?

IF YOU WANT TO READ MORE . . .

Eck, Diana L. *India: A Sacred Geography*. New York: Three Rivers Press, 2012.

Hunt, Dave. *God of the Untouchables,* Updated edition. Honolulu: Straight Street Publishing, 1999.

Mitchell, Stephen. *Bhagavad Gita: A New Translation*. New York: Three Rivers Press, 2000.

Thirumalai, Madasamy. *Sharing Your Faith with a Hindu*. Minneapolis: Bethany House, 2002.

Viswanathan, Ed. *Am I a Hindu? The Hinduism Primer*. New Delhi, India: Rupa Publications, 1992.

Notes

[1] The *Rig Veda* contains the hymns, the *Sama Veda* the melodies to be sung, the *Yajur Veda* the incantations and other instructions recited for healing, and the lesser known *Atharva Veda* which contains curses.

[2] Shankara called this concession "Saguna Brahman" ("Brahman with attributes") in Thomas A. Robinson and Hillary P. Rodrigues, *World Religions: A Guide to the Essentials,* 2nd edition (Grand Rapids: Baker Academic, 2014), 164–165.

[3] For example, Edakkandiyil Viswanathan, *Am I a Hindu? The Hinduism Primer* (New Delhi: Rupa Publications India, 1993), 32, 275.

[4] Ibid., 148.

[5] Ibid., 151.

[6] If a Hindu in America did elect to become a renouncer, they would return to India to live out their days.

[7] Laws of Manu 10:51–57 in Robert E. Van Voorst, *Anthology of World Scriptures,* 6th edition (Belmont, CA: Thomson-Wadsworth, 2008), 42. The creation of the four castes out of "Brahman" is also mentioned in the *Rig Veda* (Book 10, Chapter 90:11–12). I am quoting *The Rig Veda: An Anthology*, translated by Wendy Doniger (London: Penguin Books, 1981), 31.

[8] See examples of such discrimination and violence in Tom O'Neill's "Untouchable," *National Geographic* (June 2003): 2–31.

[9] Viswanathan, *Am I a Hindu?* makes this case, 58–59.

[10] Philip Jenkins, *The Next Christendom: The Coming of Global Christianity,* 3rd edition (Oxford: Oxford University Press, 2011), 228.

[11] Most of the idols have human-like features, but Shiva, as the god of reproduction, is represented by a "Shivalinga," a stone cylinder that is a phallic symbol.

[12] The official website for the Kumbh Mela festival is www.ujjainkumbhmela.com.

[13] A block of South Michigan Avenue in downtown Chicago was renamed "Swami Vivekananda Street" in his honor; it still bears his name.

[14] The entire mantra is four lines repeating three different names of the "divine being."

[15] www.amma.org. She was touring America as I was writing this chapter.

[16] See www.baps.org.

[17] Based on a 2011 census administered by the Indian government and reported in the article "India Has 79.8 percent Hindus, 14.2 percent Muslims, Says 2011 Census Data on Religion," in *F. India,* April 25, 2015, accessed August 4, 2016, http://www.firstpost .com/india/india-has-79-8-percent-hindus-14-2-percent-muslims-2011-census-data-on -religion-2407708.html.

[18] See Deuteronomy 9:4–6, for example.

[19] Viswanathan, *Am I a Hindu?* 5.

[20] *Bhagavad Gita* 4:11. I am quoting the translation by Paramhansa Yogananda, *The Essence of the Bhagavad Gita* (Nevada City, CA: Crystal City Publishers, 2006), 186.

CHAPTER FIVE

OUR BUDDHIST NEIGHBORS

I met Amanda and her infant son on a plane once. Her child, only six months old, was born with a whole set of medical problems that she knew would end his life before his first birthday. In our conversation that lasted as long as the flight, she told me that she and her husband had turned to Buddhist meditation to cope with their pain. As they understood it, as they learned to meditate, they would learn to detach from their feelings, if only for a few moments at a time, and find relief in detachment.

I have an older friend I'll call Ben, a Jewish son of Holocaust survivors. Ben became a Christian more than twenty years ago. But he followed a circuitous path to faith in Christ that included a stopover in the practice of what is called Nichiren Buddhism. Nichiren was a thirteenth-century Buddhist teacher in Japan who believed that the key to a meaningful life is found in chanting a certain Chinese phrase that basically affirms that the law of karma is true, and that every person has the power to control their own destiny by making good choices rather than bad ones.

Unlike Amanda and Ben, Hathai Bunyasarn says she was born into Buddhism. She came to the United States from her native Thailand to go to school here, met and married an American after college, and now makes her home in suburban Dallas, where she volunteers at the local Thai Temple. Her job is mainly to welcome visitors who drop in, most of them more curious about the exotic looking building than they are interested in Buddhism.

These are just a few of the estimated 3.9 million Buddhists in North America, who represent a small fraction of the nearly five hundred million Buddhists worldwide.[1] Buddhists are divided into three major branches and thousands of sects. But for most (though not all) Buddhists, the story of a young prince in India in the sixth century BC is where a proper introduction to the religion begins.

Significant Figures

Siddhartha Gautama (563–483 BC?)[2] is better known by his honorific title, "The Awakened One" or "The Buddha." Not all Buddhists agree on his basic life story. It was not written down until centuries after his death. Even then, ancient writers did not feel obliged to comply with the standard guidelines of modern history writing as they wrote. My Buddhist friends will tell you they are not troubled by the hazy outline of Buddha's personal life. Their faith rests in the path to enlightenment that he rediscovered and has passed down orally to his followers, not in the details of Siddhartha's story.

Siddhartha

It is said that Siddhartha was born into a "royal" family (picture a feudal lord in a rural society) in the Shakya region at the foot of the Himalayas in modern Nepal in 566 BC and died in 486 BC. (The exact years of his birth and death are disputed; some Buddhists believe he was born as early as 624.) Before his mother, Maya, learned she was pregnant, she had a dream in which a white (albino) elephant appeared, danced with her, and told her she would conceive a child who would become the savior of the world. As her due date approached, Queen Maya, following the customs of the day, traveled to her ancestral home in Lumbini (in modern Nepal) to deliver the child. She went into labor en route and gave birth in a grove of trees, experiencing almost no pain. The queen and her attendants were amazed when Siddhartha, the newborn, immediately stood up, took seven steps, and declared, "I was born to reach enlightenment."[3] Lotus blossoms sprouted magically from each footprint. Obviously, these were signs to observers that this child was extraordinary.

When Siddhartha was presented to the community, a wandering Hindu ascetic prophesied that the child would grow to be either a great king or a poor holy man like him. The prediction alarmed the king, who wanted his child to succeed him on the throne as "Shakyamuni," the leader of the Shakya tribe (another title by which Siddhartha is known). He was so intent on shielding Siddhartha from anything that might compel him to choose a spiritual path over a political career that he did not let him leave the palace. All evidence of suffering—old age, illness, and death—was hidden from his view for the first three decades of his life. Raised in isolated luxury, Siddhartha eventually married and had a child. His curiosity about life beyond the palace walls continued to grow until he demanded that his father allow him to see the world. The king eventually gave in and organized a parade for his son, the prince. Beforehand, the king cleared the city streets of all ascetics, the sick, the aged, and any dead bodies. Still, Siddhartha's eye saw all four of those things—a Hindu holy man, a sick man, an old man, and a corpse—what Buddhists call "the Four Sights." This first exposure to human suffering made a profound impression on him. He was twenty-nine years old.

Determined to find a way to escape suffering, Siddhartha said good-bye to his wife and son, left the palace, and joined a group of five Hindu ascetics who wandered from place to place, practicing an extreme form of self-denial as a means to achieving enlightenment. After more than six years of deprivation, Siddhartha was determined to make one final push for enlightenment, or to die trying. In a period of intense meditation, while sitting under a sycamore tree (called a *Bodhi* tree in Sanskrit) in a town now called Bodh Gaya (in Northern India), Siddhartha finally achieved "enlightenment": he became "awakened"—Buddha means "one who is awake"—to the ultimate realities of the universe. At that moment, the earth shook, lotus blossoms fell from the sky, and a halo encircled Siddhartha's head. The five ascetics who had followed him for more than six years were initially turned off when Siddhartha started eating and drinking like a normal person. They accused him of breaking his ascetic vows. He eventually persuaded them to join him instead, and together they formed the first Buddhist community (called *sangha*).

King Ashoka

Other significant Buddhist figures include the founders of the various sects of Buddhism described below, as well as prominent leaders who spread Buddhism in Southeast Asia. King Ashoka of India (304–232 BC), for example, renounced warfare when he learned about Buddhism and devoted the rest of his life to spreading the Buddhist message. He collected Buddhist relics (like locks of Siddhartha's hair or some of his teeth) and built Buddhist monuments, or *stupas*, like the Mahabodhi Temple in Bodh Gaya that marks the spot where Siddhartha allegedly achieved enlightenment.

Significant Beliefs

Siddhartha believed he had discovered "The Middle Way." Truth could be found neither in the life of luxury and indulgence he knew growing up nor in the extreme ascetic practices he pursued for those six-plus years after leaving the palace. Truth could be found only through emotional detachment from all material things, whether one had little or much. The logic was spelled out in his famous "Benares Sermon" delivered sometime after enlightenment in the village of Sarnath (just north of modern Varanasi, India). The "Four Noble Truths" outline that first public message.

Four Noble Truths and the Eight-fold Path

Buddha taught that

1. To live is to suffer.
2. Suffering comes from cravings that go unsatisfied. Even when a person has all she wants, she knows that such satisfaction is fleeting.
3. In order to eliminate the suffering, one must eliminate the cravings that drive it.
4. To eliminate the cravings, one must follow the Eight-fold Path.

The Eight-fold Path is the Buddhist code of conduct and consists of

1. Right views (such as the Four Noble Truths)
2. Right resolve (to extinguish all cravings)
3. Right speech (don't lie, slander, or say more than necessary, since excessive talking reflects the kind of passion that keeps people locked in the cycle of birth and rebirth)
4. Right behavior (foremost of which is avoiding killing any living thing, but includes prohibitions against cheating, stealing, and the like)
5. Right occupation (which is to become a monk, but non-monks must choose an occupation that does not harm others as the best path to being reborn as someone who might become a monk in the next life)
6. Right effort (to acquire these Buddhist virtues)
7. Right mindfulness (meaning spiritual alertness, contemplative nature, and a stoic demeanor)
8. Right meditation (as a daily practice)

Nature of the Self

Siddartha challenged the Hindu concept of Brahman-Atman, that the soul is that little "divine spark" or drop of Brahman in every living creature. He believed this idea kept Hindus locked in the cycle of birth and rebirth in pursuit of this great "something"—oneness with the Ultimate Reality, Brahman. Siddhartha taught that there is no soul, no self, and no "something" out there with which the "soul" could unite. He called his understanding of the self the *anatman*, that is "no *atman*."

Karma and Reincarnation

As in Hinduism, *karma* is the Buddhist link between deeds and consequences. Circumstances in this life are determined entirely by one's conduct in past lives. According to Hinduism, someone born into a family of privilege is obviously moving up the ladder of "reincarnation" (though my Buddhist friends prefer the term "rebirth"; read the endnote to know why).[4]

But from a Buddhist perspective, that's not entirely good. It is tempting for such a person to relish their high status and become attached to this impermanent world. The attachment will cause them to cling to life and return to another body after death.

I mentioned in the previous chapter that many people in the West have developed a fascination with reincarnation in recent decades. Surveys consistently show that around 20 percent of all Americans believe in reincarnation.[5] But those who embrace it usually speak as if reincarnation is a "good" thing.

In the East, reincarnation is not a good thing; it is an inevitable thing. To live is to suffer. Only those very few who achieve enlightenment can escape rebirth. No one (except an "awakened" person—a Buddha) knows how many past lives they have lived. Likewise, no one when they die can really know their cumulative karma "score," since no one can really know how many misdeeds from previous lives they brought with them into this life. Given that it took Siddhartha 550 lives to escape the cycle of birth and rebirth (according to his testimony), it would be presumptuous for an ordinary person to think they could escape that cycle in less time. As we shall see, many Buddhist sects promise enlightenment in different ways and through shorter paths.

Nirvana

"Nirvana" is a Sanskrit word that literally means "blown out." It refers to the state of being that one achieves when one escapes the cycle of birth and rebirth.

Buddhists liken the passion that keeps humans locked in that cycle to the fuel that ignites a Bunsen burner and keeps it lit. One must learn to turn off the fuel supply in order to extinguish the flame. When the flame is "blown out," like a candle is blown out, the person no longer returns to a body and, therefore, will suffer no more. In fact, they no longer exist.

"Extinction" is an appropriate synonym for Nirvana, at least as most Buddhist texts describe it. Buddhist scholars, on the other hand, say Nirvana is "beyond concepts" and, therefore, cannot be explained.

Three Jewels

Novice Buddhist monks take vows, pledging to "take refuge" in the "Three Jewels": "I take refuge in the Buddha, I take refuge in the *dhamma* (teaching), I take refuge in the *sangha* (the community of monks)." "Taking refuge in the Buddha" does not mean these initiates seek comfort in a living being named Buddha. When he died, Buddha ceased to exist; he reached the "Nothingness" of Nirvana. (Images of the "Reclining Buddha," that is, Buddha lying down, are intended to capture the moment of his death and reaching Nirvana.)

The *dhamma* (which is how the Sanskrit word *dharma* meaning "duty" is pronounced in the ancient Pali language of Southeast Asia) means "teaching."[6] Siddhartha's teachings and those of his followers have inspired many collections of sacred texts, and Buddhist sects are divided over which text is most authoritative. So there is no universal agreement among Buddhists on what the correct *dhamma* is.

Finally, the *sangha* refers specifically to the fellowship of monks (namely among Theravada Buddhists). In other Buddhist circles, the term applies to any gathering of Buddhists. In many Buddhist temples, visitors will see three sticks of incense burning in front of an image of Buddha. The three sticks represent the Three Jewels.

God?

Siddhartha did not believe in a Creator God, nor did he advocate the worship of any deities. The gods themselves suffer because they exist; therefore, they are no help to those who seek to escape suffering by following the path that leads to Nirvana. It is for this reason that Buddhism is sometimes labeled atheistic.

Significant Practices

Worship in Buddhist temples consists of chanting passages from Buddhist texts with worshipers seated facing either a Buddha image or, in many sects, a parchment with Buddhist writings. Meditation in various sects incorporates chanting of Buddhist scriptures or certain phrases they consider to be central. For example, Nichiren Buddhists chant "nam myoho renge kyo," a Chinese phrase usually translated, "I worship the beautiful Lotus Law." Pure Land Buddhists chant "namu Amida Butsu" ("I trust in Amida Buddha").

In some cases, practitioners believe that the vibrations of the words themselves have power to focus the mind and order one's life. On the other hand, some forms of Buddhist meditation are completely silent. Vipassana meditation, for example, teaches beginners to focus only on their own breath as a means of blocking out all other thoughts.

Some forms of meditation—silent or not—use an object to focus one's attention; the object could be an image of the Buddha. Ultimately, the goal is to be unaware of one's breath or to look through the object, to think and see only emptiness, in pursuit of the detachment that eventually leads to Nirvana.

Making Merit

The Law of Karma makes merit-making a prime concern for most Buddhists. Of course, avoiding the behaviors that bring negative karma is paramount. Positively, Buddhists seek to counter the effects of such negative karma by honoring the "Five Precepts" (which overlap somewhat with the Eight-fold Path). They are as follows:

> not killing (people or animals)
> not stealing
> not misusing sex
> not lying
> not consuming intoxicants of any kind

Other virtuous acts include giving "alms" (usually in the form of food) to monks, chanting Buddhist texts or phrases, and showing respect for Buddha images or Buddhist monks.

In practice, many Buddhists are not necessarily thinking of long-term consequences as they "make merit." A friend in Thailand may be speaking for many Buddhists when he said, "I don't make merit in order to attain something better. I do it because it gives me a sense of peace inside."[7]

Holy Days

Buddhist holy days vary from country to country. Buddhist New Year is celebrated in Theravada countries (see "Significant Sects and Developments" below) including Thailand, Burma, Sri Lanka, Cambodia, and Laos, beginning with the first full moon in April. The calendar begins with the death of Buddha 543 years before the birth of Jesus. So the year 2017 on the calendar we use in the West is the year 2560 BE (for "Buddhist Era") in those countries. Chinese, Korean, and Vietnamese people celebrate the New Year in January or early February; Tibetans celebrate about one month later. These countries do not typically use the Buddha's death as the starting point of their calendars.

Vesak or "Buddha Day" celebrates Siddhartha's birthday. Many believe he was also enlightened and died on that same day on the calendar (in our May), making Vesak perhaps the most auspicious of Buddhist holidays. In other Buddhist traditions, Siddhartha's enlightenment is commemorated on Bodhi Day (in December). In July, many Buddhists mark Dharma Day as the day when Siddhartha delivered his first sermon (on the "Four Noble Truths"). During the Obon festival (in July or August), Buddhists in China, Japan, Korea, and other countries honor their ancestors by visiting their graves and laying floating lanterns on bodies of water at night. For each holy day, special chanting services are held at the Temple with monks taking the lead and lay people sitting behind them.

Significant Sects and Developments

Buddhists believe that Siddhartha's teachings were rehearsed orally by no less than five hundred of his followers who gathered in what is considered to be the first Buddhist Council shortly after his death around 480 BC.[8] They organized their recollections into three categories: rules for monks, Buddha's sermons, and miscellaneous sayings of the Buddha. This threefold oral collection was called "Tripitaka," which means "Three Baskets"; the oral traditions were passed down from generation to generation and finally put in written form in the third century BC.

Texts that emerged much later than the *Tripitaka*, like the *Lotus Sutra* ("Flower Law") and the *Platform Sutra*, are considered more authoritative by the sects that follow them. Buddhists in Tibet (who follow the Dalai

Lama) call their holy books the *Kanjur* and *Tanjur*. Zen Buddhists believe enlightenment occurs without the benefit of words, so they revere no written text. Therefore, no single sacred text serves as the definitive scripture for all Buddhists.

Perhaps it is due to the lack of a single authoritative sacred text that Buddhism splintered into so many different factions. Most comparative religion professors name two major branches: Theravada and Mahayana, though others identify Vajrayana Buddhism (in Tibet) as a third branch. The word "Theravada" (pronounced "Tera-vada") means "the way of the elders." As such, Theravadins (as they are called) claim to represent the oldest and most orthodox form of Buddhism. Theravada Buddhism emphasizes the quest of monks to attain enlightenment with the help and support of the laity, who can only hope to acquire enough good karma to be reborn as monks in a subsequent life. Detractors who emerged within a few centuries of Siddhartha's death criticized Theravada Buddhists for stressing the clergy over the laity. Critics coined the term "Hinayana," ("Little Vehicle") to refer to this form of Buddhism that could accommodate so few. Still, Theravada Buddhism predominates Southeast Asian nations, including Thailand, Laos, Cambodia, Nepal, Myanmar, Sri Lanka, and India. It is sometimes called "Southern Buddhism."

By way of contrast, Mahayana Buddhists—"Mahayana" means "Greater Vehicle"—believe Buddha's original teaching was more inclusive, stressing the role of monks as *bodhistattvas* who delay their entrance into Nirvana in order to help others (including non-monks) find the path to enlightenment. "Mahayana" does not describe any one Buddhist sect, but instead applies to all the others that are not of the Theravada school. Mahayana sects thrive in China, Japan, and Tibet. Sometimes people refer to Mahayana Buddhism as "Northern Buddhism" for that reason. Space does not permit a full description of the various Mahayana sects. Below are brief summaries of the Buddhist sects North Americans are most likely to encounter.

Nichiren

In the thirteenth century AD, a Japanese Buddhist named Nichiren Shoshu (or Daishonen) taught that the original teachings of Buddha were best encapsulated in the text the *Lotus Sutra*. More specifically, he believed that the key to that text is in chapters two and sixteen, both of which emphasize the law of karma as the ultimate truth of the universe. Practitioners remind themselves through daily chanting that they determine their own destiny by their own behavior.

In the words of my friend Barbara, a practitioner, "Every person has the power to control their destiny by transforming, eradicating, or utilizing what may be perceived as negative into a mission for peace."[9] She and her fellow Nichiren Buddhists believe that chanting "nam myoho renge kyo" helps. The phrase is typically translated, "I devote myself to the mystic lotus law [karma]".[10] Devotees chant the phrase in groups at Buddhist Centers and in their private homes, facing a *gohonzon*, a copy of the sacred text written in Chinese characters. In their own words, "making good causes" instead of bad ones is the goal. *Nam myoho renge kyo* is more than a kind of self-talk. They believe that the sounds themselves align the chanter with this powerful force that governs the universe.

All circumstances—from a flat tire to a job promotion to a happy marriage—are the direct results of one's own actions, either in this life or in a previous life, and one's alignment with this universal law. Nichiren Buddhists, unlike other Buddhists, believe that we will always exist in bodily form; there is no escaping. "Hell" to a Nichiren Buddhist is the result of making such bad choices that one suffers only negative consequences in the here and now. "Heaven" happens when a person is clicking on all cylinders, "making only good causes," and reaping only positive rewards. "Within each moment," says Barbara, "one has the potential for the highest life-state of Buddhahood."[11]

In pre-war Japan, lay Nichiren Buddhists formed the Soka Gakkai, or the "Value Creation Society," to spread their understanding of Buddhist humanism. Soka Gakkai International (SGI) now claims more than twelve million members worldwide, with as many as three hundred thousand in the United States, operating many SGI centers in major metropolitan areas.[12] Music icons Tina Turner and Herbie Hancock and actor Orland Bloom are among the many celebrity Nichiren Buddhists.

Pure Land

Pure Land Buddhism is the most popular form of Buddhism in Japan. Founded in the twelfth century AD by a Japanese Buddhist monk named Honen, Pure Land honors a legendary Buddha named Amida, who promised that through "pure thought," the faithful may reach a western Paradise when they die. From that Paradise, they will attain the purity that will enable them to achieve enlightenment and Nirvana. The key to purity is "pure thought." The best way to achieve it is through constantly declaring one's trust in Amida Buddha by repeating the phrase "namu amida butsu"—"I trust in Amida Buddha." Practitioners chant that phrase—both in groups at Pure Land Temples and in their own homes—facing a script with those Chinese characters inscribed on it.

How often must one repeat this phrase to secure their place in Paradise? Ideally, the truly committed repeat the phrase many times daily. But Honen taught that if a person said it only ten times in a lifetime and meant it, this would be sufficient. One of his students, Shinran, questioned his master's teaching, believing the phrase to be so powerful that saying it only once would guarantee one's place in Paradise. With that conviction, he broke away from Pure Land to form the "True Pure Land" sect, a sect which has since subdivided many times over.

Vajrayana (Tibetan)

Tibetan Buddhism receives a lot of attention in the United States, though the percentage of American Buddhists who practice this form of Buddhism must be quite low.[13] But Tibet's political status (since it was annexed by China in 1959), kept in the public spotlight by the activism of celebrities like Richard Gere (among others), and by the charisma of its leader, the Dalai Lama, may give the impression that there are more Tibetan Buddhists in North America than religious censuses show. Tibetan Buddhism began in Tibet in the seventh century AD when Buddhism was mixed with the traditional religion of the region (called "Bon"). Practitioners believe it to be the true Buddhism; they call it "Lamaism" from the word "Lama" which means "superior."

Zen

The word "Zazen" is the Japanese pronunciation of the Chinese term "Zuo Chan," which means "sitting meditation." Popularly known in the West as simply "Zen," this branch of Buddhism was founded in the sixth century AD by an Indian Buddhist teacher named Bodhidharma. According to him, when Siddhartha achieved enlightenment, he actually said nothing. He did not preach on "The Four Noble Truths" or the "Eight-fold Path." He simply held a lotus flower and kept quiet until one of the five ascetics suddenly and mysteriously understood the truth Buddha had just rediscovered. To this day, Zen Buddhism emphasizes enlightenment without words, an experience known as *satori*. The key to the experience is "taming the monkey mind"—thoughts that jump from one topic to the next—through long hours of silent meditation.

Zen masters also use riddles called *koans* in an effort to free initiates from thought patterns grounded in logic or reason. Famous *koans* include, "What is the sound of one hand clapping?" or, "Does a dog have Buddha nature?" Attempts to "figure out" the verbal puzzle are wrongheaded. Instead, Zen teachers stress the importance of being "in the moment," thinking not about the past or the future but about the here and now, with full concentration, whether the activity is meditation, work, or sharing a cup of tea. Such concentration proved useful in martial arts and has been incorporated into athletics around the world by non-Buddhists.

What Makes You Not a Buddhist?

Of course, many North Americans who self-identify as Buddhists do not fully embrace the concepts and practices described above. Frustrated with that phenomenon, a Tibetan Buddhist teacher in 2008 published a book entitled *What Makes You Not a Buddhist*.[14] The author confronts those who merely dabble in Buddhism with the assertion that true Buddhists accept these four truths (not identical to the Four Noble Truths):

1. All fabricated things are impermanent and have no true essence.
2. All emotions are pain.
3. All things have no inherent existence.
4. Nirvana is beyond concepts.

Those who do not embrace these truths are, in his opinion, not real Buddhists.

THAI BUDDHISM

Textbooks on world religions focus on the generally accepted histories, beliefs, and practices of each religion. In practice, Buddhists (and other religious people) don't always follow the textbooks. Thai Buddhism serves as an example of syncretism, the blending of religions.

In Thailand, Theravada Buddhism is merged with elements of Hinduism and animism in ways that Thais themselves may not realize. For example, the "Ramakien" epic is perhaps the most cherished religious story in Thailand; many Buddhist temples depict the story line on their walls. Ramakien is the Thai pronunciation of the Ramayana story, the Hindu myth. The King of Thailand, revered by Thais, is known as Rama X, a name borrowed from Lord Rama of Hinduism. When I mentioned the Hindu connection to one Thai woman, she responded, "So they know this story in India, too?"

Evidence of animism is everywhere in Thailand. Many Thais seek protection from evil spirits through magical charms and amulets. In front of most Thai buildings, either private or commercial, those who build them also construct "spirit houses" to appease the spirits who were displaced when the new building was built. Offerings of food or incense are placed in these houses regularly.

Significant Points of Contact

A longtime missionary in Thailand told me, "We don't have to step on Buddha to lift up Christ."[15] (Given that Buddhists consider the feet to be the most unholy part of the human body, "stepping" on the Buddha would be especially offensive.) Instead, as with the other religions described in this book, we look for common ground with Buddhist "others."

Suffering may be the starting point. Christians believe that God is concerned about suffering. In fact, suffering was not part of God's original design, but entered the world as the result of sin. When a drunk driver crosses into oncoming traffic and causes an accident, his sin injures others. The cause and effect is sometimes indirect and not automatic, unlike karma, but here there is at least some common ground.

We share with Buddhists the conviction about the "impermanence of all things," but only to some extent. Paul wrote, "We fix our eyes not on what is seen, but on what is unseen. For what is seen is temporary, but what is unseen is eternal" (2 Cor. 4:18). "Impermanent" and "temporary" are virtually synonymous terms. On the other hand, Christians don't believe that all things are impermanent. Our own souls, we believe, will endure forever. Our bodies will turn to dust when we die, but in Christ we believe we will be given new "resurrection bodies," and in them our souls will return to the God who breathed life into us in the beginning.

Christians can agree that meditation is an important spiritual discipline. The method of meditation and its ultimate objective—those are different. Instead of "emptying the mind," in meditation we seek to commune with God and develop the mind of Christ.

Significant Points of Contrast

A Christian theologian describes visiting Buddhist temples in Asia where it dawned on him that the primary symbol of Buddhism is an image of Buddha in a meditative state, blissfully detached. Compare that image with what has become the most common symbol of the Christian faith—Christ *attached* to a cross—and the contrast is telling. Christ did not seek to escape suffering, but he participated in human suffering in order to free us from the sin that is at the root of all suffering.[16] As Christians, we also join with Jesus in working to alleviate suffering wherever we find it, knowing that suffering is the product of life in a broken, sinful world and not God's ideal.

When the disciples asked Jesus, "Who sinned, this man or his parents, that he was born blind?" (John 9:2), they were assuming a "blame the victim" mentality that is at least akin to karma. That is, this man's condition must surely be the result of some past misdeed, either his or his parents'. Jesus's response does not clarify the source of this man's illness, but simply says his condition presents an opportunity to display God's work in his life (John 9:3). In that same spirit, in Christ we see redemption in suffering—Christ's and our own. Generally speaking, the Bible does not make a direct connection between a particular experience of suffering and sin, although the Old Testament prophets make that case when they explain why Israel or her enemies are punished. The New Testament especially stresses how God might use suffering to build character in us, to discipline us, to shape us into the image of Jesus.[17]

The Christian understanding of "salvation by grace through faith" removes merit-making of any kind from the equation. "It is by grace you have been saved . . . not by works, so that no one can boast," Paul wrote (Eph. 2:8–9). Our good deeds are driven not by our desire *to be* saved, but by gratitude that we *have been* saved, and by our desire to participate in God's mission in the world.

Finally, Christian faith is grounded in the historical realities of God's intervention in history, the pinnacle of which is the Incarnation of Jesus. D. A. Carson points out that if someone could persuade a Buddhist that Siddhartha Gautama never lived, it wouldn't necessarily change the way they practice their faith. Buddhists do not follow a historical Buddha (though they believe him to be a historical figure); they follow the path to Enlightenment—the path Buddha had rediscovered.[18] Christians cannot say the same thing and be true to the gospel. If the life, death, burial, and resurrection of Jesus are not, in fact, historical realities, then Christian faith is reduced to a set of moral principles. Instead, "we preach Christ crucified," and, "Christ in you, the hope of glory" (1 Cor. 1:23; Col. 1:27). Paul boldly declares that "if Christ has not been raised"—in other words, if the resurrection didn't really happen—"our preaching is useless and so is your faith" (1 Cor. 15:14). If the story of Jesus is just that—a story and not history—then the Christian life would be an exercise in the pursuit of . . . well . . . nothingness.

I believe this is all about so much more: not about a great *something*, but the great *Someone* who laid down his life—suffered on our behalf— that we might be reconciled to him. And when I say "we," I mean all of us, including these significant others, our Buddhist neighbors.

TALKING TOGETHER . . .

1. Have you met individuals that remind you of Amanda, Ben, or Hathai?

2. What did you learn about the story of Siddhartha that you did not know before?

3. How would you respond to each of the "Four Noble Truths" from a Christian perspective?

4. How does the Zen approach to meditation and learning through *koans* contrast with a Christian approach to understanding and communion with God?

5. What is a Christian response to each of the four statements that Dzongsar Khyentse believes separate "real" Buddhists from people who dabble in Buddhism (in his book *What Makes You Not a Buddhist*)?

6. How can you relate the statement from a missionary in Thailand, "We don't have to step on Buddha to lift up Christ," to conversations with adherents of other religions about their spiritual heroes?

7. How might you explain to a Buddhist a Christian perspective on suffering?

IF YOU WANT TO READ MORE . . .

Khyentse, Dzongsar Jamyang. *What Makes You Not a Buddhist*. Boston and London: Shambala, 2008.

Michaelson, Jay. *Evolving Dharma: Meditation, Buddhism, and the Next Generation of Enlightenment*. Berkeley, CA: Evolver Editions, 2013.

Pine, Red. *The Zen Teaching of Bodhidharma*. New York: North Point Press, 1987.

Prebish, Charles. *Looking West: A Primer on American Buddhism*. Charles Prebish, 2011.

Zacharias, Ravi. *The Lotus and the Cross: Jesus Talks with Buddha*. Sisters, OR: Multnomah Publishers, 2001.

Notes

[1] According to the Pew Research Forum, accessed August 11, 2016, http://www.pewforum.org/2012/12/18/global-religious-landscape-buddhist.

[2] Siddhartha's birth and death dates are the subject of much debate. Some Buddhist scholars place his death in the year 543 BC, others as late as 368. For example, see Roy C. Amore and Julia Ching, "The Buddhist Tradition," in *A Concise Introduction to World* Religions, edited by Willard G. Oxtoby and Alan F. Segal, 376–439 (Oxford: Oxford University Press, 2007), 378. The discrepancy also underscores the relative insignificance of the "historical Buddha" for most Buddhists. The emphasis is on the path to enlightenment that Siddhartha rediscovered, not on the historical details of his life.

[3] There are many different versions of what the infant actually said. Some accounts say he uttered the words, "I alone am the World-Honored One," others, "I was born to reach enlightenment and free all creatures from suffering."

[4] Buddhists usually distinguish between "reincarnation" (Hinduism) and "rebirth" (Buddhism), saying the two are not identical. Given Buddhist conviction about the "self" or the "non-self," the question is what is reborn exactly if the self does not exist? The point is a person is not "reborn" as "herself" or "himself," but something of the previous existence is perpetuated in the next life. That "something" is ill-defined. Ravi Zacharias prefers the phrase "incarnated again" over "reincarnation" for this reason, in *The Lotus and the Cross: Jesus Talks with Buddha* (Sisters, OR: Multnomah Publishers, 2001), 23.

[5] From a June 15, 2015, report by Cornell University's Roper Center, accessed August 11, 2016, https://ropercenter.cornell.edu/paradise-polled-americans-and-the-afterlife/.

[6] Pali is to Buddhism what Sanskrit is to Hinduism and what Latin once was (and still is in some cases) in Roman Catholic circles—a holy language reserved for religious expression, not a language used in normal conversation.

[7] Anonymous Thai Buddhist as told to Robert Reagan, in correspondence with author January 18, 2017.

[8] Again, the exact dates of his birth and death are unknown.

[9] Barbara McBee in correspondence with author January 21, 2017.

[10] This is the translation explained on the official website www.sgi.org. Accessed on August 13, 2016.

[11] Barbara McBee in correspondence with author January 21, 2017.

[12] The statistic comes from Charles Prebish's book *Looking West: A Primer on American Buddhism* (Charles Prebish, 2011), 145.

[13] It is difficult to know how many practitioners of each Buddhist sect there may be because the U.S. Census data usually only offers "Buddhism" as an option.

[14] Dzongsar Jamyang Khyentse, *What Makes You Not a Buddhist* (Boston and London: Shambhala, 2008).

[15] Interview with Robert Reagan, Chiang Mai, Thailand, May 27, 2016.

[16] John R. W. Stott, *The Cross of Christ* (Downers Grove, IL: InterVarsity Press, 2006), 326–327.

[17] Passages such as Romans 5:3–5; 2 Corinthians 12:7–10; Hebrews 12:7–13; and James 1:2–4.

[18] D. A. Carson, "What Is the Gospel? Revisited," in *For the Fame of God's Name: Essays in Honor of John Piper,* edited by Sam Storms and Justin Taylor, 147–170 (Wheaton, IL: Crossway, 2010), 169.

CHAPTER SIX

OUR SIKH NEIGHBORS

Mandev Singh Sagoo has been employed by the same engineering firm in Indianapolis for the past twenty-five years. His coworkers, who call him "Dev," appreciate him for his work ethic, his steady, consistent, and pleasant demeanor, and his loyalty—to his family, to his friends, and to the company. According to them, he never says an unkind word about anyone. New employees are usually taken aback when they first meet Dev because of the turban he wears and his very full, untrimmed beard. Some of them assume Dev is a Muslim fundamentalist. When they ask other employees—and they always do within the first few days on the job—they learn that Dev is a Sikh, a father of three, an avid fan of the Green Bay Packers (he grew up in Wisconsin), and highly regarded by everyone in the office. None of them can explain exactly what a Sikh is, but they know that Dev believes in God and takes his faith very seriously.

Leena Kaur Takkar's coworkers say the same thing about her. Leena teaches Economics at the same public university in Arizona where she earned her PhD. She and her husband, Bik (short for Bikram), an anesthesiologist, are the parents of three teenagers. Their friends are impressed with the way the Takkars manage to juggle their many responsibilities at work and at home. Their children are well-mannered and are all at the top of their classes in school, thanks in part to their parents who are so invested in their kids' education. Bik was recently elected to the local school board, and Leena has served in the past as chairman of the junior high PTA. Nothing about Leena or Bik's wardrobe identifies them as Sikh; neither of them wears head coverings or other clothes that would reflect their India heritage. Except, that is, every now and then when neighbors will see the family piling into their SUV, decked out in traditional Indian dress, headed to a wedding at the Sikh Gurdwara where they worship.

Nimrata Randhawa has been called "Nikki" since she was a child. Born in a small town in South Carolina to Sikh parents who had immigrated to the States in the 1960s, Nikki grew up in the Sikh faith. When Nikki was twelve, her mother, knowing Nikki had a knack for numbers, put her to work as the bookkeeper at the family-owned clothing store. Nikki pursued that talent for accounting all the way to a degree at Clemson. Eventually, she became the CFO of her family's company, which by then had grown into a multi-million-dollar business. In 1996, Nikki married Michael Haley. Michael is a Methodist, Nikki was a Sikh, so they had two wedding ceremonies: one at a Methodist church and one at a Sikh Temple. As Mrs. Nikki Haley, she pursued an interest in civic policy all the way to political office, winning three terms in the South Carolina House of Representatives in the 2000s before being elected Governor of South Carolina twice, in 2009, and again in 2014. She is the first female governor in South Carolina's history and the youngest governor in the United States. Today she describes herself as a Christian, but she maintains ties to both faith communities.

"Mandev" and "Leena" are names I am giving to composite sketches of Sikh Americans I know. Former Governor Haley is a public figure and a rising star in the Republican Party.[1] They represent the worldwide community of close to thirty million members of the Sikh faith. According to the Sikh Coalition, an American advocacy group, there may be as many as five hundred thousand Sikhs in America, gathering in five hundred or more Sikh Gurdwaras (temples) across the United States.[2] Yet perhaps no religious group is more misunderstood. In the wake of 9/11, many Sikhs have been mistaken for Muslims and have been targeted for hate-crimes. Sikh men who wear the turban as a religious obligation stand out in a crowd. The unwanted attention has led some American Sikhs, especially members of the younger generation, to abandon the turban and cut their hair, while others have stood firm, wearing the turban in defense of their faith and their rights. There may be a family in your orbit that is Sikh and you didn't know it until you started reading this chapter.

Significant Figures

The founder of the Sikh faith, or "Sikhi" as it is known by adherents, is Nanak, born in 1469 to Hindu parents in the Punjab (sometimes spelled "Panjab") region of Northwest India, now on the Pakistani side of the India-Pakistan border. From an early age, Nanak was troubled by the religious divisions he witnessed, living in a corner of the world where Muslims and Hindus often collided violently. Nanak was inspired by the writings of the Indian poet Kabir, an outspoken critic of religious intolerance in general and of the Hindu caste system in particular.

When Nanak was thirty years old, he went to the local river for a traditional Hindu ritual bath, slipped beneath the water, and disappeared. Witnesses assumed he had drowned. To their great surprise, he emerged from a different location downstream three days later in a trance-like state. At first, all he would say was, "There is no Muslim and there is no Hindu." Later, he began reciting what has come to be known as the "Mul Mantar" ("root prayer") which begins with these lines: "There is only one God whose name is true, the Creator who has no fear or enmity, immortal, unborn, self-existent; by the favor of the Guru, repeat His Name!"[3]

Nanak went on to testify that during that three-day absence, he had actually ascended into the "court of God," where he had been given sacred nectar (*amrit*) to drink. He was then told to "rejoice in God's name" and to teach others to do the same. From this point forward, Sikh literature refers to him as Guru Nanak, honoring him with the familiar Hindu title.

Nanak wrote hymns that sing the praises of "one true God," hymns that were eventually collected into one book initially called "Adi Granth" (meaning "First Book"), the sacred text of the Sikhs. Those who followed the teaching of those hymns became known as "Sikhs" ("disciples").

Significant Beliefs

Nanak's epiphany about the "one true God" stands at the center of Sikh faith. Known as "Sat Nam" ("True Name"), "Ekankar" ("One Force"), and "Vahiguru" ("Awesome Wisdom"), the Divine defies human description.[4] From a Sikh point of view, too many religions speculate about the nature of God and descend into "anthropomorphisms"—that is, they attribute human characteristics to the Divine. Sikhism teaches that our duty is to remember God in practical ways: by repeating his name and by living virtuously, integrating the "outward" and "inward" aspects of life. Sikhs emphasize hard work, self-control, love of family, and service to others as the primary moral reflections of that integration of faith and life.

Shortly before his death (in 1539), Nanak was said to have named his follower Bhai Lehna as his successor, giving him the title "Guru Angad." As time passed, Sikhs came to believe that the spirit of Guru Nanak lived in all nine of his successors. When the tenth guru, Gobind Singh, died in 1708, he declared that the spirit of Guru Nanak would dwell in the sacred text itself, so the "Adi Granth" became the "Guru Granth Sahib" ("Teacher Book Revered"), the name by which Sikhs now refer to their holy book. The faithful point out that the Guru Granth Sahib is unique in that it contains hymns written by thirty-six authors, including Muslim and Hindu saints of Nanak's time. The book is the focal point of all Sikh gatherings; it is handled with great care, as if it is a living being.

Sikhism retains from its Hindu neighbors the belief in karma and reincarnation, but it teaches that people may escape the endless cycle of birth and rebirth only by "remembering God." The faithful expect to be united with God in death like a ray of light merges with pure light. Sikhs do not attempt to convert others to their faith; they believe God is tolerant of other religions and will accept all those who faithfully "remembered" him as best they could.

Significant Practices

Most Sikhs reserve a special room in their homes for their family copy of the Guru Granth Sahib. Faithful Sikhs start each day in that room, rising each morning to recite (in Punjabi) the "Japji" prayer, the first entry in the sacred text and the full version of the Mul Mantar mentioned above. (The recitation takes fifteen to twenty minutes.) Many Sikhs also gather weekly for collective worship services.

In the West, Sikhs usually meet on Sundays as a matter of convenience. (Their sacred text does not require group worship experiences, but they consider them valuable.) Sikh meeting places are called "Gurdwaras," literally "the Guru's door," since each one houses a copy of the sacred text. As worshipers enter the building, they remove their shoes and cover their heads. Inside the Gurdwara are two large rooms: the main prayer hall and a fellowship hall. In the West, many Gurdwaras also include another building with classrooms and a library where Punjabi language classes and Sikh religious instruction are offered to children in an after-school format.

Each morning at the Gurdwara, the sacred text is ceremonially brought from a side room attached to the main prayer hall and placed on a special cushioned platform in the center at the front of the room that is topped by a canopy decorated with colorful lights. The Japji prayer and other hymns are recited in the presence of the book both morning and evening. The book itself is draped in colorful cloth. During a worship service, a volunteer attendant, positioned directly behind the book, waves a fly whisk over the book every few seconds as a sign of respect.

The collective worship itself consists of two parts. As the first part, called *Kirtan*, begins, worshipers approach the Guru Granth Sahib with great reverence and bow in front of the platform, foreheads pressed to the ground. Then each worshiper places money on the lip of the platform as a means of supporting the Gurdwara, its staff, and its various functions. Men and women then take their seats on the carpeted floor—usually men on one side and women on the other—making sure that their feet are not pointed toward the book; that would be considered disrespectful.

During *Kirtan,* three musicians sing hymns from the Guru Granth Sahib, accompanying themselves with two harmonia (a pump organ) and one set of Indian bongo drums. In the *Katha* portion of the service, the book is opened and a passage is chanted aloud, usually by a Granthi (a paid caretaker of the Guru Granth Sahib), with prescribed prayers and blessings recited before and after each reading. Often an explanation of the reading will follow.

Evening services conclude with a special prayer, followed by a ceremony in which the book is returned to the bedroom where it will be kept overnight. It is considered an honor to be chosen to carry the book, resting on a cushion on one's head, and put it to bed for the night.

The practical function of the Guru Granth Sahib in daily life is illustrated by a practice called "taking *hukam*," which means opening the sacred book at random and reading the first hymn one finds to receive specific guidance for the day. The daily ritual is prescribed by the Guru Granth Sahib in the opening passage: "So how can you become truthful? And how can the veil of illusion be torn away? O Nanak, it is written that you should obey the Hukam of His command, and walk in the way of his will."[5] Every Sikh is supposed to begin the day by reading that passage and interpreting it as personal instruction for the day.

Sikhs who do not own a copy of the sacred book may read online the hukam that was read when the day began at the Golden Temple in Amritsar, India, the international headquarters of the Sikh faith. Of course, the "random reading" is not random to a Sikh believer; it is personal message from the spirit of the Guru that is said to live and breathe through the book.

Langar

The other room in the Gurdwara is called the "Langar" or fellowship hall. The meal eaten there is also called langar. The significance of the meal is best understood in the context of fifteenth century (and even modern) India, where citizens were not permitted to eat with members of another caste or religion. By contrast, all are welcomed at Langar regardless of caste or religion. Guests and members alike are served a vegetarian meal (so as not to offend vegetarian guests) while seated on the floor in rows. The meal is prepared and served by Sikh volunteers at no cost to the guests. It is often this act of hospitality that most impresses non-Sikhs who visit a Gurdwara.

Five Ks

Many Sikhs wear their religious devotion on their sleeves—literally—and on their heads. The five outward symbols of Sikh commitment all begin with the letter "k" ("*Kakaar*" in Punjabi). These are:

1. Uncut hair (called *kes*); women and men are not allowed to cut their hair. But, perhaps in reaction to Hindu "renouncers" whose uncut hair was also unkempt, Sikh men and women were instructed to keep their hair clean and combed. Men (and some women) wrap their hair in a turban for that purpose. Boys who reach puberty take pride in learning how to tie the turban, which is one long piece of cloth wrapped to contain the hair.

2. Sikhs always carry a wooden comb *(kangha)* which also represents the intention of keeping one's hair neat and clean. It is usually tucked into the hair underneath the turban.

3. A steel bracelet (*kara*) reminds the faithful of their moral obligations.

4. A small ceremonial dagger (*kirpan*) represents the commitment to vigilance in pursuit of one's faith. After the terrorist attacks of 9/11, the Transportation Security Administration (TSA) in the United States banned these religious symbols on airplanes.

5. Sikh men and women are required to wear special underpants (*kacha*) as a symbol of sexual purity.

Holy Days and Ceremonies

Most Sikh holy days mark an event in the life of one of the ten gurus. The birthday of the Guru Nanak, for example, is celebrated every November by a public reading of the entire Guru Granth Sahib from cover to cover. (It takes more than forty-eight hours to read the whole book aloud.) The ninth guru, Tegh Bahadur, was executed in 1675 by the Mughal Emperor Aurangzeb (whose father built the Taj Mahal for his late wife) for refusing to convert to Islam. The anniversary of his martyrdom, also in November, reminds followers of the price paid by their spiritual predecessors to perpetuate the Sikh faith.

Life cycle rituals take place at the Gurdwara, where predictably the Guru Granth Sahib plays a significant role. For example, families take their newborn child to the Gurdwara for the "Nam karan" or child-naming ceremony. The Granthi presides, opens the sacred text randomly (another case of *hukam*), then reads the hymn on that page. The child's name must begin with the first letter of the first word of that hymn. At Sikh weddings, the bride and groom are positioned directly in front of the Guru Granth Sahib in the main prayer hall in the Gurdwara. Hymns are sung and prayers are recited, as in any Sikh worship service. As the formal part of the ceremony nears its end, the couple walks slowly around the sacred book four times. A langar for the wedding party and guests follows. Sikh funerals include a period of mourning that features ten days of readings from the sacred text.

Significant Sects and Developments

Like so many religions described in this book, Sikh doctrine and practice developed over the years as one guru succeeded another. Sikhs note that gurus were chosen not on the basis of their lineage but based on their faithfulness.[6] When Guru Nanak named Bhai Lehna as his successor, he conferred on him the name "Angad," which means "part of me," thus establishing the precedent that each guru shares the same spirit with Nanak. The ten gurus are sometimes referred to as Nanak I, Nanak II, and so on.

Each of the ten made notable contributions that shaped modern Sikhism. Guru Angad transcribed Nanak's hymns into a new easier-to-read Punjabi script called "Gurmukhi" ("the guru's mouth"), which made the text more accessible to more people. The fourth leader, Guru Ram Das, built a reflecting pool in a village Guru Nanak used to visit, renamed the town "Amritsar" ("Pool of Nectar"), recalling the nectar ("amrit") Guru Nanak said he received when he was taken to the "court of God" during his mysterious three-day disappearance. Ram Das was succeeded by Gury Arjan Dev, who laid the foundation in Amritsar for the Golden Temple, built in the center of the reflecting pool. Known to Sikhs as "Harmandir Sahib" or "Temple of God," it is the geographical center of the Sikh faith. Arjan Dev also finished the compilation of the Guru Granth Sahib and enshrined the book in the Golden Temple. Sikh tradition says he became the first Sikh martyr when the Mughal Emperor required him to either convert (to Islam) or die.

After his death, Arjan Dev's only son, Hargobind, became the sixth guru, though he was only eleven years old. In keeping with his father's instructions, Hargobind built an army that included Sikhs, Hindus, and Muslims whose sole purpose was to defend their religious freedoms against the Mughal rulers. He established the Akal Takht ("Throne of the Timeless") next to the Golden Temple in Amritsar as the seat of Sikh political and military power.

The tenth guru, Gobind Rai, was named by his predecessor, Tegh Bahadur, before he was executed by the Mughal Emperor Aurangzeb. In response to the ongoing persecution, Gobind instituted several changes that have left an indelible imprint on Sikh faith. On New Year's Day in 1699, Gobind assembled the Sikh faithful and asked for a volunteer who would be willing to show his dedication to the faith by offering his own head. One young man stepped forward, so the story goes. Gobind took him into a tent, then emerged alone with blood on his sword as if he had beheaded the volunteer. He asked for another, then another. Five young men volunteered to die that day. In fact, Gobind had slaughtered a goat with that sword; all five men were alive and well inside the tent. This, Gobind said, was a test to see who among them would display the kind of courage such opposition required. The five men were then baptized in the "pool of nectar" that surrounded the Golden Temple; they in turn baptized Gobind. Together they became the first members of the "Khalsa" (meaning "pure"), the elite army that today refers to the most dedicated Sikhs (the ones who wear the "five k's" as symbols of devotion). Gobind conferred on these initiates the name "Singh," meaning "lion"; to the initiated women he gave the name "Kaur" or "Princess." That is why many Sikhs use "Singh" and "Kaur" as either their middle or last name.

Today thousands of Sikhs are baptized annually at the Golden Temple. The Sikh ideal is that all Sikhs should be initiated and become Khalsa, though this is considered to be an individual decision. It is likely that Sikhs you know who have cut their hair and, therefore, do not wear a turban are not considered members of the Khalsa. But they can still be Sikhs in good standing in their local Gurdwara.

The Sikh faith is led by a council of five "Jathedars," each one a representative chosen by each of the five most prestigious Sikh centers in India. They convene and deliberate at the Akal Takht in Amritsar and establish policies. The current Sikh "Code of Conduct" ("Rehat Maryada") was written by this council in the early twentieth century and is still considered the authoritative guide to orthodox Sikh faith and practice.[7] It has also been the subject of controversy within the Sikh community and a source of tension between Sikhs and the Indian government.

That tension erupted into violence in 1984 when Prime Minister Indira Gandhi sent the Indian Army to the Akal Tahkt and the Golden Temple to end a standoff with Sikh leaders who were fighting for religious freedom. The sacred precinct was desecrated, many Sikhs were killed defending it, and Sikhs all over India were attacked by non-Sikhs. The conflict further fueled the push for an independent state that faithful Sikhs intended to call "Khalistan." Today, posters with the words "Remember 1984" can be seen in many Gurdwaras. The Prime Minister herself paid a heavy price for what Sikhs considered her heavy-handedness. She was assassinated by her own body guards (who were Sikhs) later that same year. Tensions eventually subsided and the relationship between the Sikh community in India and the Indian government reached a new high when a Sikh man, Manmohan Singh, served as Prime Minister of India from 2004 to 2014.

Significant Points of Contact

In many ways, Sikhs seem to share with Christians the conviction that there is only one God and that devotion to this one true God is the focal point of our lives. The call to "remember God" that punctuates Sikh explanations of their faith resonates with us, too. "Remembering God" is more than an intellectual commitment. God is best "remembered" by those who lead virtuous lives; what is "virtuous" is what is prescribed by the Guru Granth Sahib.

Sikh hospitality is impressive and especially admirable, given the context of caste discrimination and religious infighting in which langar (the fellowship meal) was instituted. Having been on the receiving end of Sikh hospitality many times, I can verify that it achieves its stated purpose: to communicate that all are welcome to break bread with Sikhs as equals. We who are in Christ are at our best when we demonstrate such inclusiveness at our own tables.

Significant Points of Contrast

As Christians we believe God has acted in nature and history to reveal himself to humanity. In Psalm 19, David sings a hymn of praise, saying, "the heavens declare the glory of God" and "the law of the LORD is perfect, reviving the soul." In one psalm, David refers to both "general revelation" (in nature) and "special revelation" (in Scripture) through which God reveals himself. Though we cannot yet know him to the degree that we are known *by* him, God's mission has always been to reveal himself to his creatures so that we might be drawn into an intimate relationship with him. From the Sikh perspective, God reveals little more than his "true name." But we believe that God's greatest self-revealing act was to become flesh and dwell among us. In the words of the Apostle John, "No one has ever seen God, but God the One and Only, who is at the Father's side, has made him known" (John 1:18). What we see in him is the fullness of "grace and truth" (John 1:14). Paul wrote, "For in Christ all the fullness of the Deity lives in bodily form, and you have been given fullness in Christ, who is the head over every power and authority" (Col. 2:9–10).

We thank God for inspiring the sacred texts we read in the Bible. But we do not worship the Bible. My Sikh friends will tell you they do not worship the Guru Granth Sahib, but only the God Nanak worshiped. But their behavior toward the book in which they believe the spirit of Nanak dwells—bowing before it, singing and praying to it, "waking it up" in the morning and "putting it to bed" at night, treating it like the revered teacher they believe it to be—all of this would amount to "bibliolatry"—worshiping the Bible—if Christians treated the Bible in the same way. As Jesus said to a Jewish audience devoted to Torah study, "You diligently study the Scriptures because you think that by them you possess eternal life. These are the Scriptures that testify about me, yet you refuse to come to me to have life" (John 5:39–40). I respect my Sikh friends for their genuine reverence for their sacred text. But I also long for them to know this God they worship from afar who makes himself known in the person of Jesus.

TALKING TOGETHER . . .

1. Do you know any Sikhs? If yes, do the brief accounts of individual Sikhs at the beginning of this chapter match your impressions of the ones you know?

2. What features of the Sikh faith do you find noble or praiseworthy?

3. Compare the Sikh conviction about their sacred text, the Guru Granth Sahib, with your own understanding of the Bible.

4. What reminders do the Sikh build into the fabric of their day? What can Christians learn from their use of ritual and rhythm in support of their faith?

5. What do think about the historical shift within Sikhism from pacifism to a more aggressive form of self-defense in the face of persecution? What is your response to that shift from a Christian point of view?

IF YOU WANT TO READ MORE . . .

Diem-Lane, Andrea. *The Sikhs: A Brief Introduction*. Walnut, CA: Mt. San Antonio College, 2014.

Khalsa, Siri Kirpal Kaur. *Sikh Spiritual Practice: The Sound Way to God*. Winchester, UK: O Books, 2010.

Singh, Patwant. *The Sikhs*. New York: Doubleday, 1999.

Website: http://www.sikhs.org/.

Notes

[1] At the time of publication, Nikki Haley was serving as the United States Ambassador to the United Nations.

[2] According to Sikh expert, Dr. Harbans Lal, of Dallas, Texas, in correspondence with author January 22, 2017.

[3] Robert E. Van Voorst, *Anthology of World Scriptures,* 6th edition (Belmont, CA: Thomson-Wadsworth, 2008), 125.

[4] In a booklet written for non-Sikhs to explain Sikhism, entitled *Sikhi: Faith and Followers,* by Harinder Singh and others (Bridgewater, NJ: Sikh research Institute, 2013), 7, the name "Ekankar" is spelled "Ik Oankar" and translated "One Force." I have also

heard Sikhs explain that "ek" is the number one in Punjabi, "an" (the middle syllable) is actually "aum," the most sacred Hindu sound, and "kar" means "Lord," so that "Ekankar" may be translated "One-Aum-Lord."

[5] Guru Granth Sahib 1:1, in *Sri Guru Granth Sahib*, translated by Singh Sahib Sant Khalsa (Tuscon, AZ: Hand Made Books, n.d.), 1. Accessed online on April 4, 2017, http://www.gurbanifiles.org/translations/English%20Translation%20of%20Siri%20Guru%20Granth%20Sahib.pdf.

[6] Most of the ten gurus were, in fact, relatives of the ones they succeeded; many of them were young children at the time of their succession.

[7] For the current Sikh Code of Conduct, see the link at http://www.sikhs.org/rehit.htm. Accessed June 12, 2016.

CHAPTER SEVEN

OUR BAHÁ'Í NEIGHBORS

Amir Ramezani is the CFO of a physicians group in suburban Philadelphia, Pennsylvania, where he lives with his wife and four young children. Amir's family came to the United States from his native Iran when Amir was only eight years old. Three decades later, he vividly remembers that first year: how lonely he felt at school where he knew no one and spoke little English. He remembers watching his mother trying to fight back the tears, homesick for her family and friends, worried about their safety as a persecuted religious minority in the world's most populous Shi'ite Muslim nation. Fast forward to today and Amir will tell you that he feels only gratitude for the safe haven his family found here, and appreciation for the religious freedom his children will take for granted. When people learn that the Ramezani's are members of the Bahá'í faith, most smile politely and don't ask questions. Those who want to know more are impressed when Amir tells them about the Bahá'í emphasis on universal justice and tolerance, and on the unity of all religions and peoples.

Unlike Amir, Jessica Alvarez did not grow up in a Bahá'í home. In fact, her parents were not religious, though she recalls many discussions about religion around their dinner table in Sarasota, Florida. In college, turned off by the party atmosphere that surrounded her, she bonded with a fellow-student from Pensacola who was Bahá'í. She knew her friend took her faith seriously and that she attended meetings in someone's apartment about once a month, but she didn't strike Jessica as dogmatic. When Jessica started asking more questions, her friend invited her to join her at one of the meetings, which she learned were called "Nineteen Day Feasts." That sounded pretty different to her, at first. But the more Bahá'í she got to know, the more she learned about their faith, the more impressed she was with the diversity of the group, how thoughtful they were, how much time they spent in their meetings discussing an after-school literacy program they sponsored or some other noble cause. The meetings always opened with someone—and it could be anyone, since there was no clergy—reading passages worded like prayers from a little volume composed, they said, by their founder whom they called "Bahá'u'lláh." Otherwise, very little about the gatherings struck her as religious. After attending meetings regularly for six months, Jessica filled out a membership card and became a Bahá'í. There was no initiation ceremony and no fanfare. She liked that, too.

Jim Johnson came to the Bahá'í faith in a similar way. As a ninth grader, he remembers feeling disappointment with what seemed like canned answers to questions he would ask his youth pastor at the Methodist church his family attended in rural Indiana. In college at the University of Indiana where he majored in political science, he took as many religion courses as he could, fascinated and troubled all at once by the competing truth claims of the world's religions. Always a seeker, it bothered him that Christians, Muslims, Jews, Hindus, and Buddhists he met did not seem well-informed about their own religions. It was a law school classmate who gave him a book that introduced him to the Bahá'í Faith. As he read that book, it was as if the puzzle pieces all started to fit. It wasn't long before he, too, became a Bahá'í. Jim now works as chief legal counsel for a corporation in Indianapolis. On weekends, he helps organize meetings and service projects guided by his Local Spiritual Assembly, the administrative body of elected Bahá'í representatives who live in Jim's area.

These are three composite sketches of adherents of a religion that claims between five million and seven million followers worldwide.[1] In the United States, there are hundreds of Bahá'í communities concentrated mostly in larger metropolitan areas of the country. Together they advance the newest of the world's major religions. Their relatively small numbers make comparative religion scholars debate whether or not to include a chapter on Bahá'í in their textbooks. (Many of those books refer to the Bahá'í faith as one of many newcomers in chapters with titles like "New Religious Movements.") But given the likelihood that readers of this book will encounter Bahá'í, the appeal of their message in our pluralistic age, and the Bahá'í call for universal tolerance and justice, we need to learn more about our Bahá'í neighbors.

Significant Figures

From the perspective of an outsider, the Bahá'í faith began as a reform movement in Iran within Islam. Two men are considered the founders of the faith.

"The Báb"

Ali Muhammad (1819–1850) was born in Shiraz, Persia (present-day Iran), as a Shi'a Muslim. While making the pilgrimage to Mecca in 1844, he declared himself to be the mouthpiece of the "hidden imam" (the twelfth and last Shi'a imam mentioned in Chapter Three), a "gate" ("the Báb") through which the faithful could find truth. The significance of the Báb's announcement is reflected in the Bahá'í calendar which begins in the year 1844. 2017 on Western calendars is the year 174 BE (for "Bahá'í Era").

When he returned home, "the Báb" published a book entitled *Bayán*, in which he called for reforms within Islam, such as expanding access to education for more citizens, including women. He also predicted that one greater than himself would follow him and complete his work. For this reason, Bahá'í literature compares Ali Muhammad to John the Baptist, who "prepared the way" for Jesus as "the Báb" did for his successor. Those who believed "the Báb" took the name "*Bábi*," or "followers of the gate." Their numbers grew so sufficiently that the Shah, the Persian ruler, took note and began to oppress them. Ali Muhammad himself was arrested and executed for heresy (against Islam) in Persia in 1850.[2]

"Bahá'u'lláh"

Mirzá Husayn-`Alí (1817–1892) had been one of Ali Muhammad's followers.[3] As the son of a prominent government official, his embrace of the teachings of "the Báb" was a source of embarrassment to his family. But it would soon get worse. In 1852, a Bábi member was accused of attempting to assassinate the Shah. Mirzá Husayn-`Alí was imprisoned, then thrown into a dungeon in Tehran where he had an epiphany in which God revealed to him that he was, in fact, "the Beauty of God," "the Mystery of God and His Treasure, the Cause of God and His Glory."[4] Bahá'í liken the episode to God's appearance to Moses at the burning bush, the dove that descended on Jesus at his baptism, the moment of Buddha's enlightenment, and the first appearance of the angel Gabriel to Muhammad.[5]

Mirzá Husayn-`Alí kept this to himself for the next decade. Because of his high status, `Alí was not executed along with other Bábis similarly accused, but was instead banished to Baghdad. It was there in 1863, in a garden called Ridvan ("Paradise"), that Mirzá Husayn-`Alí, inspired by the vision he had in the pit in Tehran, declared himself to be the One of whom the Báb had spoken. He claimed to be nothing less than a Manifestation of God Himself. From this point forward, Mirzá Husayn-`Alí assumed the honorific name "Bahá'u'lláh" ("glory of God"); his followers became known as "Bahá'í," or "followers of Bahá'u'lláh."

Bahá'u'lláh spent the rest of his life as a prisoner of the Ottoman Empire, first in Iran, then in Turkey, and, for the last twenty-four years, in Acre (pronounced "Akko") on the Mediterranean coast of Israel, a few miles from the modern city of Haifa. In his final years, he was released from prison but kept under house arrest. There, in his house now known as Bahjí, he wrote extensively and received guests, especially Bahá'í, from around the world. Bahá'u'lláh died there in 1892 and is buried on that same property, considered by Bahá'í to be the most sacred spot on earth. It was during all those years of confinement that Bahá'u'lláh received what Bahá'í believe to be inspired revelations from God which he put in writing and which outline basic Bahá'í beliefs.

Significant Beliefs

Bahá'u'lláh taught that there is only one God (Allah), "the unknowable Essence, the divine Being, [who] is immensely exalted beyond every human attribute. . . . Far be it from His glory that human tongue should adequately recount His praise, or that human heart comprehend His fathomless mystery."[6] Yet God has revealed at least some of his attributes throughout history through "Messengers" or "Manifestations," which include Abraham, Moses, Zoroaster, Krishna, Buddha, Jesus, Muhammad, "the Báb," and Bahá'u'lláh. As the latest of these Manifestations, the words of Bahá'u'lláh are considered to be the most recent and, therefore, most authoritative. Bahá'í believe that God will not send another Manifestation for at least a thousand years.

Bahá'u'lláh taught that all of these Messengers were sent by the one God. So how do Bahá'í account for the apparent contradictions in their teachings? First, each of these religious founders brought a message from God that includes both eternal spiritual principles and social teachings that were necessary for their time and place. For example, Buddha taught what was needed in India six centuries before Christ, and Jesus revealed what the world needed to hear in his day. Second, religious adherents themselves in these different religious traditions unintentionally distort the original messages of their founders, sometimes beyond recognition. In their purer, unadulterated forms (some of which are now lost to us), they were all on the same page.

Both explanations fall under the heading "Progressive Revelation" in Bahá'í writings. This means that God has revealed himself more and more over time. Unfortunately, they argue, adherents of these religions become fixated on a literal reading of their sacred texts and miss this bigger picture they all paint of the "Oneness of God." Likewise, their teachings, though they seem different to us, all combine to form one religion. My Bahá'í friend, Todd, compares the "oneness of religion" to the many installments of the "Star Wars" movies: they are all different episodes in one unfolding story.[7] Yes, Todd acknowledges, religious people typically present their own religion as distinct from all others. But Bahá'u'lláh made it clear that they are mistaken. In his own words, "neither the Scriptures of the world, nor all the books and writings in existence, shall, in this Day, avail you aught without this, the Living Book."[8] In other words, the sacred texts of other faiths only make sense in light of the Bahá'u'lláh's writings. Therefore, believers claim that "the Bahá'í Faith is the fulfillment of all the world's religions."[9] This unity of all religions ordained by one God is part of the "Greater Covenant" God has made with humanity. The specifics of the Bahá'í Faith and the prescriptions for its perpetuation are part of the "Lesser Covenant."[10]

Any summary of Bahá'í beliefs will always include a third kind of "oneness" in addition to the oneness of God and the oneness of religion: the oneness of humanity. Inscribed on the interior walls of the Bahá'í House of Worship in Wilmette, Illinois, is this quote from Bahá'u'lláh: "Ye are the fruits of one tree, and the leaves of one branch. Deal ye one with another with the utmost love and harmony, with friendliness and fellowship." This fundamental conviction drives the diversity in the Bahá'í community which is apparent in Bahá'í gatherings, and admirable. Gender equality is prescribed by Bahá'í teaching as well. Bahá'u'lláh's son, 'Abdu'l-Bahá, wrote, "The world of humanity has two wings—one is women and the other men. Not until both wings are equally developed can the bird fly. Should one wing remain weak, flight is impossible."[11]

Bahá'í believe that individuals will continue to progress spiritually beyond death. All who choose to seek God—Bahá'í and non-Bahá'í—will grow steadily closer to God in the next life. "Hell" is reserved for those who choose not to seek God at all; it is not a literal destination, but a metaphor for the alienation from God that will be felt by the soul who chooses that path. Collectively, humanity will progress, fueled by Bahá'í insight, toward a period Bahá'í call "The Most Great Peace." God will use various means to usher in this golden age, including education for all, advances in both science and religion (which Bahá'í stress are not incompatible), universal justice overseen by a world parliament (not unlike the United Nations, but one with more authority), and a common universal language (chosen by that yet-to-be-established world parliament) which will enable the peoples of the world to communicate with each other.

Significant Practices

A faithful Bahá'í begins her day with a prayer written by the Bahá'u'lláh. Otherwise, Bahá'í are expected to abide by Bahá'í laws spelled out in Bahá'í writings. Those laws prescribe righteousness and purity as well as detachment from material things. Bahá'í do not consume alcohol, perhaps a carryover from the founders' Islamic roots. But they stress the importance of understanding the rationale behind such laws. Bahá'í value critical thinking and reason as paths to knowledge. The aim of Bahá'í faith, both individually and collectively, is the pursuit of peace and justice for all.

A minimum of nine elected Bahá'í constitute a Local Spiritual Assembly (LSA). The LSA organizes community meetings once every nineteen days in keeping with the Bahá'í calendar which consists of nineteen months of nineteen days each. The gathering, convened in members' homes and called the "Nineteen Day Feast," involves very little religious ritual. The meeting opens with prayers written by Bahá'u'lláh, the Báb, or Bahá'u'lláh's son, 'Abdu'l-Bahá. Often there will be an organized discussion of some aspect of Bahá'í faith and practice. But many meetings focus on coordinating service projects of various kinds in the community.

In cities with more Bahá'í members, Bahá'í will gather on Bahá'í Holy Days and other special occasions in Bahá'í centers they have purchased or built for that purpose. Those Holy Days include the Bahá'í New Year, known as "Naw-Ruz," which coincides with the first day of spring (March 21). "Ridvan" (pronounced "Riz-wan") takes its name from the garden in Baghdad where Bahá'u'lláh revealed his identity to his closest friends. The event is celebrated during "Twelve Days of Ridvan" beginning on April 20 or 21 each year. May 22 or 23 marks the occasion of the "Declaration of the Báb," when Ali Muhammad said he was the "Gate" who would prepare the way for Bahá'u'lláh who would follow him. The anniversaries of the births and deaths of the Báb and Bahá'u'lláh are also considered holy days.

Bahá'í have built nine "Houses of Worship" around the world to date, each one offered as a gift to the local community for spaces reserved for quite reflection and not necessarily as places of worship for Bahá'í themselves.[12] These unique buildings feature nine entrances representing the highest single number, a symbol of completeness.[13] Each morning in these "houses of worship," Bahá'í volunteers read prayers or passages from other sacred texts without commentary.[14]

The grounds are beautifully landscaped, with flowers and greenery adding to the serenity of the sites. The same is true of the two holiest Bahá'í buildings—the "Shine of the Báb" where Ali Muhammad is buried on the slopes of Mount Carmel in Haifa and the "Shrine of Bahá'u'lláh," the final resting place of Bahá'u'lláh in nearby Acre. All of these buildings are built with funds donated solely by Bahá'í; donations from non-Bahá'í are not accepted. The sites are maintained almost entirely by Bahá'í volunteers.

Significant Sects and Developments

Mirzá Husayn-`Ali's own half-brother, Azal, himself a follower of the Báb, was not thrilled when his brother identified himself as "Bahá'u'lláh" in 1863. In fact, he tried to kill him more than once and almost succeeded when he poisoned his food. Both brothers were sent into exile along with the rest of their extended family. But because of the conflict, Azal was sent to Cyprus when Bahá'u'lláh was taken to Acre, Israel. There were other Bábí who were not enamored with Bahá'u'lláh's declaration. In fact, a small group of Bábí, now known as "Azalis" (taking their name from Azal), continue the Bábí tradition in Iran and Cyprus. Otherwise, Bahá'í have avoided division, thanks to their shared conviction about the authority of Bahá'u'lláh's writings, called "Tablets," and the clear instructions about his successor.

Of all of his writings, the Bahá'u'lláh's most important work is entitled *Kitab-i-Aqdas* or *The Most Holy Book*. In its 190 verses, he affirms his identity as "the Dayspring of God's Light." "O ye leaders of religion!" he writes. "Who is the man amongst you who can rival Me in vision or insight? Where is he to be found that dareth to claim to be My equal in utterance or wisdom?"[15] Here, too, Bahá'u'lláh makes the case for the three kinds of oneness mentioned above: the oneness of God, the oneness of religion, and the oneness of humanity. The book enjoins on Bahá'í the responsibility of establishing a "House of Justice" made up of Bahá'í members, constructing houses of worship "throughout the lands," making pilgrimage to "the sacred House" (his house in Baghdad), the "Nineteen Day Feast," daily prayers, and other expectations.[16]

There are also prohibitions against common religious practices in other faiths, such as "the kissing of hands" (34), ascetic practices like those common in Hinduism (36), or shaving one's head (44), as well as prescribed punishments for offenses of various kinds.[17] Rules for marriage include the requirement of a dowry, rules for polygamy, and divorce.[18] Bahá'u'lláh specifically challenges certain Islamic practices of his day, including the custom named in the Qur'an by which a husband was allowed to divorce his wife by pronouncing three times (over a period of three months), "I divorce thee." "The Lord hath prohibited, in a Tablet," he writes, "inscribed by the Pen of His command, the practice to which ye formerly had recourse when thrice ye had divorced a woman."[19]

From an outsider's perspective, one of the most surprising features of this, "The Most Holy Book," is Bahá'u'lláh's messages to specific world leaders of his day. For example, he chastises the "Emperor of Austria" (part of the Austro-Hungarian Empire at the time) for failing to pay Bahá'u'lláh a visit when the Emperor was making a pilgrimage to Jerusalem to pray at the mosque built on the Temple Mount. "Thou passed Him by, and inquired not about Him by Whom every house is exalted."[20] He directly addresses the "King of Berlin," Queen Victoria, the Pope, and the "Rulers of America and the Presidents of the Republics therein," among others, calling on them to recognize him as a Manifestation of God.[21]

As he neared death, Bahá'u'lláh appointed his oldest son, Abbas Effendi, to succeed him as "The Servant of Baha," the meaning of the honorific title by which he is known, `Abdu'l-Bahá. Though not considered a Manifestation of God like his father, his writings are considered inspired. `Abdu'l-Bahá is credited with extending the Bahá'í faith beyond the Middle East. Granted his freedom from house arrest in 1908, `Abdu'l-Bahá was finally able to travel across Europe and as far as North America. It was there that he met with the tiny Bahá'í community in Chicago that would later construct the Bahá'í House of Worship in Wilmette. His "Tablets of the Divine Plan" outlined a strategy for spreading the Bahá'í faith around the globe. When he died in 1921, his grandson, Shoghi Effendi, succeeded him.

Bahá'í referred to Shoghi Effendi as "the Guardian of the Faith," the authorized interpreter of the Bahá'í scriptures, though his own writings were not considered inspired. Shoghi Effendi named forty-two prominent Bahá'í leaders, both male and female, as the Hands of the Cause, which moved the Bahá'í Faith in the direction of its present-day organization. Prominent among the "Hands" was his own Canadian-born wife, Mary Sutherland Maxwell, who took the name Madame Ruhiyyih Rabbani when she married Shoghi Effendi in 1937. When her husband died unexpectedly in 1957, Madame Rabbani traveled extensively for the next sixty years, visiting

Bahá'í communities around the globe. She was present at the inauguration of most of the Bahá'í Houses of Worship. The twenty-seven surviving Hands of the Cause eventually gave way to the Universal House of Justice established in Haifa in 1963 as the fulfilment of the wishes of Bahá'u'lláh. Nine elected representatives chosen by National Spiritual Assemblies around the world reside at the Universal House of Justice and constitute the governing body of the faith, interpreting the writings of its founders and devising and implementing strategies for education and expansion.

Significant Points of Contact

As Christians we, too, affirm that there is only one God. With our Bahá'í neighbors, we are sad about religious division, especially when it erupts into violence. We affirm with Bahá'í that we are all made in the image of one God. The diversity evident in the Bahá'í communities I visit is an enviable result of the deliberate eradication of prejudice as a religious obligation, which it most certainly is. More often than not, I am accompanied on these visits by a classroom full of students who do not represent as much diversity. This embarrasses me. That Sunday morning continues to be the most segregated hour in America is true because of persistent segregation among people who call ourselves "Christian."[22] But it is not what God wants.

We can appreciate the Bahá'í emphasis on a reasoned, thoughtful faith that includes, especially for converts to Bahá'í (perhaps more than for those born into Bahá'í families), their knowledge of and respect for other world religions including my own. We, too, are not satisfied with merely an inherited faith; we agree that we must own our faith by seriously examining all truth claims, including the ones that have shaped us. I have deep respect for my Bahá'í friends, all volunteers, who coordinate my visits with other Bahá'í year after year without the assistance of any paid staff.[23] There is much to admire in their egalitarian style of leadership where it seems everyone has a voice. I can appreciate, too, their simple gatherings, compelled in part by their aversion to ritual, pomp, and show.

Significant Points of Contrast

But there are significant points of contrast between Christian faith and Bahá'í teachings. Jesus's stern warnings about "many who will come in my name, claiming 'I am the Christ'" certainly apply here (Matt. 24:4), as does Paul's caution about "a gospel other than the one we preached to you," even if it is preached by "an angel from heaven" (Gal. 1:8). Of course, my Bahá'í friends have heard this one before. "All sacred Scriptures warn against false prophets," writes one Bahá'í apologist. "Do the warnings intend to discourage search, to instill fear, to teach avoidance and indifference?" he asks. "Or do they teach caution and prudence?"[24]

In fact, Jesus's words do alert us to the inevitable—that other religious figures who claim to speak for God will come and go. Their messages and their lives must be evaluated in the light of the Word who became flesh and dwelled among us. The exclusive claims Jesus makes (considered at length in Chapter One) cannot be reconciled with Bahá'í belief that Jesus was merely one Manifestation of God among many. John says of him that he was "the One and Only, who came from the Father, full of grace and truth" (John 1:14).

The Bahá'í faith represents an attempt to reconcile world religions by claiming that the Bahá'í faith fulfills them all and that the apparent differences between them disappear when understood in the light of the teachings of Bahá'u'lláh. That proposal is especially hard to accept when Buddhism is in the mix. Neither Buddha himself, an atheist, nor Buddhists would consider it flattering to refer to Buddha as "a Messenger of God." The Bahá'í interpretation relegates the distinctiveness of each of the world religions described in this book to "details," the product of a too-literal reading of all of these texts their adherents consider sacred. In some ways it is an appealing solution to all the contradictions, to say that these believers of all kinds are mistaken about what their founders intended and what their scriptures mean. But in the end, it is a condescending posture toward the billions of people who believe otherwise. The better conversation with our religious neighbors begins when we listen carefully in order to understand the differences. Only then can we make the case for Christ in a way that is respectful, informed, and persuasive.

TALKING TOGETHER . . .

1. Share with each other any encounters you may have had with members of the Bahá'í faith. In what ways do the profiles of Amir, Jessica, and Jim remind you of those encounters?

2. What do you think would be attractive about the Bahá'í faith to a spiritual seeker?

3. How should Christians respond to the Bahá'í definition of "Progressive Revelation"?

4. The Bahá'í are committed to diversity. Why? How do they understand this principle?

5. What is the Christian perspective on the "oneness" of God, religion, and humanity?

6. How would you imagine that the faithful adherents of religions described thus far in this book—Jews, Muslims, Hindus, Buddhists, and Sikhs—would respond to the Bahá'í understanding of their religions?

IF YOU WANT TO READ MORE . . .

Bahá'u'lláh. *The Kitáb-i-aqdas (The Most Holy Book)*. Wilmette, IL: Bahá'í Publishing Trust, 1992.

Bowers, Kenneth E. *God Speaks Again: An Introduction to the Bahá'í Faith*. Wilmette, IL: Bahá'í Publishing, 2004.

Momen, Moojan. *A Short Introduction to the Bahá'í Faith*. Oxford: Oneworld, 1997.

Monjazeb, Shahrokh. *Bahá'u'lláh: A Brief Survey of His Life and His Works.* Ottawa, Canada: Furútan Academy Publications, 2007.

Motlagh, Hushidar Hugh. *Bahá'í Faith: God's Greatest Gift to Humankind.* Mt. Pleasant, MI: Global Perspective, 2006.

Website: http://www.bahai.org/.

Notes

[1] According to Bahá'í websites such as http://bahaiteachings.org/. The *World Christian Encyclopedia* estimated that there were 7.1 million Bahá'í in the world in 2000. It is difficult to find accurate, current statistics on the Bahá'í population (and many other religious groups), in David B. Barrett, George T. Kurian, and Todd M. Johnson, *World Christian Encyclopedia, Volume 2,* 2nd edition (Oxford: Oxford University Press, 2001), 5.

[2] The Shah likely considered Bábís a political threat. The charge of "heresy" against Ali Muhammad provided the pretext for his execution.

[3] In deference to my Bahá'í friends who read this chapter, I am using their prescribed spellings of the names of all Bahá'í figures, including accent and breathing marks, and, as per their requests, spelling their names in full, such as Mirzá Husayn-`Ali.

[4] Shoghi Effendi, *God Passes By* (Bahá'í Reference Library at www.bahai.org/library, first published in 1944), 61. Accessed April 4, 2017.

[5] Moojan Momen, *A Short Introduction to the Bahá'í Faith* (Oxford, England: Oneworld Publications, 1997), 119.

[6] Bahá'u'lláh, *Gleanings from the Writings of Bahá'u'lláh,* translated by Shoghi Effendi (Wilmette, IL: Bahá'í Publishing Trust, 1976), 46–47.

[7] Interview with Todd Steinberg, Dallas, TX, November 8, 2016.

[8] *The Most Holy Book,* v. 168.

[9] Hushidar Hugh Motlagh, *God's Greatest Gift to Humankind* (Mount Pleasant, MI: Global Perspective, 2006), 47.

[10] According to Bahá'u'lláh's *Book of the Covenant.*

[11] Abdu'l-Bahá, *Selections from the Writings of 'Abdu'l-Bahá,* translated by a committee at the Bahá'í World Centre and by Marzieh Gail (Haifa, Israel: Bahá'í World Centre, 1978), 302.

[12] Only eight are still standing. The first one, built in Ashgabat, Turkmenistan, was destroyed by an earthquake in 1948. The remaining Houses of Worship are located in Sydney, Australia; Chicago, Illinois; New Delhi, India; Kampala, Uganda; Frankfurt, Germany; Panama City, Panama; Western Samoa; and the latest one, Santiago, Chile, which opened in 2016.

[13] Another reason the number nine is significant is that, according to Bahá'í author Kenneth Bowers, the numerical value of the Arabic word "Baha" (meaning "glory") is

nine. In *God Speaks Again: An Introduction to the Bahá'í Faith* (Wilmette, IL: Bahá'í Publishing, 2004), 219.

[14] At a morning prayer I attended at the Bahá'í House of Worship in New Delhi, India, also known as the Lotus Temple, the Bahá'í who led the short service began with a prayer written by the Bahá'u'lláh, then read passages from a Buddhist text, the Lord's Prayer (in the King James Version), Hindu scripture, verses from the Qur'an, then concluded with another prayer from the Bahá'u'lláh (translated into Hindi). In dozens of visits to the House of Prayer in Wilmette, Illinois, outside of Chicago, I have only heard Bahá'í read prayers or passages from Bahá'í writings.

[15] *The Most Holy Book*, v. 101.

[16] Ibid., vv. 30–34; v. 54.

[17] For example, a convicted arsonist must be burned to death, *The Most Holy Book*, v. 62.

[18] Ibid, v. 63–67.

[19] Ibid., v. 68.

[20] Ibid., v. 85.

[21] Ibid., v. 85–88.

[22] The famous quote is from Dr. Martin Luther King Jr. who said, in a speech at Western Michigan University, "At 11:00 on Sunday morning when we stand and sing and Christ has no east or west, we stand at the most segregated hour in this nation," December 18, 1963. See http://www.godandculture.com/blog/sunday-at-11-the-most-segregated-hour-in-this-nation. Accessed December 26, 2016.

[23] There are paid staff who work at the Bahá'í House of Worship in Wilmette, Illinois. But when I take visitors there, we are welcomed mostly by volunteers.

[24] Motlagh, *God's Greatest Gift to Humankind*, 77.

CHAPTER EIGHT

OUR JAIN NEIGHBORS

Amy Shah is a college student in Michigan majoring in micro-biology. She is looking forward to dinner with her friends tonight, although she is a little concerned that some of them who don't know her well will look at her funny when she asks the waiter her usual questions. "Do you have anything on the vegan menu that is not a tuber—a plant that grows underground (like potatoes or carrots)? Is there any soup on the menu that doesn't have any meat broth in it? Are you sure that no eggs have touched this salad?" Amy is trying to abide by the strict rules of her Jain faith that forbid her from injuring any living thing, including plants. Jains may eat fruits and vegetables that grow above ground, because in that case eating the fruit of the plant does not destroy the plant on which it grows. On the other hand, vegetables like potatoes are off limits because harvesting the potato kills the potato plant. Eggs are also considered living things. Amy is glad that at least she can go out tonight since it is summer, and the sun goes down much later this time of year. Jains are not allowed to eat after sundown since, at least in the days before electricity, people couldn't see what they were eating at night and might accidentally ingest small bugs along with their food, which also violates the Jain vow of nonviolence. The most strict Jains like Amy continue this practice even in the age of electricity.[1]

Hetali Lodaya is also a student; she's in a hurry to get to class. Since she's late, she decides to take the shortest path from her apartment on campus to the building that houses the Physical Therapy program. That means walking across the lawn, not on the sidewalk. With each step, her conscience stings her just a bit. Each blade of grass she believes is a living thing that should not be harmed. She knows such strict observance of Jain vows applies mostly to Jain monks and nuns, not to lay members like her. Still she tries her best to do no harm and wishes she had thought to ride her bike today instead.[2]

I learned much about Jainism over dinner in the home of Dr. Manoj Jain in Memphis, Tennessee. Manoj is an MD who also has a Masters in Public Health. His wife, Sunita, is also a physician. Both were raised in Jain families, they met and married in medical school in Boston, then moved south where they have raised their three children. Both are knowledgeable and passionate about their faith. Before we ate, they closed their eyes, folded their hands, and recited a brief prayer that wasn't directed at a deity but was a mantra that pays respect to Jain spiritual teachers from the distant past. There aren't enough Jain families in Memphis to build a temple. So the two dozen or so Jain families gather twice a month in homes to pray, fellowship, and encourage each other. Manoj is a member of the national board that coordinates Jain activities across North America. He has also published several books on Jain faith and practice, and he lectures on Jainism around the country.[3]

These are just a few stories about Jains in America, adherents of what they believe to be the oldest religion in the world. They will tell you, too, that Mahavira, identified by comparative religion scholars as the religion's founder, was not the founder at all, but the twenty-fourth in a line of spiritual heroes whose lives extend far back into previous eons in worlds that predate this one. The twenty-third Jain leader, they say, died about 250 years before Mahavira was born; the twenty-second died eighty-four thousand years before number twenty-three came on the scene. Jainism has relatively few adherents—fewer than five million worldwide—most of whom live in India and comprise less than 1 percent of the India population.[4] Jain websites estimate that about seventy Jain Centers in the U.S. and Canada service more than a hundred thousand Jains who make their home in North America.[5] As many as six thousand Jains attend a biennial convention in North America on the Fourth of July weekend.

Yet Jainism exerts more influence on both Indian and American culture than the small numbers would suggest. Chances are that you have heard Jain stories even if you've never heard of Jainism before now. Ever heard about the six blind men and the elephant? One version is a poem:

> *There were six men of Indostan*
> > *to learning much inclined*
> *who went to see an elephant*
> > *though each of them were blind . . .*[6]

That's a Jain parable. I know you've heard of Mahatma Gandhi whose parents were Hindus, but his mother was drawn to Jain teaching. Gandhi was inspired by the Jain's most important principle—the vow called "ahimsa" or "non-injury." Gandhi himself said it was this commitment that motivated him in his nonviolent movement for Indian independence from Britain.

Closer to home, Martin Luther King Jr. said that Gandhi became his role model for how to advocate for nonviolent change, which gave momentum to the Civil Rights Movement in America in the years that followed Gandhi's death. Even Sam Harris, the famous American agnostic and author of recent books like *The End of Faith* and *Letter to a Christian Nation* tips his hat to Jainism, calling it "the most direct and undefiled expression of love and compassion the world has ever seen."[7]

So the task here is to give an overview of this ancient faith and practice that most readers have never heard of, but one that has left its mark on the world in significant ways.

Significant Figures

World religions professors usually refer to Mahavira as the founder of Jainism. Though the details of his story are sketchy, Jains believe he was born and raised as Nataputta Vardhamana in Northeast India around 599

BC, and died as "Mahavira" or "Great Man" in 527.[8] Like Siddhartha, the Buddhist figure, Mahavira was raised in the nobleman caste in India (in the same region of India as Siddhartha, now called Bihar State), but became disillusioned with his life of luxury. At the age of thirty, when his parents died, he left home in search of enlightenment. Like Siddhartha, his quest began with extreme asceticism; he shunned clothes and shelter and ate very little.

According to one tradition, Mahavira was so determined not to harm any living being (plant or animal) that he covered his mouth with a piece of cloth (so as not to accidentally inhale bugs), strained all drinking water through a cloth (again, to filter out any tiny living beings), walked as softly as possible, and swept the path in front of himself as he walked so as not to step on any tiny creatures.

Unlike Siddhartha, there was no moment when he thought of this self-deprivation as too extreme or when he sought a more moderate "middle way." Instead, after thirteen years of the strictest kind of self-denial, at age forty, he achieved enlightenment. In that moment, he became omniscient, aware of all truth and conscious of every living thing. Having overcome all earthly, material desires, he became known as "Jina," "the Conqueror." His handful of disciples called themselves "Jains," which means "followers of the conqueror." Mahavira's self-abnegation didn't stop there. He continued to live in the forest, without a roof over his head or clothes on his back, eating very little until he died at the age of seventy-two.

Jains believe that Mahavira was not the first to live such a life and conquer all desire. He was, they say, the twenty-fourth such "Tirthankara," usually translated "ford finders," meaning enlightened ones who have found their way across the stream of existence (like a ford in a river) and reached Nirvana on the other side. Tirthankaras are not considered deities; they are "enlightened beings" who have forged a spiritual path for those who follow. Most of their stories (except for the twenty-third and twenty-fourth) are prehistoric; non-Jains would say they are "legendary" or "mythical." I mentioned the twenty-third of these Tirthankaras above, a man named Parsva who is said to have died 246 years before Mahavira was born, and Tirthankara number twenty-two who preceded Parsva by eighty-four thousand years. The first of the twenty-four Tirthankaras, called "First Master," is named Rishaba. Jains say Rishaba stood three thousand feet tall and lived to be seventy trillion years old. Obviously, the astronomical numbers are meant to astound the mind.

In India, the only Jains that stand out in a crowd are Jain monks and nuns, who vow to follow in Mahavira's footsteps and shun the basic comforts of life, and to, in Mahavira's words, "neglect [the] body and abandon the care of it. I shall with a right disposition bear, undergo, and suffer all calamities arising from divine powers, men or animals."[9] In other words, he would make no effort to protect himself against anything that might do his body harm. "Even in his thoughts," Mahavira said, "a monk should not long for a pleasant painted home filled with fragrance of garlands and frankincense, secured by doors, and decorated with a white ceiling cloth. For in such a dwelling, a monk will find it difficult to prevent his senses from increased desire and passion."[10]

A monk, he taught, should live in deserted places, in a cemetery or a forest, abstain from cooking or building a fire for any reason (since living things are killed by fire, then putting out the fire kills the fire). In the modern world, Jain monks are not permitted to drive or ride in any motorized vehicles, since engines are powered by fire and since such vehicles injure living beings. Obviously, air travel is also taboo, which creates a problem for the Jain communities outside of India who require the services of a priest. Those needs are typically met by a new class of Jain clergy who have taken lesser vows and make the journey abroad.

Significant Beliefs

The Jain worldview does not include a Creator; the world, they believe, has always existed, or as Manoj Jain puts it, "it comes from infinity and is going toward infinity."[11] There are deities like those honored in Hinduism, but they are mostly ignored. The Tirthankaras, though not divine beings, are revered as role models of how one may achieve enlightenment. Their images are worshiped in most (but not all) Jain Temples. Jains divide the world according to "jiva" ("life" or "consciousness") and "ajiva" ("non-life" or "non-consciousness"). "Jiva" includes all living things—both humans and plants—because all things animated with life have a soul. Rocks, dirt, machines, and all other nonliving things without consciousness are "ajiva."

Like Hindus and Buddhists, Jains also believe in karma, the link between deeds and consequences. But in Jainism there is no talk of "good karma" or "bad karma." All karma is bad. Karma, Jains believe, is an actual material substance that piles layers of "non-life" on one's soul and keeps the individual locked in the cycle of birth and rebirth. That is why killing any living being brings the most karma and makes the vow of "ahimsa"—non-injury—the most important Jain vow. "In this world or in the next," reads a Jain text, "the sinners suffer themselves what they have inflicted on other beings, a hundred times, or suffer other punishment. Living in Samsara [the cycle of birth and rebirth], they always acquire new karma and suffer for their misdeeds."[12]

The goal, therefore, at least for monks, is to detach completely from the material world, to live in isolation from others as Mahavira did, without clothes or shelter, eating only enough to survive, and to devote oneself entirely to meditation. Such a person may achieve liberation from reincarnation—represented in Jainism by the *swastika* symbol, which modern Jains are quick to explain has nothing to do with Hitler's misappropriation of the symbol in Nazi Germany—and reach "Nirvana."[13] Unlike the Buddhist concept of Nirvana—the nonexistence that follows being "blown out"—Nirvana in Jainism is described as "a continued isolated and changeless existence" somewhere at the top of the cosmos where the person will remain "motionless, omniscient and blissful."[14]

None of these beliefs should be held dogmatically, because in Jainism certainty is not admirable. The principle of "Anekantavada," translated as either "Non-absolutism" or "multiplicity of views," stems from the realization that people don't all share the same perspective.[15] The parable of the six blind men fits here. Each one thought he understood the nature of an elephant—that the animal was like a spear (so said the blind man who held only the elephant's tusk), a huge leaf (thought the blind man who touched the elephant's ear), a tree trunk (according to the one who put his arms around the elephant's leg), and so on. In truth, even if the six blind men compared notes with each other, they would not have an accurate or complete picture of an elephant. Jains also use the term "Syadvada" (literally "could-be-ism") in a similar way for the same reason and qualify many statements with "maybe" ("syad" in Sanskrit).[16] The recognition of the validity of what Jains often call "the multiplicity of views" resonates with many North Americans in this pluralistic age.

Jains in North America summarize these most fundamental Jain commitments lay people make in terms of three principles all referenced above: nonviolence, non-absolutism, and non-possessiveness.[17] The commitment to nonviolence is what feeds Amy Shah's veganism, and what makes Hetali Lodaya feel guilty about walking on grass, even though neither Amy or Hetali are monks. Non-absolutism or "multiplicity of views" is illustrated by the parable of the six blind men and the elephant. Non-possessiveness means, among other things, resistance to the materialism of our culture.

Jains tell a story about a man who, while wandering in the forest, was chased by an angry elephant. When he turned to run, he came face to face with a menacing demoness holding a sword. Fearing for his life, he dove into a nearby well and held fast to the reeds that grew around the mouth of the well, his legs dangling in the hole. He looked down, only to see a huge python in the bottom of well, its mouth wide open, ready for lunch. The man looked up and saw two mice chewing on the reeds that were preventing his fall. Just then the elephant, still in hot pursuit, started ramming a tree that shaded the well, dislodging a bee hive that hung from the tree. Just as the bees started stinging the poor man—you thought you were having a bad day—a drop of honey fell from the hive onto the man's tongue and gave him a moment of relief. You may think that the moral of the story is to savor the sweetness in the midst of the pain. Actually, Jains say the moral is that we should not let that one sweet moment lure us back into a place where we live to satisfy our desires. The story illustrates the allure of possessiveness that we must resist.[18]

The basic teachings of Jainism are written in a text called *Agamas* ("tradition") or *Siddhanta* ("doctrine"). Their origin and composition, however, are the subject of ongoing debate within the Jain community. This "loose canon" partly drives the divisions within Jainism described below.

Significant Practices

It is safe to say that none of our Jain neighbors in North America will live the lifestyle of Mahavira or of Jain monks. Lay Jains take only a few of the vows Jain monks take; some Jains take none, but try to honor the spirit of these vows in some way. The five vows monks take resemble the eight-fold path of Buddhism. The first and most important vow is *ahimsa*—not killing anything. It is this commitment that has brought Jainism, with its relatively few adherents, to the world stage in an age when religiously motivated conflicts capture news headlines almost every day. Jain monks take four other vows:

2. Truth telling, which leads them to insert the word "maybe" in their comments.
3. No stealing, which is interpreted by monks to mean not taking anything that was not given to them.
4. No sex (meaning no sensual pleasures and celibacy).
5. Detachment from all material things which, when fully embraced, leads to the kind of life Mahavira led.

Again, for nonmonks, honoring these vows means doing their best to do no harm (vow number one and the principle of nonviolence), speaking truthfully with humility, recognizing the limitations of human perception (vow two and the principle of non-absolutism), practicing generosity, no greed (vow three and the principle of non-possessiveness), maintaining high standards of sexual ethics (vow four), and faithfully pursuing a life of spiritual devotion (vow five).

Practically speaking, that devotion is expressed in morning prayers or chanting sessions, inspired by Mahavira, and in worshiping the Tirthankaras at Jain Temples. Jains are careful to clarify that the object of their worship is not the image of Tirthakaras per se, but the ideals those figures represent. If, in fact, Jain worship looks a lot like worship in a Hindu Temple, it is only because of undue Hindu influence on Jain practice.

On occasion, a Jain will make the news for especially rigorous practice of their faith. In October of 2016, the *Hindustan Times*, an English-language newspaper in India, reported the case of Aradhana Samdariya, a thirteen-year-old Jain girl in Hyderabad who died at the end of a sixty-eight-day fast in which she consumed nothing but water. She said she was fasting in response to the instructions of a guru who said her dedication could help her family's jewelry business prosper. Some in the Jain community in India hailed her as a hero and spiritual role model. Non-Jains have accused the parents of murder.[19] My Jain friends here insist that a true Jain would not fast for such a pragmatic, worldly purpose as the success of a business, so this case is atypical. I certainly don't want to suggest otherwise. One article on the subject suggests that on average only two hundred Jains "fast to death" each year—most of them monks—and only when death is imminent anyway.[20]

Significant Sects and Developments

The main divisions within Jainism occurred as a result of different interpretations of the life of Mahavira. Since the stories of his life and teachings weren't put in written form until centuries after his death, many Jains trace the split to that disagreement.

The oldest sect, the Digambaras, tell the story of Mahavira as I outlined it above. The word "Digambara" is usually translated "sky-clad," referring to the fact that Digambara monks do not wear clothes; that is, they "wear" only "sky." Women may not join monks in the Digambara sect; there are no Digambara nuns. In fact, according to these Jains, women may not achieve enlightenment as women; they must be reincarnated as men to enter the path that leads to enlightenment. That exclusion was likely one of the forces that led to the creation of the Svetambara or "white-clad" sect. These monks and nuns wear white robes and do not isolate themselves from others to the extent that Digambaras do. Digambaras and Svetambaras disagree on other details of Mahavira's birth, life, and death. Svetambaras also believe that the nineteenth Tirthankara was a woman; Digambaras say he was male. Predictably, Digambaras' representations of Mahavira are naked; Svetambaras show his image dressed in a loin cloth. There are other sects with fewer members who differ over matters such as the use of images of Tirthankaras (some sects reject idols), whether worshipers should sit or stand while paying homage to Tirthankaras, and so on.

For our Jain neighbors in America, the primary concern is the survival and perpetuation of their faith and culture as a minority community. Some Jains worry about the "Hinduization" of Jainism in America (as well as in India). There are far more Hindus than Jains in America; there are many more "Indian Cultural Centers" in the United States associated with Hinduism where Americans of Indian origin gather, meet, and marry. Jain organizations like J.A.I.N.A. (the Federation of Jain Associations in North America) are working to preserve the loyalty of American Jains, especially through education programs aimed at youth.[21]

Significant Points of Contact

The Jain commitment to nonviolence and, to a lesser extent, the embrace of "the multiplicity of views," point Christians to what we have in common with our Jain neighbors. There is truth in the Jain conviction about "jiva" or "life" in every living thing. The last line of the last psalm calls for "everything that has breath [to] praise the Lord" (150:6). (This doesn't mean that "everything that has breath" also has a soul.)

Jesus is plainspoken against violence toward others. "You have heard that it was said, 'Eye for eye, and tooth for tooth,'" Jesus explains in the Sermon on the Mount. "But I tell you, Do not resist an evil person. If someone strikes you on the right cheek, turn to him the other also" (Matt. 5:38–39). "Love your enemies and pray for those who persecute you" (Matt. 5:44); that line is also written in bright red letters in my copy of the New Testament. This is not the book to air out the debate between pacifism and any legitimate use of violence from a Christian point of view. But can we agree that nothing in the teachings of Jesus justifies harming another human being? With regard to plants and animals, we who are in Christ are motivated not by fear of acquiring karma and being reincarnated again and again, but by stewardship, believing that there *is* a Creator God who has entrusted us with the care of his creation.

I admire the humility of my Jain friends who are careful not to overstate truth claims. They show great restraint when they qualify their assertions with multiple "maybes." The Apostle Paul, writing under the influence of the Spirit of God, penned the famous words, "For now we see through a glass, darkly, but then face to face" (1 Cor. 13:12 KJV). Surely it is right for us, too, to resist the temptation to exaggerate what we can and cannot know, given our condition as fragile "jars of clay" that happen to contain a great treasure (2 Cor. 4:7). I also appreciate the Jain commitment to non-possessiveness that inspires their resistance to materialism. I, too, as a Christ-follower, am called on by Christ to store up treasures in Heaven, not on earth (Matt. 6:19–20).

Significant Points of Contrast

The first and most fundamental point of contrast between what Jains and Christians believe is the Creator God whose existence Jains deny. Our Maker also "breathed into" us the "breath of life, and the man became a living being" (Gen. 2:7). Plants and animals are also the work of his hands, created for his pleasure and for our responsible use, not abuse. Jesus himself "came eating and drinking," according to his critics (Matt. 11:19). He was no vegan. We know he participated in Passover, which would have meant that he consumed lamb.[22] Jesus taught that God cares for "the birds of the air" and "the lilies of the field" (Matt. 6:26–29), yet we are not forbidden from consuming plants and animals. In a different context, Paul wrote, "If I take part in the meal [that included meat] with thankfulness, why am I denounced because of something I thank God for?" (1 Cor. 10:30). A few verses before, Paul points to the biblical reason we are free to do so: "The earth is the Lord's and everything in it" (1 Cor. 10:26, quoting Ps. 24:1). Our starting point is the Creator; good stewardship is a basic ethic.

Our Creator has also taken the initiative to make himself known to his creatures. Those who quote the parable of the six blind men to make the point that we cannot know everything and that what we know we cannot know with certainty don't mention the king who called those six poor men together. I know it is a parable and not a historical account. But what kind of king (like the king who convened that imagined meeting) thinks it is fun to watch six blind people grope in the dark trying to figure out the nature of an elephant? How cruel to make a spectacle of these men and their limitations![23] Jesus said, "I am the light of the world. Whoever follows me will never walk in darkness, but will have the light of life" (John 8:12). And the same man (Paul) who wrote "for now we see through a glass, darkly" (1 Cor. 13:12) boldly declared to those philosophers on Mars' Hill, "Now what you worship as something unknown I am going to proclaim to you" (Acts 17:23).

As with Hinduism and Buddhism, in Christ we do not believe that the "karma" that results from our misdeeds goes on a permanent record that can only be expunged through our virtuous living over thousands of lives. Nor do we believe that the kind of self-denial that represents an ideal in Hinduism and Buddhism and is at its most extreme in Jainism actually fulfills God's purposes for us, his creatures. As Christians, we seek the spiritual transformation that comes only through our cooperation with the Holy Spirit who indwells us. When I read Mahavira's "Rules for Monastic Life," I can't help but think of this admonishment from Paul:

> Since you died with Christ to the basic principles of this world, why, as though you still belonged to it, do you submit to its rules: "Do not handle! Do not taste! Do not touch!"? These are all destined to perish with use, because they are based on human commands and teachings. Such regulations indeed have an appearance of wisdom, with their self-imposed worship, their false humility and their harsh treatment of the body, but they lack any value in restraining sensual indulgence. (Col. 2:20–23)

Instead, Paul continues, we "set [our] hearts on things above, where Christ is seated at the right hand of God" (Col. 3:1). Yes, Paul also goes on to say, "you died, and your life is now hidden with Christ in God" (Col. 3:3). We are not our own; we have been bought with a price. Therefore we seek to glorify God in our bodies. That doesn't mean we starve them or shun clothes and shelter. It does mean that we get our priorities straight, that we seek first his Kingdom and his righteousness, and entrust the rest to him. It means that with Paul, we learn "the secret of being content in any and every situation, whether well fed or hungry, whether living in plenty or in want." And here is the secret: "I can do everything through him who gives me strength" (Philip. 4:12–13).

May we be good role models for all of our neighbors, including our Jain friends, fleshing out in front of them what the life of contentment looks like when Jesus Christ is its source.

TALKING TOGETHER . . .

1. Sam Harris believes Jainism to be "the most direct and undefiled expression of love and compassion the world has ever seen." Now that you've read this chapter, what do you think led Harris to that conclusion?

2. How does the Jain understanding of karma differ from that of Hindus and Buddhists?

3. What is a Christian perspective on the three basic Jain principles of nonviolence, non-absolutism, and non-possessiveness?

4. Given that all truth is God's truth, what truths can we glean from the parable about the six blind men and the elephant and the story about the man who seeks shelter in a well when chased by an enraged elephant?

5. The Book of Psalms ends on this note: "Let everything that has breath praise the LORD" (150:6). After reading this chapter, how do you hear that verse now?

6. Jains and Christians prioritize denial of self, but their reasons for doing so are very different. How should a person practice this important principle?

IF YOU WANT TO READ MORE . . .

Chandanaji, Acharya, and Vastupal Parikh. *Walk with Me: The Story of Mahavira —A Remarkable Revolutionary*. Toronto, Canada: Peace Publications, 2009.

Jain, Yogendra. *Jain Way of Life: A Guide to Compassionate, Healthy, and Happy Living*. Boston: JAINA, 2007.

Jain, Manoj, Laxmi Jain, and Tarla Dalal. *Jain Food: Compassionate and Healthy Eating*. Germantown, TN: Manoj Jain and Laxmi Jain, 2005.

Website: http://www.jaina.org/.

Notes

[1] Amy Shah, "Jain Food Struggles in America," *Huffington Post*, January 12, 2016, accessed December 27, 2016, http://www.huffingtonpost.com/amy-shah/jain-food -struggles-in-am_b_8961854.html. Manoj Jain estimates that less than 1 percent of Jains in North America are as strict as Amy in their observance of the restriction against eating after sundown. In correspondence with the author February 5, 2017.

[2] Hetali Lodaya, "Ahimsa in the Small Things: A Jain College Student's Approach To Nonviolent Living," *Huffington Post*, June 17, 2013, accessed December 27, 2016, http:// www.huffingtonpost.com/news/cultivating%20nonviolence/.

[3] Manoj Jain in interview with author February 4, 2017, Memphis, TN.

[4] According to the 2001 census by the Indian Government, ttp://censusindia.gov.in /Census_And_You/religion.aspx. Accessed December 27, 2016.

[5] Such as http://www.jainsamaj.org/ and www.jaina.org.

[6] John Godfrey Saxe, "Blind Men and the Elephant," accessed May 17, 2017, http:// www.allaboutphilosophy.org/blind-men-and-the-elephant.htm.

[7] Sam Harris, *Letter to a Christian Nation* (New York: Vintage 2006), 11.

[8] These are the traditional dates. Some Jain sources list the birth and death dates as 540–468 BC, which would make him a contemporary of Siddhartha Gautama (Buddha).

[9] From the "Kalpa Sutra," as quoted in Robert E. Van Voorsts's *Anthology of World Scriptures*, 6th edition (Belmont, CA: Thomson-Wadsworth, 2008), 113.

[10] Quoted in Van Voorst, 118.

[11] Manoj Jain in correspondence with the author February 5, 2017.

[12] Quoting from the Jain text "Sutrakritanga" in Van Voorst, 117.

[13] The swastika or hooked cross with its four arms represents the four possible levels of reincarnation for living beings: a demonic being, a subhuman living thing (like a plant or animal), a human, or a holy heavenly being.

[14] Ninian Smart, *The Religious Experience*, 5th edition (Upper Saddle River, NJ: Prentice-Hall, 1996), 63.

[15] For a more thorough explanation, see the Jain World website at http://www .jainworld.com/book/shramanmahavirajainism/ch5.asp.

[16] According to the New World Encyclopedia at http://www.newworldencyclopedia .org/entry/Syadvada. Accessed December 28, 2016.

[17] For example, Yogendra Jain, *Jain Way of Life: A Guide to Compassionate, Healthy, and Happy Living* (Boston: Federation of Jain Associations of North America, 2007), 12–18.

[18] The story and its interpretation is found in *Eerdman's Handbook to the World's Religions* (Grand Rapids: Eerdmans, 1994), 210.

[19] Srinivasa Rao Apparasu, "'Don't Interfere': Jain Leaders Tell Activists as Girl Dies Fasting for 68 Days," Hindustan Times, October 11, 2016. http://www.hindustantimes .com/india-news/don-t-interfere-jain-leaders-tell-child-rights-activists-after-girl-s-death /story-905BfchczLKGGwKu5KgT7N.html. Accessed December 28, 2016.

[20] Julie McCarthy's "Fasting to the Death: Is It a Religious Rite or Suicide?" NPR's "Morning Edition," September 2, 2015. http://www.npr.org/sections/ goatsandsoda/2015/09/02/436820789/fasting-to-the-death-is-it-a-religious-rite-or -suicide. Accessed February 7, 2017.

[21] See for example, "Can Jainism Survive in the 21st Century?" by Sulekh Chand and Yashwant K. Malaiya, February 7, 2015, accessed December 28, 2016, http://www .herenow4u.net/index.php?id=82539.

[22] Since the destruction of the Temple in Jerusalem, lamb is no longer included in a Jewish Passover seder; a lamb bone is placed on the seder plate in memory of the sacrificial system. But in Jesus's day, the Temple still stood, and he would have eaten lamb at Passover.

[23] Manoj Jain believes this is a misinterpretation of this parable, stretching the application in a way that was not intended, in correspondence with the author February 5, 2017. Others make the same point I am making here including Leslie Newbigin, *The Gospel in a Pluralist Society* (Grand Rapids: Eerdmans, 1989), 9, and more recently Timothy Keller, *The Reason for God: Belief in an Age of Skepticism* (New York: Dutton, 2008), 8.

CHAPTER NINE

OUR NATIVE AMERICAN NEIGHBORS

Ladonna Brave Bull Allard is the founder and director of the Sacred Stone Camp established in 2016 on property her family owns in a corner of North Dakota. LaDonna is also a writer and the Historic Preservation Officer for the Standing Rock Sioux Reservation that straddles the border between North and South Dakota. Recently, she made national news as one of the organizers of the protest that led the U.S. Army Corps of Engineers to change its plans and reroute the Dakota Access oil Pipeline around what LaDonna and her fellow-Standing Rock Sioux consider to be sacred land.[1] They refer to themselves as "protectors," not "protestors." Their concern was not only that the pipeline could pollute the local water supply, but that the pipeline's path through Sioux-owned land, especially burial grounds, amounted to one more violation among many of previous agreements with U.S. authorities. LaDonna feels the injustice deeply and personally. Her great-great-grandmother survived what historians call the Whitestone Massacre in September 1863, in which more than three hundred

Dakota Indians were killed by the U.S. Army while they were feasting together after a successful buffalo hunt.[2]

I met James Bilagody in his hometown on the Navajo Reservation in Tuba City, Arizona, where he was born and raised and where he teaches Native culture at the same public schools he attended as a child. James sings original Navajo songs, he writes new ones, he has appeared in movies about Native America, and he often speaks to groups of visitors who want to know more about Navajo Traditional Religion, or as the Navajo call it, "The Way of Beauty." He speaks with reverence about the "Holy People"—the spiritual beings from whom he believes the Navajo, or the Diné, as they call themselves, descend. They are an important part of the worldview James and many others work to preserve, a worldview that values balance and harmony between nature and spirit.[3]

Stanford Addison is an Arapaho chief who makes his home on the Shoshone-Arapaho Reservation in Ethete, Wyoming. He and his wife live in a small frame house with a crucifix on the wall and a sweat lodge in the backyard. The small lodge, which consists of tarps and skins draped over poles, is formed in the shape of a turtle. Inside, the fire-heated stones and buckets of water create the steam that inspires the name. Addison, who is Roman Catholic, says he and his friends pray in the sweat lodge several times a week. "Prayer is more intense in the lodge," says Addison. "Last time I was in church it seemed like everybody was trying to appear to everybody else and not to the Creator. In the sweat you can't see each other so we believe we appear to God."[4] Unlike commercial sweat lodges that cater to non-Native Americans, Addison does not charge guests who wish to "sweat" with him.

To accurately represent with these three profiles the spiritual lives of the estimated two million Native Americans and Native Alaskans subdivided into the nearly six hundred distinct tribes that are "federally recognized" by the U.S. Bureau of Indian Affairs is difficult.[5] Even that language is problematic. Other Native Americans, like the residents of Mashpee, Massachusetts, to name only one group, for a number of reasons are not "federally recognized," and therefore their efforts to reclaim their native land on Cape Cod have not been successful.[6] This is just one of many factors that make this chapter especially difficult to write. Who qualify as "Native Americans"?

Another and more painful reason this task is difficult is the long and sad history of injustice against North America's original peoples—a history that includes genocide, forced relocation and assimilation, and broken treaties. That tale of tears (which includes more than one "Trail of Tears") makes this and any other attempt to describe Native American culture or religion especially sensitive.

Another complication is that over the last three centuries, many of the distinct features of the hundreds of tribal groups that once inhabited this continent have been erased. The heading "Native American Religion" gives the false impression that we are talking about a single phenomenon rather than a "best-we-can-come-up-with" label for the common themes that recur in many Native American cultures.

In recent decades, the conversation is made even more complicated by the fascination of many non-Native Americans with Native American Indian spiritual practices, even though it seems that most such "outsiders" only experiment and dabble. Maybe you have heard of "dream-catchers," "kachina dolls," and "vision quests." Perhaps you have even spent time in a "sweat lodge" somewhere, in search of a spiritual experience. What motivates the dabblers? Is it a sense of guilt over these awful injustices of the past (and present)? Or are some motivated simply by their boredom with other more familiar forms of spirituality?

You should know that to at least some Native Americans, this curiosity-driven exploration feels like yet another case of exploitation of their resources, in this case, spiritual ones.[7] It also makes some Native Americans resistant to Christianity and makes others who believe in Jesus and his resurrection reluctant to call themselves Christian. I write these words fully aware that as a white male Christian, I am running the risk of offending any Native American readers who think this overview is not truly representative of their experience. Once again, by asking several Native Americans from different backgrounds to preview this chapter before publication, I have tried to minimize that very real possibility.

In the undergraduate course I teach on World Religions, and in most textbooks on the subject, Native American religions are surveyed in a chapter with a title such as "Traditional Religions" or "Indigenous Religions." In the past, these religions were grouped together under the label "animism" (from a Latin word that means "spirit"). I prefer the more current heading "traditional religion," because it underscores the fact that the religions under discussion here are not perpetuated by a written sacred text, but by oral traditions and rituals passed down from one generation to the next. Yes, all of our religious experiences—in fact, most of our human experiences in general as groups of people—include "traditions" or practices we repeat as part of "our" heritage (whoever "we" are). But these religious traditions deserve their own chapter.

I should pause here for a full disclosure moment: The traditional religion with which I am most familiar is not Native American, but the one in which I was immersed for a decade of my life as a missionary among the Kalenjin-speaking peoples of rural Kenya. On the one hand, I have tried to resist the temptation to reframe Native American spirituality in the African terms I know best. On the other hand, this chapter is also aimed at understanding our neighbors from Haiti, Nigeria, the islands of the South Pacific, and many other parts of the world—neighbors whose cultural heritage is rooted in one of the many traditional religions still practiced on all of the inhabited continents. It is hard enough to generalize responsibly about the hundreds of Native Americans religions in North America; it is harder still to group them together with all other Traditional Religions from around the globe and describe them all in one chapter. But, with that major disclaimer, here we go.

Significant Figures

The most significant figures in Native American religions (and other traditional religions) are spiritual beings and the human mediators between those spirits and individuals or groups of people. At the top of the hierarchy in many of these worldviews is a Supreme Being, known as "Wakan Tanka" or "Great Spirit" among various Sioux tribes, "Manitou" also translated "Great Spirit" among the Algonquin, or among the Creek, "Hisakitaimisi," which translates to "Breath Holder" (a personal favorite).

In some cases, the "Great Spirit" is credited with creating the world and sustaining a certain moral order by punishing wrongdoers and rewarding the righteous. In other cases, Native Americans say such names (Wakan Tanka and Manitou) do not describe personal beings, but serve as labels for the "Great Mystery," perhaps more like energy, that fills the universe and animates every living thing. This "Great Spirit" is evident in the winds, the clouds, in thunder and lightning. Similarly, the Navajo speak of Tsohanoai, "the Sun God," and his consort, "Estsanatlehi," translated "Changing Woman," as an important heavenly pair, but my Navajo acquaintances say these are not "Supreme Beings" in the same way monotheists conceive of a Creator God.[8] Most traditional religious cultures also believe in a "trickster" character, a spirit being who is up to no good, often represented by an animal such as the coyote (because this trickster displays shifty coyote-like qualities).

The vast majority of the other traditional religions of the world, from the Aztecs of South America to the Zulu of South Africa, worship a single Creator who made the world, then retreated from it, usually, they say, because he took offense at some human behavior.[9] These "fall myths" (so-called in comparative religion because of the biblical account of the sin of the first couple in the Garden of Eden) are a thread that runs through Native American religions as well. To some observers, they represent attempts to explain why some adherents perceive the Creator to be distant. To others, he is not remote, but is very present. Still, most agree that this Creator left the day-to-day operation of nature in the control of lesser spirits or ancestors.

Spirit beings include both ancestors—that is relatives who are now deceased—and non-ancestors. More often than not it is the non-ancestral spirits, or "nature spirits," who control the wind and weather and the natural resources on which communities depend, from hunting grounds to cultivated fields. It is this belief that inspires festivals like the annual Green Corn Ceremony celebrated among the Cherokee and the Seminole at harvest time to honor the agricultural spirits who blessed the harvest. "Kachina" spirits of the Hopi and Zuni tribes in the Southwest, represented by "kachina" dolls, are considered responsible for sustaining crops among those people groups. Not surprisingly, these spirits are represented in the ceremonial dances of these peoples by men dressed in kachina masks. Ancestral spirits, unlike nature spirits, are those deceased relatives who are still believed to be part of the extended family. They are invited to all ceremonies and consulted for their input when the family or tribe faces important decisions.

Religion scholars call the leaders of such ceremonies "shaman," a term borrowed from the indigenous people of Siberia.[10] "Medicine man" became the more popular English designation for these men and women who act as mediators between the spirit world and people. More often than not, shaman are the offspring of shaman—that is, the wisdom and skills of shamanism are passed on only within certain families. Of course, each traditional religion has for shaman its own ideas, titles, hierarchies, roles, and tools that vary widely. Many shaman serve as mediums, believing their bodies can be taken over by ancestral spirits, who then communicate with those around them through the shaman while he or she is in a trance-like state. They are also healers and herbalists, using a wide variety of healing techniques, some of which are named below.

There are also historical figures who are significant because of the roles they played in the conflicts between Native Americans and the former Europeans (my ancestors) who occupied their homeland.

Significant Beliefs

Native American and other traditional religious worldviews do not accept what secularism assumes, that there is a great divide between "physical" and "spiritual" reality, between the visible and invisible worlds. On the contrary, the key to well-being is organic harmony between spirit and body, understanding that the so-called "natural world" is permeated through and through by spiritual beings and spiritual truths. The ideal relationship between nature and spirit is symbolized by the circle. The Oglala Sioux chief Black Elk famously said, "Everything an Indian does is in a circle, and that is because the power of the world always works in circles, and everything tries to be round."[11] It is no accident that dwellings—from tipis to hogans, to sweat lodges—are built round, or that ceremonial participants dance in circles that represent harmony.[12]

Disharmony brings disease that must be cured by restoring wholeness, not by killing germs. Broken relationships between the "Great Spirit," nature spirits, ancestors, and their descendants (who still live in bodies) leads to trouble. So remembering, honoring, and nurturing those relationships is of utmost importance. There is also a sense of kinship between humans and animals on which the humans depend. For example, some hunters feel compelled to warn the deer or bird they are about to kill, not to give it opportunity to flee, but as a show of respect.[13]

That kinship is often reflected in one version or another of "totemism," an English word that derives from the Ojibwa term for a "brother-sister relationship." For the most part, "totemism" is the system whereby a given culture keeps straight who belongs to what family, clan, or cluster of clans. In some cultures, the totem is an animal that symbolizes the clan, much as a surname distinguishes one family from another in other cultures. Where the totem is an animal, that animal cannot be killed by members of that family. Myths or legends that involve that animal and a human family or tribe may be represented in that culture's art, as they are on totem poles. Totem poles are not worshiped; they are not idols. They are unique ways of preserving the folklore of a given clan. It brings a smile to my face when I think about how American sports teams choose a mascot as a symbol, often an animal (such as a bison or a tiger), unwittingly adopting a sanitized type of totemism.

Americans have been exposed to "Disneyfied" versions of some of these core beliefs through animated features like "The Lion King" with its ancestor veneration (Rafiki, the shaman, to adolescent Simba regarding his deceased father Mufasa, "He lives in you!"), "Pocahantas," and "Colors of the Wind" with its organic worldview ("every rock and tree and creature has a life, has a spirit, has a name"), and more recently "Moana" with its traditional religious mythology (an amalgamation of creation and fall stories from the Pacific Islands).

Significant Practices

Individual religious practices range from simple morning prayers directed to the east wind, to healing rituals for the sick. Among the Navajo, for example, a shaman creates a "sand painting" (using corn pollen and other organic materials) of a specific sacred figure or pattern on the floor and has the patient lie on it while he or she sings sacred prayers. The sweat lodge mentioned above, that originated with the Dakota, has now been adopted by other Native American groups as a means of purification, prayer, and healing. Individuals may also seek the will or favor of the spirits through various forms of divination, such as the "shaking tent" ceremony among the Anishinaabe or the "trembling hand" ceremony among the Navajo.

"Medicine men" preside over rites of passage that mark the four major life transitions—birth, puberty, marriage, and death. In these rituals, shaman interact with spirits through sacred songs, dances, and other spiritual practices. At birth, children are usually assigned names based on some natural object the family or tribe values (a plant or animal), but may also receive an ancestral name, reflecting a belief in a type of reincarnation that is not clear or uniform from tribe to tribe. Children may be assigned different names as they grow older, based on an accomplishment or a characteristic they have displayed.

The rite of passage from puberty to adulthood may involve an organized ordeal. Among some tribes, a young man (and occasionally a young woman) goes on a "vision quest." In one version, the initiate spends several days alone in the wilderness, deprived of food, drink, and sleep, awaiting the appearance of a "guardian spirit" that may take the form of a hawk or a deer. A mystical message is communicated from that spirit to the initiate, who returns with a deep sense of connection to the animal that represents that spirit.

The famous "Sun Dance" practiced by many Plains tribes is another example of an ordeal that likely began as a rite of passage from puberty into adulthood. Today others join in. In this painful ceremony, participants insert small pieces of wood into their pectoral muscles, then attach ropes from those wooden pieces to a pole in the center of the ceremonial space. While others sing and dance, these initiates move back and forth, up and down, putting pressure on those points where the ropes are fastened to their chests. The ceremony can last hours, even days. The goal for the initiate is to free himself from the pole by leaping backwards until the wooden pegs are ripped from his flesh. The chest wounds result in a scar that the initiate will show with pride in future Sun Dances.

In traditional religious cultures, marriages are still arranged between families rather than between the two individuals getting married. The joining of two families or clans is a deeply spiritual occasion that calls for dancing and the blessings of the ancestors. Burial customs also vary widely but typically follow strict rules about who may touch the body of the deceased and how it should be disposed. In most Native American cultures, a clan other than the clan of the deceased handles the body so that the family in mourning may not be ritually defiled.[14] Often, feasts follow funerals as a way to honor the dead and settle any debts he or she may have left unresolved.

But where do the spirits of the dead reside? No clear answer to that question can be given for all Native American groups. Some believe the souls of the dead travel to a region "to the southwest," others believe they wait "among the stars" until they are reborn as their descendants' children. Answering the question is not of primary concern in Native American cultures, whose worldviews are rightly described as more "this-worldly" than "other-worldly."[15] That means traditional Native Americans, like practitioners of other indigenous religions, are more preoccupied with harmony in the here and now than they are with speculation about life after death.

In many Native American ceremonies, smoke from a pipe plays an important role. Agreements are sealed when two parties smoke the pipe together, making sure to draw the smoke from the pipe to their faces using their hands. In other ceremonies where the pipe is used, the ritual leader blows smoke in all four directions, invoking the blessing of the all-pervasive "Great Spirit."[16]

Significant Sects and Developments

Much of what I have described so far is the product of the mixing of different Native American tribal customs that was the result of the U.S. government's policies of "resettling" the Native population. In many cases, tribes interacted who had not done so before. Subsequent developments are almost all related to their attempts to survive. Armed struggles, like those led by the Sioux chief Sitting Bull (1831–1890), including the famous Battle of the Little Bighorn in 1876, were occasionally successful and offered faint hope of either victory over the white man or at least peaceful coexistence.

One of the most famous efforts to repel the foreigners and restore Native American religion and culture was led by a Paiute from Nevada named Wokova, also known by the name Jack Wilson (1856–1932). Wokova claimed to have a vision in which he was told how to end the encroachment of the white man and restore the native heritage. If his own people would work hard, be honest, and stop their feuding, he prophesied that white people would be removed, the ancestors would return, and so would their lost herds of buffalo. These events would be hastened by what came to be called the "Ghost Dance." The dance caught on among other tribes, including the Lakota, who gathered a large crowd for a Ghost Dance on the Pine Ridge Reservation near Wounded Knee Creek in South Dakota in December 1890. Participants brought with them bows and arrows they intended to use to shoot the buffalo they expected to return. Seeing the weapons, some members of the U.S. cavalry panicked and fired the first shots in a massacre that killed more than three hundred men, women, and children. Ghost Dances were banned by the U.S. government until the 1930s.

Faced with no other options, many Native Americans gradually accepted assimilation with the majority non-Native culture. According to the most recent 2010 U.S. Census, 5.2 million U.S. citizens are of Native American descent. Yet, as noted above, the Federal Bureau of Indian Affairs places the number closer to two million, since they count only members of "federally recognized tribes." Evidently, many Native Americans have not "enrolled" (the word used by many Tribal Councils) as members of a particular tribe. Those who have enrolled and who live on or near a reservation tend to be the most likely to preserve their indigenous religion to one degree or another.

Of course, many have embraced Christianity, sometimes in syncretistic ways. The Native American Church is the most prominent example of such a denomination. Established as a formal organization in Oklahoma in 1918, the Native American Church blends Native American spirituality with Protestant Christian beliefs and practices. They are best known, for better or for worse, for consuming "peyote," an edible cactus with hallucinogenic qualities. From the Native American Church's perspective, the visions one sees while under the influence of peyote are divinely inspired. The ceremony, organized to benefit someone who is suffering in some way, is usually an all-night gathering that takes place around a fire in a tipi. Also known as the "Peyote Road," the Native American Church is a loose association of like-minded groups who claim thousands of members, coordinate legal defenses of religious freedom (to ingest peyote as part of their religion), and try to identify other organizations of non-Natives who, in their view, hide behind the Native American Church's name to consume peyote illegally.

Significant Points of Contact

I don't remember reading the story of the Recabites before I moved to Africa. This small nomadic tribe is mentioned only in Jeremiah 35.[17] God points them out to Jeremiah as role models of obedience, in stark contrast with the children of Israel at the time. According to Jeremiah's account, the Recabite's greatest ancestor, Jonadab, forbade his people to drink wine, plant crops, or live in permanent shelters. They abided by these strict rules for generations and did not budge from them when God himself had Jeremiah invite representatives of the tribe into the Temple courts and offered them wine. "To this day," God tells Jeremiah, in praise of the Recabites, "they do not drink wine, because they obey their forefather's command." He makes his point in the very next line: "But I have spoken to you again and again, yet you have not obeyed me" (35:14). In other words, God praises this obscure group of people for holding fast to their honorable traditions simply because they are honoring the instructions of their ancestor.

In that spirit, I find much that is praiseworthy about traditional religion. The appeal of the Native American Church with its Christian influences (minus the peyote) testifies to the common ground on which we stand. Like most of our Native American neighbors, we believe in a Creator God who is all-pervasive. Like Paul who endorsed the quotation of a pagan poet on Mars' Hill, we agree that "in him we live and move and have our being." Christians can learn from the holistic view of nature and spirit at the core of the Native American worldview. Too many of us have bought into the ancient Greek dualism carried on in modern secularism that separates the world into very different realms—one material and one spiritual. How often do we pray, "Lord, please grant us not only physical blessings, but spiritual ones as well"? We should pray like Paul: "May God himself, the God of peace, sanctify you through and through. May your whole spirit, soul and body be kept blameless at the coming of our Lord Jesus Christ" (1 Thess. 5:23). What we call "physical blessings"—health and wealth—are actually "spiritual" because they come from God. The harmony between all of God's creatures, human and non-human, is envisioned as part of the ideal world of the future where "the wolf and the lamb will feed together" (Isa. 65:25).

Much more could be said about a proper biblical theology of the environment and our role in it as stewards. Spending time with Native

Americans makes me more aware of the truth that we live in a world in which "everything that has breath praise[s] the LORD" (Ps. 150:6). I am impressed, too, with the strong family ties that have bound traditional Native Americans together, bonds that by the forces of secularism and materialism are strained to the breaking point as these people live in other communities.

Significant Points of Contrast

The first and most significant point of contrast between Christianity and Native American religion in particular is the way the Creator is described. He is not the same as the "Great Spirit" who created the world, but then left it in the invisible hands of lesser spirit beings. We may speak of the "Great Spirit" to our Native Americans friends as a place to begin, because "he has not left himself without testimony" (Acts 14:17), and many acknowledge that testimony. He is near to us, not distant. David testifies in his own sacred songs, "He is our God and we are the people of his pasture, the flock under his care" (Ps. 95:7), and more personally, "You know when I sit and when I rise; you perceive my thoughts from afar" (Ps. 139:2). He is intimately familiar with us, invested in all the details of our lives. And once again, he has made himself known most recently and most definitely in the Word who "became flesh and made his dwelling among us" (John 1:14).

In Christ we also acknowledge that there are spiritual forces in the universe that we do not fully understand. Paul believed these forces oppose us: "Our struggle is not against flesh and blood, but against the rulers, against the authorities, against the powers of this dark world and against the spiritual forces of evil in the heavenly realms" (Eph. 6:12). We do not deny the presence of such entities. Do nature spirits exist? Is it possible for the living to communicate with the dead? The Bible does not write off all such beliefs as "superstition." There is no indication, for example, that Saul did not actually converse with Samuel (who had recently died) through a medium, the "witch of Endor" (1 Sam. 28). But the Bible prohibits such attempts at communication and all other forms of divination (see, for example, Leviticus 19:26).

I well remember sharing that passage with a Christian brother who had become fascinated with New Age "spirit guides," consulting them daily for direction. I did not feel compelled to tell him such things are not real, but only that those forms of spirituality are filled with deception (thus Paul's characterization above of "the powers of this dark world" and "the spiritual forces of evil in the heavenly realms"). We should have nothing to do with them. Instead, we trust in God's Spirit for the guidance we need. That commitment also precludes any help we may seek from ancestral spirits.

I mentioned above that Native American religions, like other traditional religions of the world, are prime examples of "this-worldly" worldviews. They are much more concerned about well-being in the here and now than in the afterlife. In Christ, we seek balance between the two. On the one hand, Jesus teaches us to pray, "Give us today our daily bread" (Matt. 6:11), and he assures us that God is concerned about providing us with enough to eat, drink, and wear. But we are told not to worry about such things (Matt. 6:25–34). We are also told, "set your minds on things above, not on earthly things" (Col. 3:2), to follow in the footsteps of great people of faith who "were longing for a better country—a heavenly one" (Heb. 11:16), and to live our lives "as aliens and strangers in the world" so that our neighbors will "see [our] good deeds and glorify God on the day he visits us" (1 Pet. 2:11–12). We understand why Paul would say he "would prefer to be away from the body and at home with the Lord" (2 Cor. 5:8), but we don't disconnect from our responsibilities here and pine for Heaven. Like Paul, "we make it our goal to please [the Lord], whether we are at home in the body or away from it" (2 Cor. 5:9).

Sadly, many Native Americans and other traditional religious practitioners around the globe continue to resist the gospel, which still represents to some the "white man's religion" and the oppression that came with it. It may be only because of the kind of "good deeds" Peter had in mind, offered with Christ-like humility and service to our Native American neighbors, that Jesus's claims might be reconsidered and embraced.

TALKING TOGETHER . . .

1. What major stereotypes about Native Americans did this chapter challenge?

2. Those who study comparative religions consider Native American religions to be a traditional religion. Why is this category helpful, and what are the dangers in grouping religions together under this kind of label?

3. How can those of us who are not Native American overcome the barriers that stand between many Native Americans and the gospel, partly as a consequence of centuries of oppression at the hands of our ancestors?

4. Discuss an appropriate Christian response to this statement: Native American and other traditional religious worldviews do not accept what secularism assumes, that there is a great divide between "physical" and "spiritual" reality, between the visible and invisible worlds.

5. Do you believe that divination is real? Can mediums actually communicate with the dead? What is a biblical response to those kinds of spiritual phenomena?

6. What can we learn from the Recabites whose story is told in Jeremiah 35?

IF YOU WANT TO READ MORE . . .

Hiebert, Paul G., R. Daniel Shaw, and Tite Tiénou. *Understanding Folk Religion: A Christian Response to Popular Beliefs and Practices.* Grand Rapids: Baker Books, 1999.

Locke, Raymond Friday. *The Book of the Navajo,* 6th reprint edition. Los Angeles: Mankind Publishing Company, 2005.

Niehardt, John G. *Black Elk Speaks, The Complete Edition.* Lincoln and London: University of Nebraska Press, 2014.

Smith, Craig Stephen. *Whiteman's Gospel: A Native American Examines the Christian Church and Its Ministry Among Native Americans.* Winnipeg, Canada: Indian Life Books, 1997.

Notes

[1] As of this writing, the future status and route of the pipeline is uncertain.

[2] LaDonna Brave Bull Allard, "Why the Founder of Standing Rock Sioux Camp Can't Forget the Whitestone Massacre," in *Yes! Magazine* online post, September 3, 2016, http://www.yesmagazine.org/people-power/why-the-founder-of-standing-rock-sioux -camp-cant-forget-the-whitestone-massacre-20160903.

[3] James Bilagody in interview by author January 26, 2017, in Tuba City, AZ.

[4] In Julia Roller, "Native and Christian: Sweat Lodges in Wyoming," https:// journalism.berkeley.edu/projects/nm/julia/index.html.

[5] Population figures according to the website of the Bureau of Indian Affairs, https:// www.bia.gov/WhoWeAre/index.htm. The 2010 U.S. Census reports that 5.2 million Americans identified themselves as American Indian or Alaska Native, either solely or in combination with another ethnicity. Of this total 2.9 million identify as American Indian or Alaska Native alone. See http://www.census.gov/prod/cen2010/briefs/c2010br-10.pdf.

[6] See relevant articles on the Mashpee Wampanoag website, http://www .mashpeewampanoagtribe.com/blog/?p=870.

[7] For example, see this critique by Johnny P. Flynn, "New Age Tragedy in Sedona: Non-Indians in the Sweat Lodge," in the online publication *Religion Dispatches*, October 12, 2009, published by University of Southern California, Annenberg, http:// religiondispatches.org/new-age-tragedy-in-sedona-non-indians-in-the-sweat-lodge. For a more strongly worded statement against such exploitation, see the "Declaration of War Against Exploiters of Lakota Spirituality" published in 1993 by the American Indian Cultural Support network, at http://www.aics.org/war.html.

[8] Some religion scholars (such as Warren Matthews, *World Religions*, 5th edition, Belmont, CA: Thomson-Wadsworth, 2007, 26) use the term "henotheism" to describe Native American religion. Henotheism is the belief in one Supreme God who presides over a pantheon of lesser gods.

[9] Among the Kalenjin of Kenya, for example, one version of the "fall" story is that "Asis" (the Creator) drew so close to a house where a woman was stirring corn meal that her spoon slipped and she accidentally poked Asis in the eye with it. Offended, Asis withdrew from human beings and only returns on occasion.

[10] According to Winfried Corduan, *Neighboring Faiths: A Christian Introduction to World Religions*, 2nd edition (Downers Grove, IL: InterVarsity, 2012), 246.

[11] In John G. Niehardt, *Black Elk Speaks, The Complete Edition* (Lincoln and London: University of Nebraska Press, 2014), 121.

[12] William A. Young, *The World's Religions: Worldviews and Contemporary Ethics*, 3rd edition (Boston: Prentice Hall, 2010), 41.

[13] John Lame Deer, a twentieth-century Sioux shaman, once said, "When we killed a buffalo, we knew what we were doing. We apologized to his spirit, tried to make him understand why we did it." Quoted by Christopher Partridge in *Introduction to World Religions* (Minneapolis: Fortress Press, 2005), 121.

[14] In Navajo tradition, non-Navajo are asked to handle the body of the deceased. Corduan, *Neighboring Faiths*, 259.

[15] I know that "this-worldly" and "other-worldly" don't sound like technical terms, but they are.

[16] Willard G. Oxtoby and Alan F. Segal, eds., *A Concise Introduction to World Religions* (Oxford: Oxford University Press, 2007), 33.

[17] The "house of Recab" is mentioned in 1 Chronicles 2:55 as a family descended from the Kenites, a foreign tribe eventually attached to Judah. The Recabites featured in Jeremiah 35 may be descendants of these Kenites.

CHAPTER TEN.

OUR CHINESE NEIGHBORS

Yuxi (yoo-shee) Chen teaches physics at a major public university in upstate New York. Born and raised in New York City, Yuxi studied at MIT where he met his wife, Jennifer, who was a fellow-graduate student there. Jennifer and Yuxi live with their two young children in a neighborhood full of young families much like theirs. Yuxi loves (in this order) his family, his students, his colleagues, the New York Knicks—even in their worst seasons—and authentic Italian food.

Canwen Xu (Shoo) says she lives in two worlds—one Chinese and the other American. Born in China, her parents moved to the United States when Canwen was only two years old and settled in the upper Midwest. Canwen is now eighteen and lives in Boise, Idaho, where she recently completed her freshmen year of college. Canwen is used to the questions people ask about her name and her family's origins. "How did you get your name?" Her answer: "My parents gave it to me; how did you get yours?" "Where are you from?" Her standard answer: "Boise." Often the next question is,

"Where were you from *before* you moved to Boise?" People seem surprised when she responds, "We moved here from South Dakota; before that we lived in North Dakota." Unsatisfied with that answer, sometimes her interrogator will then ask, "Have you ever lived farther away than that?" Her answer, "We lived in Texas for a while." Of course, these strangers are asking about her ethnicity, but they don't want to be so direct.[1]

Yu Kuang began to call himself "Howard" when he came to the States and realized Americans had difficulty pronouncing his name. Before coming here, Yu studied engineering in China and worked for the large engineering firm that oversaw the construction of the Three Gorges Dam on the Yangtze River in Hubei Province, the dam that produces more electricity than any other hydro-electric facility in the world. Like most of his friends, Yu grew up in a home that was not religious. He remembers that every morning after the Chinese New Year, his grandparents would burn incense and fake money for their ancestors. His grandmother told him once that she had a dream in which her late father told her he needed the money. Howard's own parents didn't participate in the brief ritual. He was aware that other families and their kids would go to cemeteries on what was called "Tomb Sweeping Day" ("Qing Ming Jie") to do the same ritual, clean the tombstones, and pick up trash.

In school, Howard was introduced to the writings of Confucius. He remembers that his parents gave him a copy of the *Tao-te-Ching* to read at home, thinking that it would help him develop good morals. Once in college, an American English teacher invited Howard to a Bible study at the teacher's apartment. Initially he wasn't interested in the Bible or in learning more about Christianity, but he agreed to go because this was the first time in his life as a student that a teacher extended friendship. The teacher-student relationship back home is a very formal one. At first Howard thought the Bible stories were silly, like myths, and he didn't understand how intelligent people could believe them. But over time, the warmth and hospitality of his teacher softened his heart and opened his mind. At the age of twenty he declared his allegiance to Jesus and was baptized. Wanting to know more, he applied for a scholarship to study the Bible in the United States to be better equipped to minister to his fellow-Chinese back home. He received that scholarship, made his way to Arkansas, and is now a student at the university where I teach.[2]

The stories of these three people illustrate how difficult it is to generalize about the experience of people of Chinese ancestry in America. Many Chinese Americans were born here—children, grandchildren, and great-grandchildren of those who immigrated generations ago. Others were born in China, or Hong Kong, Taiwan, Singapore, or elsewhere, but were raised here. Still others, like Howard, are here on student visas or work permits and intend to return to their homelands. It is difficult to generalize about the religious experiences of any of our Chinese neighbors. I know nothing about the religious commitments of Yuxi or Canwen. Howard's spiritual journey I know because he is one of my students.

According to the 2010 U.S. Census, 3.8 million people who were born in China reside in the United States. That figure does not include the many more—maybe millions more—who are of Chinese ancestry but were born here. Of those 3.8 million who were born in China and then moved here, nearly half of them live in just two states: New York and California. Forty-six percent of Chinese immigrants in America live in just three U.S. cities: New York City, Los Angeles, and San Francisco.[3] These statistics reflect a dramatic increase in immigrants from China as well as other parts of Asia following the passage of the Immigration Act of 1965, which eased restrictions that had made it difficult for Asians to enter the States previously.

Given those challenges, the best I can do here is to outline in broad terms the religious landscape in China, namely the People's Republic of China where the largest number of new Chinese immigrants, guest workers, and students originate. Some of our Chinese neighbors who hail from nations such as Hong Kong, Singapore, or Taiwan will relate to some of these descriptions; others less so. In no way do I suggest that what I summarize here applies to all people of Chinese ancestry any more than an outline of the Christian faith would apply to all people whose ethnic origins trace back to Africa, Asia, Europe, North America, or South America.

Significant Figures

It may be difficult for Americans to appreciate the significance of the fact that the history of China is told with reference to a long and mostly unbroken chain of dynasties stretching from the legendary Huangdi, "The Yellow Emperor," whose reign—so the story goes—began in the year 2698 BC (on our calendars) and ended in the year 1912 when the last Emperor died and a Chinese republic was established. That year—2698 BC—is the year "zero" on the traditional Chinese calendar. I am writing these words at the beginning of the year 2017, which (after the Chinese New Year in January) is the Chinese year 4715 AH for "Anno Huangdi," "the Year of Huangdi."[4]

Why begin with Emperors as "significant figures" if the last one died more than a hundred years ago? The answer lies in the fact that the Emperor was considered divine and that his piety, expressed mainly in the veneration of ancestors and the appeasement of spirits, was considered crucial to the nation's well-being. Therefore, loyalty to the head of state was a religious obligation that persisted (ironically) during and after the upheaval caused by Mao's avowedly atheistic "Cultural Revolution" and the subsequent reforms initiated by the Communist government of the People's Republic of China. Expressing dissent or attempting to operate outside government boundaries is (mostly) not considered virtuous and threatens the welfare of the people.

Lao-zi and Confucius

Among historical religious figures, two rise to the top as the most influential. The first is Lao-zi, a name which means "Old Master." Though the details of his life are obscured by legend, scholars generally agree that he lived and died in the sixth and fifth centuries before Christ, which would make him a contemporary of Siddhartha Gautama (Buddha) and of Confucius, the second most important Chinese religious figure. According to one legend, Lao-zi met Buddha when he traveled to India, and he occasionally sparred with Confucius over philosophical questions.[5] Lao-zi worked as a government archivist. This gave him access to books that he cherished until he eventually authored one himself.

On that alleged journey to India, the guards at the Great Wall compelled him to record his wisdom in writing before they would let him pass. It was then and there that he wrote the *Tao-te-Ching*, "The Way and Its Power," in a single sitting. In it he extoled the virtues of following "the Way," not through harried activity, but by practicing stillness. In fact, the authorship of this important book was attributed to Lao-zi only in hindsight.

More than that, long after his death, Lao-zi was revered as a spiritual teacher, his images were worshiped, and temples were built in his name. The earliest record we have of the book he allegedly wrote dates only as far back as 240 BC, and its author was anonymous.[6] But I will follow convention and attribute it to Lao-zi when I speak of the *Tao-te-Ching* and the worldview it describes.

"Confucius" is the Latin name first used by Jesuit missionaries to China to refer to the second of these two most important religious figures. In China he is known as "Kung-fu-tzu" or "Master Kung." The outline of his life is told with a greater degree of confidence than that of Lao-zi. Master Kung was born in the year 551 BC in Lu State, now part of the modern Chinese province of Shandong, and he died in 479. Because of his love for learning, he was considered to be a child prodigy in his hometown. As an adult, he worked as a government magistrate where, like Lao-zi, he was exposed to literature more than the average person of his day.

Through reading, he learned about the earliest days of the Chou (Joo) dynasty (1120–221 BC), the one still in power during his lifetime. But the books he read, such as the *Book of History*, the *Book of Odes*, the *Book of Rites*, and the *Spring and Autumn Annals*—now considered Chinese classics—made Master Kung think of that ancient period more than five hundred years before he was born as the "Golden Age" in Chinese history. Back then, he read, the Chinese language was more uniform from region to region. In Confucius's time, a Chinese citizen from the north could barely communicate with someone from the south. Not only had the language been more standardized, the ancient culture seemed richer, the poetry more beautiful, the people more faithful in keeping ancient rituals honoring divine beings and ancestors, families were more orderly, and the general etiquette was more proper.

Confucius was also more impressed with the historical government officials he read about than he was with the ones he served in his lifetime. Two reforms he pushed the most in his writings were that rulers should be chosen on the basis of merit, not heredity, and that the true aim of government should be to promote the welfare of the people more than serving the interests of the governing officials. A teacher at heart, Confucius resigned his government post while still in his fifties, then spent ten years as a traveling sage, promoting his reforms around the country. Disappointed with the reception he received, he returned home feeling like a failure.

He spent the last five years of his life writing his memoirs and producing updated editions of those classics he loved. His own words of wisdom are recorded in the book entitled *The Analects* or "Lun Yu" ("Collected Sayings"). He would be surprised to know that eventually, the Han dynasty (which began in 206 BC) would adopt his teaching as the official state philosophy and that Master Kung himself would, like Lao-zi, be revered as a spiritual teacher, people would worship his image, and temples would be built in his honor.

Of course, after Lao-zi and Confucius came many significant figures who revised their teaching, philosophers whose refinements deserve to be mentioned (and are) in textbook treatments of Chinese religions. The influence of these two overlapping philosophies is still felt in modern China, despite the attempts to eradicate them in the twentieth century.

Mao Zedong

Mao Zedong (1893–1976) was the eradicator-in-chief. Born in Hunan Province, the young Mao was first exposed to Marxism while working in the Peking University library—an interesting connection to Lao-zi and Confucius who were both inspired by the books they read. He cofounded the Chinese Communist Party in 1921 and took control of the government in 1949 in the chaos that followed World War II. Internal squabbles within the Communist Party leadership led to the "Cultural Revolution" in 1966, in which Mao purged the party of those not loyal to him, burned churches and temples—Taoist, Confucian, and Buddhist—closed schools, and reasserted his authority as the party Chairman.

Conservative estimates put the number of Chinese victims of these purges at more than one million. His "Little Red Book" was compulsory reading for every Chinese citizen. When Mao died in 1976, the Cultural Revolution effectively ended. Deng Xiaoping (1904–1997) succeeded Mao and presided over the economic reforms that have continued to open China to the rest of the world (despite the Tiananmen Square protests of 1989). He and his successors also relaxed their grip somewhat on the philosophical and religious aspects of life in China.

Significant Beliefs

Religion in modern China blends elements from four different sources: Traditional Religion, Taoism, Confucianism, and Buddhism. The traditional religion that was present before these other, more formal religions or philosophies emerged, includes a belief in a Supreme Being. He was called by different names: "Shang-di" which means "Above Emperor," as in "The King Above," and "Tian," which usually translates as "Heaven," and originally referred to as the ultimate Divine Being but was gradually identified with an impersonal moral force. In some cases, "Tian" is shorthand for the universe itself. But, as in Native American religions and other traditional religions described in the previous chapter, this Supreme Being faded in importance over time and left the control of the day-to-day operation of the universe to lesser spirits, namely ancestors.

Ancestor veneration and appeasement persist in modern China, mainly among senior citizens in rural areas. Two kinds of spirits require attention. "Shen" are the benevolent spirits which include nature spirits that dwell in rivers, mountains, and forests, as well as departed ancestors whose blessing their descendants seek and whose needs they must meet (as when Howard's grandmother burned paper money at her dead father's request). According to the traditional belief, when people die, they join the shen. "Gui," often translated as "ghosts," are the malevolent spirits that live in desolate places such as deserts and threaten harm if not appeased.

Yin and Yang

Fundamental to Chinese traditional religion is the concept of "Yin" and "Yang," the twin forces that fill the cosmos and represent qualities like light, strong, and male ("yang") to name a few versus dark, weak, and female ("yin"). Before you get your feelings hurt by the apparent sexism in that little sampling, keep reading. All such qualities are necessary and all must be kept in perfect balance. The picture of yin-yang (next page) says as much: the curved line (as opposed to a straight line) that separates the opposite forces and the appearance of a black dot in the white part and a white dot in the black part—these are not accidental. The ideal is not one or the other but balance between the two.

FIGURE 1. YIN-YANG SYMBOL

Related to yin-yang is the concept of "Chi" (also spelled "qi"), which may be translated "universal energy" or "vital force." Maintaining the proper balance and flow of this energy through the body is essential to health. Most forms of Chinese traditional medicine are designed to adjust or regulate chi in one way or another. "Tai Chi" (literally "the way of chi") is an exercise routine that aligns the practitioner's own body with nature's chi. Chi is a foundational element in "Feng shui," a method of organizing one's home to maximize the flow of energy and to remove any unseen obstacles that restrict it.[7]

Finally, embedded in the traditional Chinese worldview is a sense that life is cyclical. The Chinese do not traditionally speak of karma as Hindus, Buddhists, or Jains do, but there is a strong sense that cycles repeat themselves and that there is harmony in this endless turning of the wheel. The Chinese calendar is based on twelve-year cycles repeated five times in a sixty-year period. The Chinese, like so many other adherents of traditional religions, do not imagine "timelines" but time circles.

The Tao

Speaking of timelines, we cannot know exactly when the concept of "the Tao" ("the Way") became an integral part of the Chinese worldview. I mentioned above that the oldest references to the *Tao-te-Ching* date to 240 BC, but we have reason to believe the idea was in circulation centuries before then.

What exactly is the Tao? The opening verse of the *Tao te-Ching* shows why that is such a tricky question to answer: "The Way that can be told is not an unvarying way. The names that can be named are not unvarying names."[8] In other words, the Tao that can be described in words is not the true Tao. This doesn't keep scholars from trying. It is, they say, "the correct flow of things in proper harmony," "the cosmic force behind all phenomena," "the inexpressible Way of Reality of which no one can speak," or "a way of life in conformity with the nature of the universe."[9]

Bottom line is that the Tao defies description. It (not he or she) will reveal itself to you when you learn to be still. Taoism is the effort to master the appropriate stillness. Taoist philosophy emphasizes the "Law of Return" ("Fu") whereby eventually all things will return to their original, pristine, and natural condition—"the state of the uncarved block"—if we human beings can leave it alone and literally let nature take its course. "See, all things howsoever they flourish return to the root from which they grew. This return to the root is called Quietness; Quietness is called submission to Fate; what has submitted to Fate has become part of the always-so."[10] The appropriate response to this truth is "actionless action" ("wu wei"), which usually takes the form of meditation through which a person is more equipped to practice moderation in all things (as opposed to over-planning or over-reacting to circumstances).

Confucian Ideals

My Chinese friends agree that much of what is considered virtuous in China today is actually the realization of the ideals of Confucius, though he was not given the credit for being a primary source of Chinese ethics during the Cultural Revolution. He is best known for two major ethical principles: "ren" ("reciprocity") and "li" ("propriety").

"Ren" means doing what is best for others. "Do not impose on others," Confucius wrote, "what you yourself do not desire."[11] Sound familiar? Comparative religion professors call it "the Silver Rule," since it states in the negative what Jesus's "Golden Rule" says more positively (in Matthew 7:12). As for "propriety," Confucius's *Analects* are filled with his ideas about what was and was not proper, covering everything from the right way to eat to the correct way to make a bed.

His emphasis on family loyalty—what scholars label "filial piety"—brought the two concepts of "reciprocity" and "propriety" together and focused on the five relationship pairs he believed were most important for the stability and well-being of every person. First and foremost is the father-son relationship. Fathers should show their sons kindness; sons must be loyal to their fathers, no matter what. When that relationship is proper, it will trickle upward and outward to positively influence a right relationship between a husband and wife (husband should be righteous, wife should be obedient), between an older brother and his younger brother (elder brother should be gentle, younger brother should be humble), between any older person and any younger person (elder should be considerate, youth should defer to their elders), and eventually inspire the right relationship between the ruler and his subjects (ruler should be benevolent, subject should be loyal). Confucius believed the breakdown of these family relationships would bring about the demise of the whole nation.

In modern China, the value placed on reciprocity is best seen perhaps in what Chinese call "Guan-xi" (GUAN-shee), translated "connections" or "relationships." In many ways, success in life—from securing a job to finding an apartment—is dependent on how well a person can build and maintain a network of connections, then work the system. That is the pragmatic side of the Confucian ideal.

Buddhism in China

Buddhist missionaries from India brought Buddhism to China as early as the third century before Christ. The language barrier made the translation of Buddhist concepts from Sanskrit to Mandarin challenging; the result was that Buddhist fundamentals were reinterpreted in ways that fit Taoism. A more orthodox version of Buddhism eventually thrived in China, though it faced periods of suppression as a foreign religion whenever a Taoist or Confucian Emperor was in power.

Today the branches of Buddhism that are most popular in China are "Tendai" (sometimes spelled "Tiantai") and "Chan" (called Zen elsewhere). For many Chinese, Buddhism only enters their life at death; Buddhists funerals strike some of my Chinese friends as more appealing than the alternatives.

We cannot underestimate the impact of decades of official atheism on all of these beliefs. Reliable statistics are hard to find, but my Chinese informants tell me that most of their friends are not religious. They are preoccupied instead with building careers and attaining wealth.

Significant Practices

Books like this one attempt to separate the elements of any given culture for the sake of analysis. But in practice, these beliefs are all smashed together. To be sure, secularism, the product of official atheism, shapes Chinese culture today more than any other factor. But, in my opinion, daily life in the People's Republic of China is regulated more by the teachings of Confucius than by any of the other *religious* influences, often more than Chinese people themselves may realize.

Confucian ideals are Chinese ideals. Traditional religion is still very evident, especially in the popularity and prominence of diviners. Many Chinese citizens rely on various forms of divination or "fortune telling" when faced with a decision or when curious about the future. The ancient diviners' manual, the *I Ching* or "The Book of Changes," is famous around the world. The formations created when short sticks and long sticks are thrown on the ground (in the more contemporary version, a series of coins are tossed instead) tell the skilled diviner what message to relay to the client who seeks their counsel.

Ancestor veneration, though not as common as before, is still part of life, especially for older people in rural areas. But it touches everyone during the annual Chinese New Year and Spring Festival celebration (late January or early- to mid-February) when some estimate that as many as half of the Chinese population travel home, causing tremendous congestion in the national transportation system and massive traffic jams. The "Reunion Dinner" on the Eve of the celebration is to Chinese culture what Thanksgiving is in America. Underneath this mass migration every year and behind many of the rituals connected to it are filial piety and ancestor veneration, even if for some participants the connections have been forgotten.

Taoism operates more behind the scenes, contributing to the worldview of many Chinese more than it is reflected in daily practice. But travelers to China will certainly witness people in the park doing Tai Chi. Various forms of meditation may be attributed to the Taoist ideal of "actionless action." Many Buddhist temples have been rebuilt in recent decades, an indication of renewed interest, especially in the forms of Buddhism that are most popular in China.

Significant Sects and Developments

In the decades since the Cultural Revolution, the Chinese government has allowed a slow thaw in its relationship with formal religion. This has led to a revival of sorts of Taoism, Confucianism, and Buddhism. At the same time, Muslims in the West among the ethnic Uighurs and religious cults including Falun Gong have made international news for incidents of brutal suppression.[12] The government seems to have loosened, though not eliminated, some of the restrictions on Christian movements. In a 2016 speech, current Chinese President Xi Jinping called on the Communist Party of China (CPC) to exert more control, not less, on the country's religious institutions to ensure that they "serve socialism."

As it stands now, Christian groups in China must operate under the authority of the government-led Three Self Patriotic Movement (TSPM) and its sister institution, the China Christian Council. These bodies oversee the so-called "Sinification" of Christian theology—that is, making sure that Christian teaching is appropriately Chinese, not foreign. The government is especially nervous about what it perceives to be politically-minded activism disguised as Christian propagation.[13] Many of the small independent Protestant groups have chosen not to come under the umbrella of the TSPM. The government seems to mostly ignore these groups as long as they avoid large gatherings and steer clear of politics. That 2016 speech may indicate a change.

Best estimates put the number of Christians of all stripes in China as high as one hundred million.[14] Hard data is hard to come by, given the reluctance some Chinese Christians feel to identify themselves as Christians. A 2010 Pew Research report showed there were 67 million Christians in China, including 58 million Protestants and 9 million Catholics. According to that report, 35 million (or 52 percent) belong to the independent "underground" churches.

If those numbers are correct, it would suggest that China has experienced a 10 percent increase in the number of Christians every decade since

1979 and is on track to have more self-proclaimed Christians than any other nation on earth by the year 2030.[15] Many Chinese Christians dream of much more than survival. The mission of the "Back to Jerusalem" movement, to give one example, is "to evangelize the unreached peoples from [the] eastern provinces of China, westward toward Jerusalem."[16] Members of that movement display remarkable faith and courage in the face of opposition as they pass through Muslim-majority nations to take the gospel back to where it began. In many ways, Christian believers from China are less encumbered by the suspicion attached to Christian missionaries from the West.

Significant Points of Contact

There is much to respect about a nation and people that maintained for nearly three millennia a traditional religion that at least initially included a belief in a Supreme Being and an admirable code of ethics. We cannot let the politics of the last one hundred years blind us to the richness of Chinese culture, grounded as it once was in a spiritual worldview. A key element of that worldview for many was (and is) the concept of "the Tao," the force that fills the universe but otherwise defies definition. Yet those who translated the New Testament into Chinese use the term in John 1:1: "In the beginning was the Tao, and the Tao was with God, and the Tao was God." Obviously, Christians more knowledgeable than I am see in the Tao a significant point of contact.

Another part of Chinese tradition and culture we can appreciate is the family loyalty and the emphasis on proper relationships that begin at home and spread upward and outward to society at large. In China, a person's "first" name is their family name. In other words, if I were Chinese, I would introduce myself first as "Cox" and only later as "Monte." We reverse that order in the Western half of the world because of individualism. I am first "Monte," and only secondarily a member of the "Cox" clan. (Sorry, Mom.) Western Christians have to overcome this "rugged individualism" that in us inspires self-reliance and not interdependence, keeping it to ourselves instead of confessing our sins to one another, going it alone rather than pursuing "the fellowship of the Holy Spirit." We could learn much from the group mentality of our Chinese neighbors.

Significant Points of Contrast

The atheism taught in schools and reinforced in Chinese public institutions fuels the materialism that captivates so many people, including many of our fellow-Americans and, if we're honest, many of our fellow-Christians. Spiritual conversations with a Chinese neighbor will not likely center on the residue of Taoism, Confucianism, or Buddhism that touches them here and there, but on the basic questions of why we believe what we believe. When the seed of the gospel lands on soft soil, cultivating that soil will typically require at least some apologetics communicated in an atmosphere of warmth and friendship.

For more religiously minded Chinese, the syncretism that I described above is accepted without critique. Yet Jesus demands exclusive devotion to him that does not leave room for bits and pieces of Taoism or Buddhism, though there are certainly virtues Confucius promoted, like the reciprocity of "The Silver Rule," that are also Christian virtues. But in Christ, it is not a self-serving, "you scratch my back, I'll scratch yours" kind of reciprocity. Because of Christ, we "do nothing out of selfish ambition or vain conceit, but in humility consider others better than [ourselves]" (Philip. 2:3). We depend on each other, just as the eye needs the ear and the foot needs the hand (1 Cor. 12:12–26). The goal of our interaction, in Paul's words, is "unity in the faith and in the knowledge of the Son of God" (Eph. 4:13). It is into that kind of Christ-centered web of relationships that we invite our Chinese neighbors.

TALKING TOGETHER . . .

1. How do the spiritual journeys of Yuxi, Canwen, and Howard connect (or not) with personal encounters you have had with people from China?

2. What, if anything, do you find true and admirable about the insights attributed to Lao-zi and Confucius?

3. Does the "yin-yang" concept capture any truth we embrace as Christians?

4. How does the Taoist commitment to "actionless action" square with the biblical teaching to "be still and know that I am God"?

5. What are lessons Christians need to learn from the group orientation of non-Western cultures?

6. What are some ways that we can encourage and support the growing Christian movement in China?

IF YOU WANT TO READ MORE . . .

Confucius. *The Analects of Confucius.* Translated by D. C. Lau. New York: Penguin Books, 1979.

De Mente, Boyé Lafayette. *The Chinese Mind: Understanding Traditional Chinese Beliefs and Their Influence on Contemporary Culture.* Tokyo: Tuttle Publishing, 2009.

Waley, Arthur, translator and editor. *The Way and Its Power: Lao Tzu's Tao Te Ching and Its Place in Chinese Thought.* New York: Grove Press, 1958.

Wenzhong, Hu, Cornelius N. Grove, and Zhuang Enping. *Encountering the Chinese: A Modern Country, An Ancient Culture,* 3rd edition. Boston and London: Intercultural Press, 2010.

Notes

[1] Canwen Xu, "I Am Not Your Asian Stereotype," TedxTalk Boise, Idaho, April 29, 2016, on YouTube at https://www.youtube.com/watch?v=_pUtz75lNaw.

[2] Interview by author with Yu Kuang, December 16, 2016, Searcy, Arkansas.

[3] Data source is www.migrationpolicy.org/chinese. Accessed December 17, 2016.

[4] In this chapter, I will mostly use the "pinyin" system of writing Chinese words in English characters, developed by the Chinese government in the 1950s to replace the older "Wade-Giles" system named for its nineteenth-century British creators. That is when "Peking" became "Beijing" and "Mao-Tse-tung" became "Mao Zedong."

[5] The dialogues between Lao-zi and Confucius are also legendary, described in the collection of Taoist writings known as *Zhuangzi*.

[6] According to the introduction written by Arthur Waley in *The Way and Its Power: Lao-tzu's Tao Te Ching and Its Place in Chinese Thought*, translated and edited by Arthur Waley (New York: Grove Press, 1958), 86.

[7] Feng shui is a complex system based on the chi that relates to the five basic elements: fire, earth, water, metal, and wood, the colors that correspond to each element, and the chi that flows through different kinds of shapes as well.

[8] *Tao-te-Ching*, 1:1, translated and edited by Arthur Waley in *The Way and Its Power*, 141.

[9] So say in order Winfried Corduan, *Neighboring Faiths: A Christian Introduction to World Religions*, 2nd edition (Downers Grove, IL: InterVarsity Press, 2012), 393; S. A. Nigosian, *World Faiths*, 2nd edition (New York: St. Martin's Press, 1994), 188; Roger Eastman, *The Ways of Religion: An Introduction to the Major Traditions*, 2nd edition (New York: Oxford University Press, 1993), 197; and George W. Braswell Jr., *Understanding World Religions*, revised edition (Nashville: Broadman and Holman Publishers, 1994), 73.

[10] *Tao-te-Ching* chapter 16, in Waley's translation of *The Way and Its Power*, 162.

[11] *The Analects*, 15:24, translated by D. C. Lau (New York: Penguin Books, 1979), 135.

[12] For example, on the 2009 uprising among the Uighurs and the Chinese government response at the time, see "The Riots in Xinjiang: Is China Fraying?" in *The Economist* online, June 9, 2009, at http://www.economist.com/node/13988479. On the suppression of the Falun Gong, see James Griffiths, "Why China Fears the Falun Gong," in *The Los Angeles Times* online, July 14, 2014, at http://www.dailynews.com/general -news/20140714/why-china-fears-the-falun-gong.

[13] Brent Fulton, "China Reveals What It Wants to Do with Christianity," in *Christianity Today* online, April 28, 2016, accessed on December 17, 2016, http://www .christianitytoday.com/ct/2016/april-web-only/china-reveals-what-it-wants-to-do -christianity-xi-jinping.html.

[14] According to the World Christian Database, it is as high as 108 million. As reported in the 2011 Pew Report entitled "Global Christianity—A Report on the Size and Distribution of the World's Christian Population," December 19, 2011, 99. See http://www .pewforum.org/files/2011/12/ChristianityAppendixC.pdf. Accessed December 19, 2016.

[15] According to Eleanor Albert, "Christianity in China," in *Council on Foreign Relations* online, May 7, 2015.

[16] See the Back to Jerusalem website, https://backtojerusalem.com.

CHAPTER ELEVEN

OUR SHINTO NEIGHBORS

Manabu Sakane works as a corporate executive for Nissan North America in Franklin, Tennessee. A graduate of Osaka University, Sakane-san (as his colleagues in Japan call him) began his career at Nissan in 2002 and has worked his way up the corporate ladder to his current position. He and his wife, Michiko, moved to Tennessee five years ago. Although there is much they miss about home—their families, the food, the ease of getting around, and the general feeling of security—they are learning to appreciate the openness and spontaneity of their new American friends. Lately, they've been talking about starting a family. The thought of giving birth in America makes Michiko nervous, since she is not as familiar with the American medical system. She and Manabu also have questions about raising a child in a foreign country. They feel torn between their loyalty to Manabu's company and their longing for home.

William Lee Rand is the Founder and Director of the International Center for Reiki Healing near Detroit, Michigan, where he offers training classes in the healing techniques of Reiki. Introduced by Japanese teacher Mikao Usui (1865–1926) in the 1920s, Reiki is based on belief in a universal energy (called "Reiki") that permeates everything. Rand believes that a person "attuned" (his word) to its power can tap into it to heal others and themselves. The primary method of healing is a kind of therapeutic touch; Rand teaches students where to place the hands on the body of a patient to release the energy that heals. Rand himself discovered Reiki in 1981 after dabbling in astrology, rebirthing exercises, hypnotherapy, and other sorts of metaphysical practices that are not part of the mainstream approach to medicine in America.[1] Today, he travels the world doing Reiki workshops and maintains a website designed to educate others about Reiki.

Reuben Habito is a World Religions professor at the Perkins School of Theology at SMU in Dallas. Originally from the Philippines where he served as a Catholic priest, Habito later studied theology at Tokyo University, where he developed an interest in Eastern spiritual practices. While teaching at SMU, Habito established the Maria Kannon Zen Center in Dallas, which derives its name from a combination of the Virgin Mary and a Buddhist female figure known in Japan as Kannon. The center operates in space provided by the White Rock United Methodist Church in Dallas. According to their website, the center's mission is to teach Zen practice to people from various backgrounds and faiths in order to "cultivate wisdom and compassion in their daily lives and in their relationships in society and the whole world."[2] Habito himself, like many visitors to the center, is still a practicing Roman Catholic, but he is convinced that Zen has much to offer for those who seek spiritual formation at a deeper level.

I realize that I have started this chapter on religion in Japan by profiling three people, only one of whom is Japanese. But the influence of Japanese forms of spirituality is apparent in their stories, with the exception of the Japanese corporate executive who would not describe himself as religious. The religion and culture of Japan have made an impact on American life much more than the numbers of Japanese in America might suggest. An estimated 1.3 million people of Japanese ancestry were in America as of 2010, a 12 percent increase since 2000. California and Hawaii are home to America's largest Japanese-background populations, with close to eight hundred thousand people.[3]

I know of no data that reveals the religious inclinations of these members of our society. So in this chapter I won't be giving an overview of the faith of our Japanese neighbors. On the other hand, recent polls on religion in Japan show that 84 percent of its 127 million citizens choose "Shinto" as their religious affiliation, 71 percent claim Buddhism, less than 2 percent select "Christian," and nearly 8 percent choose "other."[4] If the math is giving you trouble, understand that many Japanese practice both Shintoism and some form of Buddhism, so they will check both on surveys. To muddy the waters even more, I should also mention that, according to a 2012 Gallup poll, 31 percent of Japanese citizens identified themselves as atheists and 57 percent said they were "religiously unaffiliated."[5]

As in China where many people combine elements from four main religious sources—traditional religion, Taoism, Confucianism, and Buddhism—in Japan, people observe Shinto rituals on certain occasions and Buddhist rituals on others. The difference is, as Winfried Corduan explains it, in China the four main religious ingredients are mixed together in one bowl; in Japan they are all on the same tray, but kept in separate compartments, with one space labeled "atheism."[6] Of course, a Japanese person knows the difference between a Shinto shrine and a Buddhist temple; they may frequent both for different purposes. Once again, the focus in this chapter is not on the faith commitments of Japanese Americans, but on religion in Japan as most Japanese experience it there, and on the elements of that experience our newest Japanese neighbors here likely have brought with them.

Significant Figures

Japan traces its history as a nation back to a legendary first Emperor, Jimmu Tenno, who ascended the throne, they say, in the year 660 BC. Fast forward almost two thousand seven hundred years to Emperor Akihito, current occupant of the Japanese throne, the son of Emperor Hirohito of World War II fame, and the 125th Emperor in that unbroken chain. Jimmu Tenno was believed to be a descendant of Amaterasu, the sun goddess, and was, therefore, divine. On this end of the timeline, Hirohito was forced by the victorious Allies to renounce his divine ties. His son, Emperor Akihito, however, retains in modern Japan the mystique of someone who is more than a figurehead and who still serves in some ways as the leader of Shintoism.

In that long line of rulers, a few stand out for significant parts they have played in the story of religion in Japan. Emperor Tenmu, who ruled in the seventh century AD, commissioned the writing of the *Kojiki*, "The Record of Ancient Matters," which was completed in 712, twenty-five years after his death. Historians speculate that the Emperor felt threatened by the growing popularity of Buddhism and Confucianism, brought to Japan by emissaries from China and Korea in the century before him. The book was an attempt on his part to solidify a uniquely Japanese identity by putting in writing Japanese religious traditions that were neither Buddhist nor Confucian. The term "Shinto" had not yet been coined to describe Japanese traditional religion, but the *Kojiki* recorded the myths that formed the core of those traditions.

The religious landscape shifted again during the Tokugawa period (1603–1867) when a series of fifteen "shoguns," the first named Ieyasu Tokugawa, took charge of Japan and made the Emperor a figurehead. These shoguns were served by the "samurai," a title drawn from a Chinese word that means "servant," who adopted the warrior code called "Bushido" (literally "the way of the warrior"), a mixture of mental discipline borrowed from Zen Buddhism, ethics drawn from Confucius, and Japanese patriotism.

When the young Emperor Meiji came to power in 1867, he assumed the authority his predecessors had relinquished when the shoguns took over. Emperor Meiji is credited with "modernizing" Japan by opening the country to industry and welcoming other influences that were considered foreign before. (Moviegoers may recall the mostly fictionalized version of Emperor Meiji portrayed in the 2003 movie *The Last Samurai*, starring Tom Cruise.) Meiji also initiated reforms that established "Shinto" as the official state religion. The Meiji Constitution of 1889 specified that

1. Shinto is not a religion, but supersedes all religions as an expression of Japanese patriotism.
2. All Shinto shrines are government property and the priests who serve there are government employees.

3. The head of Shinto is the divine Emperor.[7]

Many historians, both Japanese and non-Japanese, attribute the nationalistic fervor that led Japan into World War II to Meiji's reforms. Incidentally, Emperor Hirohito, who declared war on the United States, was Meiji's grandson; he died in 1989, exactly one hundred years after his grandfather's constitution was passed.

With regard to religion, post-war Japan went through a reactionary phase that saw a decline in Shintoism, an upsurge in interest in Christianity (perceived as the religion of the conquerors, right or wrong), and a dramatic increase in the number of "new religions" (or what others would label "cults"). Gradually, preoccupied with rebuilding the nation, Japan slid into the secularism that characterizes it today. Miho, my guide on a tour at the base of Mount Fuji, added this disclaimer after explaining the traditional spiritual connections to "Fuji-san": "But we Japanese are not very pious."

Since this is the "Significant Figures" section, I must mention the "kami," or "deities," and the Shinto priests who serve them. The translation of the term "kami" is problematic. Usually translated "gods," the kami are, in fact, any and all superior spiritual beings and the energy they produce. "Kami" inhabit natural landmarks, such as mountains, streams, and trees, much like nature spirits in the worldview of other traditional religions. The pantheon of Japanese "gods" and "goddesses" are also referred to as "kami," as are ancestral spirits. In fact, what I am calling "Shinto" (from the Chinese words "shen" for benevolent spirits and "dao" for "way"), the Japanese call "kami-no-michi," or "the way of the kami." "Kamikaze" pilots during World War II were given that name—"divine wind"—because of the belief that the spirit ("wind") of the kami accompanied them to their deaths on their suicidal missions. Shinto priests mediate between kami and the people, although such mediation is usually only necessary on special occasions like births, weddings, funerals, and national holidays. Otherwise, individuals approach the kami at home without the help of a priest.

Other significant figures in Japanese religion are those Buddhist teachers such as Honen, Kukai, Nichiren, and Eisai, to name a few, who centuries ago modified the sects of Buddhism they embraced to make them more Japanese.

Significant Beliefs

Conviction about the "kami" is the foundation of Shintoism. Their role in creation itself is clear in the Preface to the *Kojiki*:

> I, Yasumaro [the author], say, when chaos had begun to condense, but force and form were not yet manifest, and nothing was named, nothing done, would could know its shape? Nevertheless, Heaven and Earth first separated, and the Three Deities [Kami] began creating. The Passive and Active Essences then developed [yin and yang], and the Two Spirits became the ancestors of all things.[8]

(Sounds a bit like Genesis 1, doesn't it?) The creative "Three Deities" (kami) are not named, but the "Two Spirits" are Izanagi and Izanami, the first divine couple, whose children include the Sun ("Amaterasu"), the Moon ("Tsukiyomi"), and the god of storms, "Susa-no-wo." Of those, Amaterasu is arguably the most important. The first Emperor is considered her offspring. Her divine symbol, the sun, is represented by the large red dot on the Japanese flag. The Shinto Shrine in Ise, Japan, where Amaterasu is worshiped, is considered by many Japanese to be the most sacred site in the country.

Once a person dies, they join their fellow kami in the realm of the departed. Yet, as in other traditional religions, the ancestors are very much present with their embodied descendants. They must be honored and, at times, appeased. As we shall see below, many Shinto religious practices are aimed in the direction of the ancestral kami. For example, the Yasukuni Shrine is a Shinto worship site in Tokyo that honors more than two million kami of Japanese soldiers who have died in battle since the 1800s, including fourteen Japanese military leaders who were convicted of war crimes committed during World War II. A visit to the shrine, like the one made by Prime Minister Shinzo Abe in December of 2013, is considered a religious act and offends leaders of nations like China, Korea, and the United States, who suffered greatly because of Japan's aggression.[9] The Yasukuni complex includes a museum full of World War II memorabilia and an angle on the events before, during, and after the war that is quite different from the one students in the West learn in school.

The nature kami who reside in mountains, streams, forests, rocks, and trees also demand respect. Rice farmers organize Shinto rituals at key moments on the agricultural calendar to seek the blessing of the kami who oversee the fields, the water supply, the weather, and therefore the success of the harvest. Japanese culture is well-known for its emphasis on living in harmony with nature rather than trying to conquer it, precisely because humans and nature are bound together, for better or for worse, by the presence of the kami.

Following the tsunami that struck Japan on March 11, 2011, a prominent Japanese official in Tokyo surprised many of his countrymen when he attributed the disaster to the kami. "The Japanese people must take advantage of this tsunami to wash away their selfish greed. I really do think this is divine punishment."[10] The official later apologized. But he likely expressed what many Japanese believed. The official tied the calamity to spiritual impurity, underscoring the fact that ritual purity, achieved through ceremonial washings and the avoidance of tabus, is of utmost importance in Shintoism.

It is difficult to summarize the beliefs of the 71 percent of Japanese people who say they practice Buddhism, given the differences in the Buddhist sects that claim the most adherents in Japan. Each of the Japanese leaders of these sects put a uniquely Japanese stamp on them. Pure Land Buddhism (described in Chapter Five) is perhaps the most popular form, but it is split into hundreds of smaller sects, each one teaching a variation on the religion as Honen, the twelfth-century Japanese Buddhist monk, and his disciple, Shinran, understood it. All of them trust in "Amida Buddha"—not the personal figure of Siddhartha, but the concept of "Universal Buddhahood"—to lead them after death to a "Pure Land" somewhere to the west of Japan where, in that purer place, they will be able to achieve enlightenment. The emphasis on purity derives from Shintoism. I visited the headquarters of one "splinter group" in Kyoto known as "Otani-ha," whose massive and beautiful temple is called "The Eastern Temple of the Original View," a reference to the "original view" of Shinran, whom they consider the proper interpreter of *True* Pure Land Buddhism. This one sub-sect of True Pure Land Buddhists claims 5.5 million members.

Nichiren taught his brand of Buddhism in thirteenth-century Japan, convinced that the Buddhist text called *The Lotus Sutra* was the only authoritative Buddhist teaching. As I mentioned in Chapter Five, Nichiren Buddhists chant a Japanese phrase that is usually translated, "I bow down to worship the mystic law of the Lotus Sutra." Nichiren's spiritual descendants have become known for their aggressive attempts to proselytize, even among other Buddhists. Their numbers are growing in the United States.

Kukai learned the Shingon ("True Words") Buddhist tradition in China and brought it home to Japan in the ninth century, pointing to a primordial figure called "Vairocana" as the ground of all being itself and the key to truth. Eisai, yet another twelfth-century figure, brought Zen Buddhism to Japan from China where he learned it, along with the tea that, he discovered, helped keep devotees awake during long hours of "zazen," "sitting meditation."

I once visited the Sanjusagendo Temple in Kyoto which houses 1001 images of "Kannon," a female Buddhist "bodhisattva" (one who delays their entrance into Nirvana in order to guide others) in the longest wooden building in Japan. "Kannon" worship was also brought from China, where the same figure is called "Guanyin." It is this female spiritual hero that SMU Professor Habito combined with the Virgin Mary when he established the Maria Kannon Zen Center in Dallas.

Each of these cases illustrates the Japanese propensity for taking a religion or philosophy that originated elsewhere and making it their own.

Significant Practices

It is helpful to me to think of Shinto in action within four different categories: State Shinto (sponsored by the government), Shrine Shinto (Shinto practices that take place at a Shinto Shrine or "Jinja"), Domestic Shinto (what Japanese people practice at home), and Sectarian Shinto, an interesting label applied by the Japanese government to "new religions" it allows but tries to absorb under the larger Shinto umbrella.

State Shinto

State Shinto officially ended with the Japanese surrender at the end of World War II and the public renunciation by the Emperor Hirohito of his divine connections, an announcement the Allies required the Emperor to broadcast on Japanese radio. The government would no longer fund Shinto shrines or pay the priests that served in them.

Decades later, many of those same Shinto shrines—including the two-thousand-year-old Ise Shrine dedicated to Amaterasu, the Meiji Shrine that honors the kami of the Meiji Emperor and his wife, and the Yasukuni Shrine honoring the kami of Japanese war dead, to name just a few I have visited personally—function like National Monuments. The priests and others who work there do, in fact, receive federal funding, and, as I mentioned above, the current Emperor Akihito fills the role of the national Shinto leader.

Shrine Shinto

Shrine Shinto is also called "Jinja," because the building itself where the Shinto rituals take place is called Jinja. The entrance is marked by a unique gate called a "torii" (to-ree-HEE), easily recognized by its simple construction: two upright pillars made of wood holding two horizontal crossbeams, one above the other. The gate is intended to separate "a Shinto sanctuary from the secular world and [marks] the entrance to a sacred world."[11] Guests bow twice before they pass through the gate.

On the other side, the path, often lined with figures of animals who serve as symbolic guardians, leads visitors through a grove of trees that is also considered sacred. Traditionally, worshipers are supposed to stay to the right or the left of the path instead of walking in the center, believing that the middle of the path is reserved for the invisible kami themselves. Worshipers then come to an ablution fountain, where they use a dipper to pour water on their hands and rinse their mouths for the sake of ritual purity. As the shrine itself comes into view, the path curves to the left; a straight path strikes the Japanese as too direct and therefore improper.

The shrine building, typically made of wood, can be a simple structure or an elaborate one.[12] A long rail marks the front of the shrine proper, usually with a wooden box where visitors place donations or offerings. Guests do not proceed beyond that point. After putting the offering in the box, visitors may ring a bell that hangs from a rope and signals to the kami the presence of the worshipers. Practitioners bow twice before the kami, then clap their hands twice (with about one second between claps). Then they may stand and offer silent prayers. The inner sanctuary of a Shinto shrine houses relics that were associated with the kami (ancestors) who once lived there or built that shrine. In smaller neighborhood shrines, these relics (called "shintai") are taken out of the building once a year and paraded through the streets in a special container as a way to honor the kami.

Close to the shrine are vendors selling amulets of all kinds and ancestral tablets the purchaser will place in their home as good luck charms and as a way to honor their own ancestors. Another stand sells wooden prayer plaques on which the visitor may write prayer requests. At a popular shrine like the Meiji Jinja in Tokyo, guests will see these prayers for health, peace, and prosperity written in languages from around the world and hung for display. There it is the blessing of the Meiji kami the prayers invoke. The smaller neighborhood shrines play a larger role in daily life. Newborns are presented to the neighborhood kami there. Offerings of rice, sake, seafood, fruits, or candy are routinely left at the threshold by those who live in that neighborhood.

Domestic Shinto

Domestic Shinto inspires the faithful family to keep images or symbols of their deceased loved ones in a cabinet called a "kamidana." There they routinely place offerings like those left at neighborhood shrines to honor their ancestors and secure their blessings. Given the number of Buddhists in Japan, it is also common to find a "Butsudan" in the same room as the kamidana. The Butsudan looks like a TV cabinet; inside is placed either an image of Buddha or a scroll with sacred Buddhist writing on it, depending on the form of Buddhism practiced by the homeowner.

Other practices that would fall under the heading "Domestic Shinto" include the life-cycle rituals common in other traditional religions. A month-old baby is presented to the neighborhood kami at the local shrine for their blessing on the child's health. Families also pay a visit to that same shrine every year on November 15, known in Japan as the "Shichi-Go-San Festival." Shichi-Go-San are the numbers seven, five, and three in Japanese. In the years they turn three and seven (for girls) or three and five (for boys), young children are presented once again to the kami, but this time they are dressed in traditional Japanese clothes—a kimono for girls and "haori" jackets and "hakama" pants for boys. On the occasion, parents give their kids special "1000 Year Candy" ("chitose-ame") as a symbol of long life.

My Christian friends in Tokyo told me that the "Shichi-Go-San" Festival is a time when many Christians feel especially left out. Some churches have organized special assemblies on November 15 to bless the children who are seven, five, and three. Missionaries label a ritual like that a "functional substitute"—that is, a Christian version of a traditional practice minus the spiritual elements they cannot embrace. The practice is somewhat controversial among Japanese Christians.

The traditional rite of passage from puberty into adulthood has faded almost completely in modern Japan. Weddings once took place in private homes as simple rituals involving the two families of the newlyweds. The Meiji Restoration saw more Japanese citizens organizing formal wedding ceremonies at Shinto Shrines with Shinto priests officiating. This trend has continued; wealthier Japanese will often get married (or at least pose for wedding pictures) at major national Shinto Shrines. And, curiously, many Japanese brides choose to wear bridal gowns they associate with "Christian" weddings.

Funerals in Japan often follow Buddhist traditions. Japanese may bury or cremate the dead. A period of mourning lasting forty-nine days is not uncommon. The number is significant; Tibetan Buddhism teaches that the period of limbo between death and the next reincarnation is no longer than forty-nine days. If the deceased is to re-enter another womb and be reborn, it will happen, they believe, within that forty-nine-day window.

In some ways, the festivals that honor the dead are more important than funerals. New Year's Day is arguably the most important national holiday in Japan. Families gather for four days between December 31 and January 3, eat special foods, and engage in ritual activities, some of which have Buddhist roots. It is traditional for families to visit a Shinto Shrine together during those days to ask the kami for blessings in the New Year.[13]

During the annual Obon Festival (July-August), which is actually borrowed from Buddhism, Japanese believe that their ancestors return to this world to visit relatives. Traditional lanterns are hung at the front door to welcome them. Families visit graves, where they make offerings of food. At the end of Obon, people place floating lanterns in rivers and lakes to guide ancestors back home. Once again, Christians in Japan wrestle with the extent to which they can participate. One group of church leaders told me that they feel they do well to drive relatives to and from Obon activities, help serve the meals or take photographs, but they cannot join in the parts of the Festival aimed more directly at the kami.

Significant Sects and Developments

I described above the emergence of Shintoism as a distinct religion only in response to the appeal of alternatives such as Buddhism and Confucianism. Religion scholar Ninian Smart puts it this way: "Shinto was the early religion of Japan. It forms a substratum of belief and practice that remains to this day."[14] The resilience of Shintoism is apparent in its resurgence after World War II, when as many as 10 percent of the Japanese people turned to Christianity, at least for a season. In the decades that followed, however, the number of Christians sank back to pre-war lows and remains at only 1 percent of the population today. The biggest barrier to Christian faith, according to Japanese church leaders I asked, is the obligation to honor one's ancestors, which is at Shinto's core.

New Religion Movements in Japan

The "New Religions" that are classified by the government as "Sectarian Shinto" fit here as relatively recent developments. With hundreds of sects, some large and some small, I can only offer a representative sampling and point to common features. Tenrikyo, one of the largest of these "new religions," was founded by Miki Nakayama (called "Oyasama" by Tenrikyo members) in 1838 when, according to her, "God the Parent" ("Oyagami" in Japanese, known previously as the kami "Tenri-o-no-Mikoto") inhabited her body as a "Shrine of God" and revealed to her that all humankind could know him and the "Joyous Life" he offers.[15] Blending some elements of monotheism with Japanese traditions, Tenrikyo members focus on sweeping away the mental "dust" (what Christians would call "sin") through "daily service." Headquartered in Tenri, near Nara, Japan, the Tenrikyo Church has organized almost seventeen thousand local congregations in Japan and claims a worldwide membership of two million.

Seicho No Ie preaches a similar message. The sect claims 1.6 million members worldwide, with more than half of them residing outside of Japan. Founder Masaharu Taniguchi (1893–1985) first published a magazine in 1930 by that title, "Seicho No Ie," which believers translate as "Great Universe." In that and later publications, Taniguchi taught that all human beings are God's offspring (he called God "Buddha") and that the key to health and prosperity is realizing one's identity in relationship with this Ultimate Reality. The main path to this realization is through meditation techniques taught by Seicho No Ie "ministers." In worship gatherings, the focal point is not an image but a written script called "Jisso" or "true image," based on the conviction that the truth about this greatest of "kami" cannot be conveyed by a statue.[16]

Reiki, the sect mentioned at the beginning of this chapter, represents another type of "new religion" that is not atypical in Japan. The word "Reiki" combines two words: "Rei" ("God") and "Ki" ("life force," called "chi" or "qi" in China). Founded by Mikao Usui (1865–1926) as a healing technique, the invisible but potent Reiki energy is manipulated through the placement of the hands on the body in specific ways. In this way, its power is released to bring healing to the body and soul. Reiki claims to supplement but not replace other forms of medicine, and it does not require practitioners to leave whatever religion they practiced before they learned about Reiki.[17] In fact, there are Christian groups in the United States and elsewhere that promote Reiki as an appropriate spiritual application of the "laying on of hands." There are other Christians who oppose the practice as syncretistic or worse.[18]

One notorious "new religion" called Aum Shinrikyo ("Om Supreme Truth"), shortened to "Aum" in conversations in Japan, was founded by Shoko Asahara in the 1980s. Mixing Hinduism, Buddhism, and Christianity, Asahara claimed to be both the Christ and the first enlightened person since Buddha. His doomsday predictions put him on the Japanese government radar, which only fueled his anti-government message. His followers were convicted of several attacks on Japanese citizens in public places, most infamous of which was the release in the Tokyo subway system in March of 1995 of a deadly nerve gas that killed twelve people and injured thousands more. Asahara and twelve other members were sentenced to death for the crime and still await execution. Two new spinoff groups—Aleph and Hikari No Wa—carry on the spiritual legacy of Aum as legal but "dangerous" religious bodies.[19]

Most of these "new religions" have in common a single founder who had an epiphany of some kind, a tight organizational structure, a this-worldly focus (on health and prosperity), and remnants of Shintoism mixed into their faith and practice. Their growth initially represented the disillusionment with the older religions that Japanese people believed failed them during the war. Today, their proliferation may be a reflection of the spiritual hunger many Japanese people have been unable to suppress in a very secular culture.

I should mention one more development among our Japanese neighbors closer to home. The U.S. policy decreed by President Roosevelt's Executive Order 9066 two months after the Japanese attack on Pearl Harbor authorized the forced relocation of people of Japanese ancestry. In all, one hundred twenty thousand people, many of them born on American soil, were forced into ten "internment" camps around the country and remained there until the end of the war, some even a year after the war. Recognizing the grave error only in hindsight, President Reagan signed the Civil Liberties Act in 1988 which paid survivors of the internment camps twenty thousand dollars each. Needless to say, the whole episode left its mark on these neighbors of ours whose parents and grandparents had to endure it.

Significant Points of Contact

As with other traditional religions around the world, there is much to admire about Japanese tradition and the culture it shaped. God designed the family to be a source of stability, security, and belonging. Family is all of those things in Japan. Allegiance to family that extends even to the realm of the dead is the building block of a culture of loyalty in which, for example, employees will work long hours for the same company for their entire career.

The *Kojiki* repeats a popular legend that illustrates that virtue in the extreme. The Emperor Yuryaku, traveling in the countryside, sees a young, attractive peasant girl named Akawi-ko. Smitten by her beauty, he tells her, "Do not marry a husband. I will send for you." So she waits . . . for eighty years without being summoned by Yuryaku. The Emperor, still alive, had forgotten the encounter with the young girl, who was now an old woman. In the end, compelled to prove to him how loyal she had been her entire life, she presented herself at the Emperor's palace. "I had quite forgotten the former event!" he confessed. "Meanwhile, ever faithfully awaiting my commands, you have vainly let pass by the years of your prime. This is very pitiful."[20] Though he did not marry her, he praised her for her loyalty and rewarded her with riches.

This loyalty that begins at home and extends outward to the larger society also engenders the ethic of responsibility, for which Japan is famous. Secularism has not eroded it. Public spaces in Japan are spotless and virtually free of crime. A wallet or purse accidentally left on the train will most likely be handed over to the authorities, who will return it to its owner. A general atmosphere of politeness and mutual respect pervades the work place, the park, the train station, and the restaurant.

Significant Points of Contrast

The family loyalty that is so admirable has an underside. The fundamental Japanese orientation seems to be this-worldly. Interactions with the kami are preoccupied with receiving their assistance in some way and, therefore, appear at times to be manipulative. In other words, we honor the ancestors (and other kami) because of what they can do for us, not solely because they are worthy of honor. To some extent, that same dynamic is reflected in the pragmatism (as opposed to others-focused altruism) of interpersonal relationships in Japan.

As a Christian, I am grateful for my heritage. I recognize the truth repeated often in the Bible that my own parents' faithfulness to the Lord blesses me and those who come behind me "to a thousand generations" (Ex. 20:6). But I do not seek the blessing of my deceased ancestors directly, and my primary motivation for interacting with others cannot be what I can receive from them, but it must be how I might glorify God in those relationships. The secularism that is increasingly entrenched in Japan (with 57 percent of the Japanese claiming no "religious affiliation") helps drive the workaholism that actually harms families and leaves the soul hungry. "What good will it be for a man," Jesus said, "if he gains the whole world, yet forfeits his soul?" (Matt. 16:26). Surely it is this spiritual void that accounts for the appeal of Japan's "new religions." We can pray that God will use the inner longings of those who seek to fill that void to inspire many of our Japanese neighbors to give the gospel of Jesus Christ a fresh hearing.

TALKING TOGETHER . . .

1. What surprises you most about religion in Japan as outlined in this chapter?

2. What makes the polls about religious belief and practice in Japan so confusing to Westerners? How might that reaction be changing in the pluralistic environment of North American culture?

3. What, if anything, do you find admirable about Shintoism?

4. What do you think about the four broad categories of Shintoism?

5. How would you evaluate practices such as Reiki when Christians embrace them as potentially effective therapies?

6. How can allegiance to family, highly valued in Japan, be both a good and a bad thing?

IF YOU WANT TO READ MORE . . .

Davies, Roger J., Osamu Ikeno, eds. *The Japanese Mind: Understanding Contemporary Japanese Culture*. Tokyo: Tuttle Publishing, 2002.
Hillsborough, Romulus. *Samurai Tales: Courage, Fidelity, and Revenge in the Final Years of the Shogun*. Tokyo: Tuttle Publishing, 2010.

Kenji, Kato. *Shinto Shrine: Bilingual Guide to Japan*. Translated by Christopher
Cooling and Yanagita Takamichi. Tokyo: Shogakukan, 2016.

Norbury, Paul. *Culture Smart: Japan! The Essential Guide to Customs and
Culture*. London: Kuperard, 2011.

Notes

[1] Trevor Courneen, "The Healing Power of Reiki," in *Newsweek On-line*, February 28,
2016, accessed January 4, 2017, http://www.newsweek.com/healing-power-reiki-430143.
See also Rand's website at www.reiki.org.

[2] The website for the Maria Kannon Zen Center is http://www.mkzc.org.

[3] According to Asia Matters for America website, http://www.asiamattersforamerica
.org/japan/data/population. Accessed January 6, 2017.

[4] According to "Japan," in *ReligionFacts.com*, October 28, 2016, accessed January 6,
2017, www.religionfacts.com/japan.

[5] As reported by Matthew Coslett, "Japan: The Most Religious Atheist Country," in
GaijinPot online, February 8, 2015, accessed January 7, 2017, at https://blog.gaijinpot
.com/japan-religious-atheist-country.

[6] Winfried Corduan, *Neighboring Faiths*, 2nd edition (Downers Grove, IL:
InterVarsity, 2012), 423.

[7] I am indebted to Winfried Corduan, *Neighboring Faiths*, 429–430, for his summary
of the Meiji Restoration.

[8] Excerpted from the Preface to the *Kojiki*, in Van Voorst's *Anthology of World
Scriptures*, 6th edition (Belmont, CA: Thomson-Wadsworth, 2008), 183.

[9] Report by Ed Payne and Yoko Wakatsuki, "Japanese Prime Minister Abe Visits
Controversial Yasukuni War Shrine," on *CNN* online, December 28, 2013, accessed
January 7, 2017, http://www.cnn.com/2013/12/25/world/asia/japan-pm-war-shrine.

[10] Barbara Bradley Hagerty, "After Tsunami Japanese Turn to Ancient Rituals," on
National Public Radio's "Morning Edition" program, March 17, 2011, accessed January 8,
2017, http://www.npr.org/2011/03/17/134597421/after-tsunami-japanese-turn-to-ancient
-rituals.

[11] Kato Kenji, *Shinto Shrine: Bilingual Guide to Japan*, translated by Christopher
Cooling (Hitotshubashi, Japan: Shogakukan, 2016), 15.

[12] The Ise Shrine dedicated to Amaterasu is rebuilt from scratch every twenty years
as a way to maintain its purity. New trees are cut down, shaped, and shipped to the site,
and the reconstruction, which last occurred in 2013, is identical to the previous one.

[13] Haruka Masumizu, "A Guide to New Year Traditions in Japan," in *Japan Today*
online, December 31, 2016, accessed January 8, 2017, https://www.japantoday.com
/category/arts-culture/view/a-guide-to-new-year-traditions-in-japan-2.

[14] Ninian Smart, *The Religious Experience,* 5th edition (Upper Saddle River, NJ: Prentice Hall, 1996), 155.

[15] See the Tenrikyo International website at http://www.tenrikyo.or.jp/eng.

[16] See the official website at http://www.seicho-no-ie.org/eng.

[17] According to the American website www.reiki.org. Accessed January 11, 2017.

[18] For the pro-Reiki view, see http://www.christianreiki.org; for the opposing view (which I endorse), see the official statement by the United States Conference of Catholic Bishops entitled "Guidelines for Evaluating Reiki as an Alternative Therapy," March 25, 2009, http://gnm.org/wp-content/uploads/PDFs/Reiki-evaluation-guidelines-2009 .pdf. If you are interested in reading a more personal (and negative) critique from a one-time practitioner, see this post at https://reikiandchristianity.wordpress.com. Accessed January 11, 2017.

[19] Article by Kuchikomi, "Aum Spinoffs Still Out There," in *Japan Today* online, Sept. 20, 2016, accessed January 7, 2017, https://www.japantoday.com/category/kuchikomi, 41.

[20] From the *Kojiki* as quoted by Van Voorst in *Anthology of World Scriptures,* 6th edition (Belmont, CA: Thomson-Wadsworth, 2008), 188.

CHAPTER TWELVE

BOOKENDS:
WHAT I HAVE LEARNED

On April 16, 2007, a very troubled student at Virginia Tech shot and killed thirty-two classmates in what became known as the Virginia Tech Massacre. The following April, I was attending a Sabbath service in a synagogue in Dallas when William Gershon, formerly the senior rabbi for Congregation Shearith Israel, mentioned the massacre in his morning message. He recalled a meeting between the Dalai Lama and several Jewish leaders that took place in New Jersey years before, in which the Tibetan Buddhist leader asked the Jewish representatives about the "secret" to their survival. "His Holiness" believed members of his own spiritual community, especially Tibetan Buddhists in exile, could learn something from the Jewish people.[1]

Rabbi Gershon was not present at that meeting and did not know how those Jewish leaders answered the Dalai Lama's question. But if he had been present, he said, he would have pointed the Buddhist leader to two sources of Jewish resilience: memory and hope. Jews, he said, are purposeful and intentional about remembering their past, including the sad, even tragic moments. Jewish Holy Days commemorate defeats as well as victories. "Sitting Shiva" after the death of a loved one compels the grieving survivors to reminisce about the departed. Memory helps them go on. And because of hope, the children of Israel anticipate a brighter future. At the end of Passover, he reminded the congregation, participants exclaim together "Next Year in Jerusalem," expressing out loud the possibility that the Messiah might come between now and next year, rebuild the Temple, and gather Jews from the diaspora to convene in the Holy City to celebrate Passover together.

Memory and hope. I knew I was hearing something true and profound. Because it was the Sabbath, I could not take notes until we had left the building. But I have repeated those words many times since then. It was one moment among many others when I heard a core truth in a non-Christian place of worship. That no longer surprises me. Truth comes from the same divine source regardless of who repeats it. Sometimes truth follows a circuitous route and overcomes serious obstacles before it can surface in such a setting. But it often does surface.

Significant Points of Contact: Truth Is Truth

I have had that same feeling in other places of worship. In the mosques I have frequented, I am impressed by the symbols of submission I see—from the prayer posture (prostrate on the ground, face down, in submission to Allah), to the American teenagers I meet who can already recite the Qur'an word for word in Arabic, a language they cannot converse in, to the women I see in public wearing the head scarf that will identify them as members of America's Muslim minority. Remember, the word "Islam" means "submission." But it is much more than a word to my Muslim friends.

In Hindu, Buddhist, and Sikh temples I have visited, I am struck by the evidence of commitment I see to the goals these neighbors pursue, dedication that in some cases requires hours of sitting on the floor in silence or in meditation in what would be uncomfortable positions to me. In parts of the world where Traditional Religions predominate—from the outback of Australia to Native American reservations in the United States to the tribal region of Kenya I once called home—I feel a deep sense of appreciation for the traditions that preserve (some with more success than others) a worldview that is ancient, when I myself live in a culture obsessed with anything and everything "new."

I identify with the sentiments of Peter Feldmeier who teaches courses in theology and world religions at the University of Toledo. In his book *Encounters in Faith: Christianity in Interreligious Dialogue*, Feldmeier explains how decades of scholarly interactions with non-Christians have made him more aware of important aspects of his Christian faith. He describes, for example, how learning from mystics has given him appreciation for those mysteries of life in Christ which we cannot reduce to logical analysis.[2] Learning from priests, rabbis, imams, gurus, and shaman has helped him understand the role God calls on Christian mediators to fill. Studying Judaism, Islam, Hinduism, Buddhism, Chinese, and other "indigenous religions" has, he says, deepened his own relationship with God.[3]

Acknowledging what we might learn from our non-Christian neighbors is not the same as claiming that all religions are alike. That is the conventional wisdom of our relativistic culture. Television programs like Oprah's "Belief" and Reza Aslan's "Believer" assume a posture of "neutrality" toward all religions in order to defend the idea that religion—any religion—is good. Kinnaman and Lyons, responding to Oprah's "Belief" (which they were invited to screen before it was broadcast), write that

> the basic notion being conveyed was that all faith is good, no matter which one you choose. This was a *fair* thing, but not a *true* one [italics theirs]. And while all faiths contribute to a lot of good in the world, not all beliefs can be true. They each have ultimate claims that contradict the others. . . . Good faith Christians must be wary of these distortions. The message that all faiths are true is pluralism as its worst. Instead of respecting diverse points of view (confident pluralism), this relativizes competing beliefs and suggests none of them are actually true; they are just good ways to become more "spiritual."[4]

Obviously, I have shown my hand throughout this book. I have written as an unapologetic follower of Christ. I believe that people of conviction can communicate with each other in a way that is respectful and informed without resorting to the mushy relativism that, in fact, minimizes the differences between believers of all kinds by ignoring what those believers themselves say they believe.

Significant Points of Contrast: Jesus the One and Only

I have spent most of my adult life immersed in the study of world religions, first as a missionary in rural Africa, then later as a student and professor of world religions. Those experiences built the backdrop against which I am learning to appreciate the beauty of Christ in comparison to the alternatives. Here are some of the features of the Christian faith I find most unique.

A Story

Without exception, the sacred texts of the world's religions are filled with philosophical insights and guidelines for living. The Bible contains both, but they are interspersed throughout this collection of documents, all bound in this single volume, and assembled on a framework of a story from start to finish.

That story begins with creation, then explains the origins of the people of Israel and their calling as God's mediator nation to the world. Their inspired wisdom and God's messages to Israel's prophets before, during, and after seasons of exile round out the first half of the larger story and prepare the reader for the coming of the promised Messiah. The Gospels provide testimony about him from four different camera angles. Acts of the Apostles helps us understand how his first followers interpreted his instructions to them to take his message to the rest of the world. The epistles address the churches they established around the Mediterranean Sea, each letter written to a specific group with particular issues as they tried to figure out what it meant to follow Jesus together. The story ends with Revelation, which gives the reader a preview (mostly) of stories yet to be told.

I have learned that the narrative nature of the Bible is surprising to new readers, especially ones familiar with other sacred texts. Yes, other scriptures include stories, from the account of "Yusef" (Joseph) in Egypt (chapter 12 in the Qur'an) to the saga of Arjuna and his chariot driver, Krishna, in the Gita. They are primarily collections of hymns, prayers, or words of instruction, with stories here and there. The Bible is an epic story that includes instruction. But that story purports to be more than simply "a story."

Grounded in History

In my early years in Africa, I struck up a friendship with a Peace Corps volunteer who lived in our small town. In one conversation (among many), I had the impression that he was warming up to the possibility that the Christian faith might be true. He expressed appreciation for the values he saw in us: a moral center, a clear sense of purpose, and hope for a life beyond the grave. Then he stopped me in my tracks when he said, in so many words, "You don't have to convince me that it would be nice to be a Christian. But if it isn't true, it isn't true." I think he was right. I was trying to show him all the benefits of life in Christ, but he was not persuaded that the story of Jesus on which my Christian life (and yours) rests is founded on facts. To him it is merely one "story" among many other "stories," none of which are verifiably true. I was probably not alone in my approach to evangelism back then, highlighting the perks of the gospel as the reason to embrace the gospel. But if it isn't true, it isn't true.

Those who preached this gospel from the beginning were convicted that Jesus of Nazareth was who he claimed to be—God in the flesh, the Incarnate Word. The four Gospels claim to be recording testimony from eyewitnesses telling what they saw and heard. Luke's intentions are clear from the beginning:

> Many have undertaken to draw up an account of the things that have been fulfilled among us, just as they were handed down to us by those who from the first were eyewitnesses and servants of the word. Therefore, since I myself have carefully investigated everything from the beginning, it seemed good also to me to write an orderly account for you, most excellent Theophilus, so that you may know the certainty of the things you have been taught. (Luke 1:1–4)

John saves his purpose statement for the end, but makes the same case:

Jesus did many other miraculous signs in the presence of his disciples, which are not recorded in this book. But these are written that you may believe that Jesus is the Christ, the Son of God, and that by believing you may have life in his name. (John 20:30–31)

It may be the same John who begins an epistle to first-century Christians appealing to this same historical foundation for faith when he writes:

That which was from the beginning, which we have heard, which we have seen with our eyes, which we have looked at and our hands have touched—this we proclaim concerning the Word of life. The life appeared; we have seen it and testify to it, and we proclaim to you the eternal life, which was with the Father and has appeared to us. We proclaim to you what we have seen and heard, so that you also may have fellowship with us. And our fellowship is with the Father and with his Son, Jesus Christ. We write this to make our joy complete. (1 John 1:1–4)

Just ten days after the Ascension he says he witnessed, Peter stood on the Day of Pentecost and said to his fellow-Jews in Jerusalem, "Men of Israel, listen to this: Jesus of Nazareth was a man accredited by God to you by miracles, wonders and signs, which God did among you through him, as you yourselves know" (Acts 2:22). In that pivotal message, he went on to make the case that Jesus was crucified, not because he was overpowered by opponents stronger than him, but because he understood God's redemptive purpose for the cross. Then, unlike King David, who was buried in Jerusalem and whose tomb they could still visit, Jesus came out of the tomb alive on the Sunday that followed that "Good" Friday. Peter's closing argument went like this: "God has made this Jesus, whom you crucified, both Lord and Christ" (Acts 2:36). Once again, in a letter that bears his name, a letter addressed to a Christian audience, Peter writes:

We did not follow cleverly invented stories when we told you about the power and coming of our Lord Jesus Christ, but we were eyewitnesses of his majesty. For he received honor and glory from God the Father when the voice came to him from

the Majestic Glory, saying, "This is my Son, whom I love; with
him I am well pleased." We ourselves heard this voice that came
from heaven when we were with him on the sacred mountain.
(2 Pet. 1:16–18)

Paul, too, staked his faith to historicity when he wrote, "If Christ has not
been raised, our preaching is useless and so is your faith" (1 Cor. 15:14). A
few verses later he adds, "If only for this life we have hope in Christ, we
are to be pitied more than all men" (1 Cor. 15:19).

None of that "proves" that the testimony about Jesus is, in fact, historically reliable. I believe that case can be made, has been made, and should
be made.[5] The point here is that, according to the foundational documents
on which the Christian faith rests, there is no Christian faith without the
testimony of those who knew Jesus personally. My Buddhists friends would
not say that their faith and practice collapse without a "historical Buddha."
Their faith rests in their experience that Buddhism (whichever form they
practice) works, that its truths become apparent only when one follows the
path the Buddha rediscovered and experiences them in his or her own life.
Our Hindu, Jain, Sikh, Native American, Chinese, and Japanese neighbors
share a similar point of view. Many of our Jewish friends, on the other hand,
especially the observant ones, do believe God revealed his will to Moses
and that those words, both written and oral, are recorded in the Hebrew
Bible and in the Talmud. (As Christians, we agree that the written portions of the Old Testament are the words of God composed with human
partners inspired by his Holy Spirit.) Likewise, our Muslim neighbors are
convinced that Allah did, in fact, communicate his word through the angel
Gabriel to Muhammad off and on for twenty-two years. Theirs is a faith
based on history. But the accounts of those revelations to Muhammad are
not corroborated by witnesses. No one but Muhammad ever saw the angel
Gabriel reciting the Qur'an.

I don't mean to suggest that our faith rests solely on the testimony of
others. To be sure we can (and should) add our "testimony"—that is, our
experiences of walking with Jesus in our time—to the testimony of those
original eyewitnesses. But we should not hesitate to do what they did: stake
our faith to this, the most important piece of history ever recorded.

Centered on the Incarnation

The center of that history (or a little to the right of the center if you're holding a Bible in your hands) is the "Word [who] became flesh and made his dwelling among us" (John 1:14). We believe that at the pinnacle of history, when God wanted to communicate his nature and will to humanity, he did what one does when there is a really important message to deliver: he delivered it in person. But as Ravi Zacharias points out, Jesus did more than deliver a message. Jesus *is* the message. "He did not just proclaim the truth. He said 'I *am* the truth'" (italics his).[6]

This is the main reason I react negatively when I hear people describe themselves as "New Testament Christians." The way I hear it, that phrase minimizes the significance of what we have in Christ. The New Testament is not just an updated version of the Old Testament with modified rules and regulations. What we have in Christ is more revolutionary than that! The Word did not become new words; the Word became flesh and dwelled among us. We may call ourselves "new covenant" Christians if we like, but that is redundant. There really is no other kind of Christian.

Peter Feldmeier points out that it is in the Incarnation that Creator and creation are brought together in a way that is unique among world religions. Yes, in Hinduism, "avatars" of Vishnu have come and gone, and our Baha'i neighbors believe that multiple "Manifestations" of God have appeared over the centuries. But the Christian claims about the Incarnation are unique. First, we believe he has appeared only once in the flesh, that he is "God the One and Only" (John 1:18). Second, we believe that through the Incarnation, God has "provided the means for human nature to participate in the divine."[7] Third, the "divine" we participate in is not an impersonal force or energy into which we may one day—after thousands of incarnations in flesh—be absorbed, like atman returns to the Brahman from whence it came. No, because the Word became flesh, and this Word was with God in the beginning and is, in fact, God, we know that the God we serve is a Being (John 1:1). So our response to him is personal.

> For we do not have a high priest who is unable to sympathize
> with our weaknesses, but we have one who has been tempted
> in every way, just as we are—yet was without sin. Let us then

approach the throne of grace with confidence, so that we may
receive mercy and find grace to help us in our time of need.
(Heb. 4:15–16)

We draw near to God through Christ because we know he is approachable.
We know he is approachable because he dwelled among us in the flesh.

The Foolishness of the Cross

None of the religious founders whose biographies are summarized in the
preceding chapters died in shame and humiliation at the hands of their
opponents. All religions have had their martyrs. But only in the Christian
story is the execution of the faith's founder interpreted as an act of atonement and a means of redemption. No wonder this surprise ending was
considered "a stumbling block to Jews and foolishness to Gentiles" (1 Cor.
1:23)! For reasons I explained in Chapters Two and Three, it still is a stumbling block to Jews and Muslims, and it makes no sense to adherents of
other religions. How could this case of capital punishment in an otherwise
obscure place in an ancient time be the key to unlocking the mysteries of
the universe? Because by surrendering his life, Jesus illustrates the self-sacrificing love of God.

Jesus made it clear that it was *self*-sacrificing; he was not overpowered
by his opponents. "The reason my Father loves me is that I lay down my
life—only to take it up again. No one takes it from me, but I lay it down
of my own accord. I have authority to lay it down and authority to take
it up again" (John 10:17–18). When the Roman governor Pilate suggested
otherwise, Jesus set him straight. "You would have no power over me if
it were not given to you from above" (John 19:11). And he understood
that God would somehow, through his death, "ransom" others, that by his
wounds, we would be healed, that he would endure for us the punishment
we deserved because of our sin, and that by his own blood we would be
granted access to God's holy Presence. The driving force behind all of it
was love.

That Jesus's followers are called upon to follow in his steps and demonstrate the same kind of self-sacrificing love is also clear: "This is how we
know what love is: Jesus Christ laid down his life for us. And we ought to

lay down our lives for our brothers" (1 John 3:16). The focus on love may not seem unique to Christians. Feldmeier writes, "Every great religion recognizes the power and importance of love, but Christianity has made it core."[8] I'm not sure that he's right about "every religion," when so many of them teach that avoiding attachments of all kinds is the key to escaping suffering. Love is surely one of those attachments. But he is certainly correct that in Christ, love is at the center of the gospel about God who "so loved the world that he gave his one and only Son" (John 3:16). Only in Christ do we speak of a God who *is* love: "Whoever does not love does not know God, because God is love" (1 John 4:8). The cross is a demonstration of the love of God inherent in his nature.

The Hope of the Resurrection

No other religion claims that its founder came back to life after death and walked with his followers as Jesus did for forty days post-resurrection. Once again, to Christians there is no room for a "spiritualized" resurrection story that reduces a literal historical event to a mystical appearance to a few of his close followers in something like a dream sequence. "If Christ has not been raised" . . . you know the rest of it. The Gospels present the resurrection and Jesus's post-resurrection encounters as historical events. The oldest written account of Jesus's resurrection is not in the Gospels but in one of Paul's letters in which the apostle appealed once again to eyewitness accounts that verified the facts (1 Cor. 15:3–8).

Of course, Christians are not alone in their belief in life after death. Both Jews and Muslims believe human beings will encounter God after we die, that either punishment or Paradise awaits us. Many of the other religions assume that multiple births and rebirths precede the ultimate and desired after-life experience, either the absorption of the "atman" into Brahman or the relief of being "blown out" like a candle, thus ending the cycle of birth and rebirth and the chronic suffering. In Christ, we anticipate the recreation of our bodies which, we are told, will be transformed and made fit for immortality. "So will it be with the resurrection of the dead. The body that is sown is perishable, it is raised imperishable; it is sown in dishonor, it is raised in glory; it is sown in weakness, it is raised in power; it is sown a natural body, it is raised a spiritual body" (1 Cor. 15:42–44). Though we don't know the details, Christ "will transform our lowly bodies so that they may be like his glorious body" (Philip. 3:21). At that point "what is mortal may be swallowed up by life" (2 Cor. 5:4).

We who are "transformed" in this way will not constitute a mass of undifferentiated "souls" (a la Brahman). In some ways, we will retain our individuality; otherwise it would be impossible to tell that the "multitude" assembled in Heaven on that day includes people "from every nation, tribe, people and language, standing before the throne and in front of the Lamb" (Rev. 7:9). We do not lose our distinctiveness, but only the selfishness and other forms of sin individualism inspires when it is not tempered by submission to God and by the realization of how much we need each other. Apparently, based on this vision of the future in Revelation 7, we will also retain some indicators of our ethnicities. But the animosity they often produce—all the sinful "us and them" stuff—will melt away in the heat and light that comes from the Presence of a holy God who abides forever with a made-holy people. This reconciliation is a key feature of the resurrection hope we preach.

The Promise of the Holy Spirit

No other faith promises that the Divine Being himself will reside within the bodies of the adherents. We who are in Christ are living the fulfillment of the prophecy God made through Ezekiel: "I will put my Spirit in you and move you to follow my decrees and be careful to keep my laws" (36:27). Yes, the "atman" that animates the body of a Hindu is understood as a tiny drop of Brahman, but that Brahman is an impersonal force, not the invisible but potent presence of a Person. The Holy Spirit is the "Living Water" that Jesus promised to the woman at the well (John 4:10–14) and to "whoever believes in me" (John 7:37–39). He is "the Counselor, the Holy Spirit," whom the Father would send in Jesus's name (John 14:26). It is through our cooperation with God's Spirit that we experience the spiritual transformation that renews and sanctifies us, that empowers us to put to death the misdeeds of the body and brings true spiritual freedom and produces in us the fruit that characterizes people who experience intimacy with God.[9]

The Christian faith is a story uniquely grounded in history and centered on the Incarnation. We proclaim the foolishness of the cross and the love on display there, embracing the hope of the resurrection and the transforming power of the Holy Spirit.

Our "None" Neighbors

When the Pew Forum released its findings in October 2012 on religious life in America, the results were different enough from those of previous surveys that the report drew national attention.[10] National Public Radio aired a week-long feature entitled "Losing Our Religion: The Growth of the 'Nones.'"[11] *USA Today* and *Huffington Post* chimed in.[12] What people of faith found alarming is that the number of Americans who checked "none" on religious affiliation rose in five years (between 2007 and 2012) from 15 percent to 20 percent; one-third of adults under thirty claimed no religious affiliation.[13] Among the religiously unaffiliated, 88 percent said they are not even looking (for religious faith). Many of them might identify with Jonathan Rauch, who described himself not as an atheist or agnostic but as an "apatheist"—he just doesn't think about God or religion.[14] That label might resonate with Hazel, one of the lead characters in the 2014 movie, *The Fault in Our Stars*. When her boyfriend, Gus, who, like Hazel, is afflicted with a terminal disease, asks her if she believes in an afterlife, she says she doesn't know. His response is, "Then what's the point?" to which she replies, "What if there is no point?"[15]

The Pew Research findings were in line with previous surveys and publications including the American Religious Identification Survey (2009), Christian Smith's *Souls in Transition: The Religious and Spiritual Lives of Emerging Adults* (2009), and David Kinnaman's *You Lost Me: Why Young Christians Are Leaving Church* (2011), to name a few.[16] Christian authors have scrambled to suggest ways we might reverse the downward trends. In his 2014 book, *The Rise of the 'Nones': Understanding and Reaching the Religiously Unaffiliated,* James Emery White, for example, counsels the church on how to stop the hemorrhaging of its members, especially those 18–29 years old.[17] But what do the numbers really mean? As Kinnaman and Lyons observe, "When you give people a chance to mark 'not affiliated' or 'none,' but you've never offered that option in the past, you don't have any way of tracking a hypothetical increase."[18] We certainly can't assume that all of these "nones" reject spirituality altogether. Many consider themselves "spiritual but not religious."[19]

Robert Fuller wrote a book with that title, *Spiritual but not Religious*. In it, he outlines common themes among these neighbors:

- That there is an experiential core common to all religions, a core that is usually described as a kind of "energy."
- That human beings have unlimited spiritual potential that must be actualized to achieve success in life.
- That experience, not truthfulness, is the proper way to test any worldview.
- That spirituality has more to do with a general openness to multiple spiritual realities than a commitment to a particular creed.
- That those who are "spiritual but not religious" are highly suspicious of any organized religion.
- That the figure of Jesus, if he is mentioned at all, is seen as a highly evolved spiritual being who can help us in some way in our spiritual evolution.[20]

Even Sam Harris, the best-selling atheist, has published a book on what it means to be "spiritual" minus religious affiliation.[21] It makes sense to me why books that explore spiritual themes apart from the orthodoxy of any specific religious tradition—like *Eat, Pray, Love* (2006) and *Life of Pi* (2001)—resonate with this population; both were bestsellers.[22]

From a Christian perspective, these trends reflect a stubborn inner longing that God has hard-wired into human beings. Motivational speakers like Tony Robbins tap into it, filling the vacuum created by the rise of secularism and the demise of religion. Robbins's six-day "Date With Destiny" seminars blend pop psychology and religious-sounding themes and package them like revival meetings of the past, with Robbins delivering the content like a televangelist, complete with testimonials and musical numbers that are interspersed at the peak emotional moments for maximum effect. As I watched the "Date With Destiny" documentary with my wife, we both thought, "Wow! People are really hungry for something that rings true, something that makes them feel valued, from a messenger who seems authentic and spiritual at the same time."[23] As Dallas Willard put it, "The soul will strike back," especially when it is starved for spiritual substance.[24]

Bookends: Grace and Truth

Our interactions with *these* non-Christian neighbors must also be respectful and informed if we hope to have any chance of being persuasive. Jesus embodies what meaningful interaction requires. John says of him that he was "full of grace and truth" (1:14). It moves me to see that combination of grace and truth fleshed out in Jesus's dealings with others. If we confine ourselves to John's Gospel alone, we see it in Jesus's response to his own mother's request (John 2), to Nicodemus (John 3), to the woman at the well (John 4), to the lame man he heals at pool of Bethesda (John 5), to a hungry crowd (John 6), to the woman caught in adultery (John 8), to the man born blind (John 9), and on and on. In each case, he spoke truth with grace. We represent him well only when we reflect the same combination.

We don't see it only in John's account. Jesus models grace and truth from start to finish. The bookends of Jesus's earthly life are telling. He entered the world in a manger and breathed his last on a cross. From these two word pictures (and many others in between), we learn much about what it means to engage "others" as Jesus did. If we learn anything from the Incarnation (and surely there is more to learn than I will ever understand), it is that God wants to be with us. He won't share in our sinful behavior. But he has covered great distance to be with us. And if we learn anything from the cross (and there is so much to learn), at the very least we know without a doubt that God himself is willing to lay down his life that we might be reunited with him.

The question I must ask at the end of this book about our non-Christian neighbors is this: Do these significant others in your circle of influence know these two things about you? Can they tell that you want to be with them and that you are prepared to lay down your life for them? If your honest answer is "probably not," then I'm pretty sure the information in this book will not help. But if the answer is "yes," then thank God for you! You are giving off the aroma of Christ. May God bless our relationships with our neighbors and reconcile us—all of us—to himself.

TALKING TOGETHER . . .

1. How do you respond to Rabbi Gershon's message about "memory and hope" and keys to the resilience of our Jewish neighbors?

2. In addition to values and practices such as submission, meditation, and tradition, what other values stand out to you as truly valuable as you reflect on these non-Christian religions?

3. Cox makes the case for the uniqueness of the gospel with this statement: "The Christian faith is a story uniquely grounded in history and centered on the Incarnation. We proclaim the foolishness of the cross and the love on display there, embracing the hope of the resurrection and the transforming power of the Holy Spirit." What touches you most about the uniqueness of the gospel against the backdrop of the alternatives?

4. What have you read in this chapter that you think might help you in conversations with "nones" you know—the growing number of people who claim no religious affiliation?

5. In what ways do you feel more equipped to share your faith with others now that you have read this book?

IF YOU WANT TO READ MORE . . .

Corduan, Winfried. *A Tapestry of Faiths: The Common Threads Between Christianity and World Religions.* Downers Grove, IL: InterVarsity Press, 2002.

Feldmeier, Peter. *Encounters in Faith: Christianity in Interreligious Dialogue.* Winona, MN: Anselm Academic, 2011.

Fuller, Robert C. *Spiritual But Not Religious: Understanding Unchurched America*. Oxford: Oxford University Press, 2001.

Harris, Sam. *Waking Up: A Guide to Spirituality Without Religion*. New York: Simon and Schuster Paperbacks, 2014.

Tennent, Timothy C. *Christianity at the Religious Roundtable: Evangelicalism in Conversation with Hinduism, Buddhism, and Islam*. Grand Rapids: Baker Academic, 2002.

Volf, Miroslav. *Flourishing: Why We Need Religion in a Globalized World*. London and New Haven, CN: Yale University Press, 2015.

White, James Emery. *The Rise of the 'Nones': Understanding and Reaching the Religiously Unaffiliated*. Grand Rapids: Baker Books, 2014.

Zacharias, Ravi. *Jesus Among Other Gods: The Absolute Claims of the Christian Message*. Nashville: Word Publishing, 2000.

Notes

[1] Ari L. Goldman, "Dalai Lama Meets Jews from Four Major Branches," in *New York Times*, September 27, 1989, accessed March 22, 2017, at http://www.nytimes.com/1989/09/26/nyregion/dalai-lama-meets-jews-from-4-major-branches.html.

[2] Peter Feldmeier, *Encounters in Faith: Christianity in Interreligious Dialogue* (Winona, MN: Anselm Academic, 2011).

[3] Ibid., 261–262.

[4] David Kinnaman and Gabe Lyons, *Good Faith: Being a Christian When Society Think You're Irrelevant and Extreme* (Ada, MI: Baker Books, 2016), 230.

[5] Including these personal favorites: Michael J. Wilkins and J. P. Moreland, eds., *Jesus Under Fire: Modern Scholarship Reinvents the Historical Jesus* (Grand Rapids: Zondervan, 1995); Craig Blomberg, *The Historical Reliability of the Gospels* (Downers Grove, IL: InterVarsity Press, 1987); Gary R. Habermas, *The Historical Jesus: Ancient Evidence for the Life of Christ* (Joplin, MO: College Press, 1996); and Lee Strobel, *The Case for Christ: A Journalist's Personal Investigation of the Evidence of Jesus* (Grand Rapids: Zondervan, 1998).

[6] Ravi Zacharias, *Jesus Among Other Gods: The Absolute Claims of the Christian Message* (Nashville: Thomas Nelson, 2002), 89.

[7] Feldmeier, 280.

[8] Ibid., 281.

[9] The passages I have in mind are, in this order, Titus 3:3–7; 2 Thessalonians 2:13; 1 Peter 1:2; Romans 8:12–13; 2 Corinthians 3:7–18; Galatians 6:22–25.

[10] "'Nones' on the Rise: One-in-Five Adults Have No Religious Affiliation," The Pew Forum on Religion and Public Life, October 9, 2012, 9. www.pewforum.org.

[11]"Losing Our Religion: The Growth of the 'Nones,'" "Morning Edition," National Public Radio, January 13, 2013.

[12]Cathy Lynn Grossman, "The Emerging Social, Political Force: 'Nones,'" *USA Today* online (October 9, 2012), http://www.usatoday.com/story/news/nation/2012/10/09/nones-religion-pew-study; Sean McCloud, "Nones, Somes, and the Combinativeness of American Religious Practices," *Huffington Post* online (February 28, 2015), http://www.huffingtonpost.com/sean-mccloud/nones-somes-and-the-combinativeness-of-american-religious-practices.

[13]"'Nones' on the Rise," 9–10.

[14]Jonathan Rauch, "Let It Be," *The Atlantic Monthly* (May 2003), 34.

[15]"The Fault in Our Stars," 20th Century Fox, 2014.

[16]Barry A. Kosmin and Ariela Keysar, "American Religious Identification Survey 2008," www.americareligionsurvey-aris.org; Christian Smith, *Souls in Transition: The Religious and Spiritual Lives of Emerging Adults* (Oxford: Oxford University Press, 2009); David Kinnaman, *You Lost Me: Why Young Christians Are Leaving Church* (Grand Rapids: Baker, 2011).

[17]James Emery White, *The Rise of the 'Nones': Understanding and Reaching the Religiously Unaffiliated* (Grand Rapids: Baker Books, 2014).

[18]Kinnaman and Lyons, *Good Faith*, 220.

[19]"'Nones' on the Rise" reports that of the 46 million religiously "unaffiliated" Americans, 68 percent say they believe in God and 37 percent classify themselves as "spiritual but not religious" (9–10).

[20]Robert C. Fuller, *Spiritual but not Religious: Understanding Unchurched America* (Oxford: Oxford University Press, 2001), 10, 63, 68, 73, 75–77.

[21]Sam Harris, *Waking Up: A Guide to Spirituality Without Religion* (New York: Simon and Schuster Paperbacks, 2014).

[22]Elizabeth Gilbert, *Eat, Pray, Love* (New York: Penguin, 2006); Yann Martel, *Life of Pi* (Toronto: Knopf, 2001).

[23]Joe Berlinger, "Tony Robbins: I Am Not Your Guru," Netflix Original documentary, March 14, 2016.

[24]Dallas Willard, *Renovation of the Heart: Putting on the Character of Christ* (Colorado Springs: NavPress, 2002), 204.

SIGNIFICANT

OTHERS

SIGNIFICANT
UNDERSTANDING OUR NON-CHRISTIAN NEIGHBORS
OTHERS

MONTE CO

SIGNIFICANT
UNDERSTANDING OUR NON-CHRISTIAN NEIGHBORS
OTHERS